NORMAN MAILER

A COLLECTION OF CRITICAL ESSAYS

Edited by
Leo Braudy

Prentice-Hall, Inc. *Englewood Cliffs, N. J.*

A SPECTRUM BOOK

Library of Congress Cataloging in Publication Data

BRAUDY, LEO, comp.
    Norman Mailer.

    (A Spectrum book)
    1. Mailer, Norman.   I. Title.
PS3525.A4152Z6   813'.5'4   72-2673
ISBN   0-13-545533-2
ISBN   0-13-545541-3 (pbk.)

Quotations from Norman Mailer's *The White Negro* (copyright © 1957 by Dissent Publishing Associates) are used by permission of the author and City Lights Books.

Quotations from Norman Mailer's *Advertisements for Myself* (copyright © 1959 by Norman Mailer) are used by permission of the author, G. P. Putnam's Sons, and Andre Deutsch Ltd.

Quotations from Norman Mailer's *Cannibals and Christians* (copyright © 1966 by Norman Mailer) are used by permission of the author and the author's agents, Scott Meredith Literary Agency.

Quotations from Norman Mailer's *The Armies of the Night* (copyright © 1968 by Norman Mailer) are used by permission of the author and The New American Library.

Quotations from Norman Mailer's *Of a Fire on the Moon* (copyright © 1969, 1970 by Norman Mailer) are used by permission of the author, Little, Brown and Company, and the author's agents, Scott Meredith Literary Agency.

10   9   8   7   6   5   4   3   2   1

PRENTICE-HALL INTERNATIONAL, INC. (*London*)
PRENTICE-HALL OF AUSTRALIA, PTY. LTD. (*Sydney*)
PRENTICE-HALL OF CANADA, LTD. (*Toronto*)
PRENTICE-HALL OF INDIA PRIVATE LIMITED (*New Delhi*)
PRENTICE-HALL OF JAPAN, INC. (*Tokyo*)

Contents

Contents

Acknowledgments

I would like to thank all those people who helped me emerge from the thicket of publishers' permissions with a minimum of scars, especially Diana Trilling and Norman Mailer. Michael Cowan did me the tremendous favor of writing an original essay especially for this collection. I would also like to thank Jon Lear and David Lehman for their comments on the introduction, Ellen Chesler and Steve Weisman for their long-distance research, Lilia Tchistoganow for her typewriter, Vincent and Jane Crapanzano for their manuscript-preserving service, Dorothy McGahee for her prodding and willingness to read rough drafts whenever they were finished, and Norman and Elsa Rush for needing to be convinced.

L. B.

Introduction
Norman Mailer: The Pride of Vulnerability

by Leo Braudy

What uneasy impetuousness to take a writer in the midst of his career, at the height of his productivity and renown, and attempt to assess what in his work will have permanent value after the literary controversies about the living man have receded from criticism into biography or cultural history. And how in particular could the literary body of Norman Mailer play host to such abrupt critical timelessness? Beginning with *Advertisements For Myself* (1959), Mailer has so concertedly placed his personal character and beliefs at the center of his work that the disentangling of work and man, a process that seems so important to our current definition of lasting literary value, becomes an almost impossible task. Propelled by the dynamic of personal reference, Mailer does not stand still to be evaluated and critically categorized; tags hung on him at various stages in his career, such as "war novelist" or "Jewish novelist," seemed peculiarly irrelevant when they were first minted and are even more misleading now.

Mailer himself has been little help to his prospective critics. Although he is often accused of excessively seeking fame and publicity, Mailer has paradoxically enough pursued this success by successively alienating whatever audiences he had achieved by his earlier work. He resisted the great popular and critical triumph of *The Naked and the Dead* (1948), which brought him fame and wealth at the age of twenty-five, and immediately proceeded to try to find his own way. The dream-like, allegorical mood of *Barbary Shore* (1951), his next novel, seemed to many critics and readers a betrayal of the naturalistic method of *The Naked and the Dead*. More than ten years later, similar complaints about "lack of verisimilitude" would be dusted off for similarly outraged reactions to *An American Dream* (1965). The first impulse of many critics on being faced with a new

1

work by Mailer has therefore been to consider his career a series of disjunctures held together thinly by his raucous public personality.

Mailer himself courts such critical reactions by his belief, as stated in *The Armies of the Night* (1968), that he should change his style for each project; he abandons completely the literary good manners that lie in developing a single theme, style, or set of characters. Mailer instead forces the interested reader and critic to accept this seeming discontinuity as essential to an understanding of his career, demanding an exploration of the complex imagination that manipulates the public Mailer rather than a retreat to the barer but surer ground of notoriety and literary gossip. Despite the many attacks on both his work and his character, Mailer has never taken the easy path of repeating past success. His effort to grapple continuously with his work, setting up a constant interplay between himself and whatever project he is engaged in, has made him at once the most protean and the most archetypal of American authors, producing since *The Naked and the Dead* more than fifteen separate volumes including novels, essays, journalism, poetry, and a play, as well as three movies. It was twenty years before *The Armies of the Night* brought Mailer anything like the literary success and understanding that greeted *The Naked and the Dead*. Yet in the meantime Mailer never compromised his own sense of what ought to be done in a particular work.

The dynamic of such a process is often as fascinating as any individual work within it. Although each of Mailer's works has a literary and intellectual unity of its own, it also fits into an ongoing career that at any moment may reject both the style and the ideas of earlier expressions. Mailer never seems content with previously held positions, just as he will never give up a belief merely because he is one of the only people holding it, whether the belief is revolutionary socialism in the midst of the Cold War, or biological determinism in the midst of Women's Liberation. What Norman Podhoretz said of Mailer in 1959 holds true today: "He must always work everything out for himself and by himself, as though it were up to him to create the world anew over and over again in his experience." [1] Podhoretz speaks here about Mailer's ideas, but his remarks apply also to Mailer's literary expression of those ideas. In fact, the critic's problem is *not* to separate the personal posturing

1. "The Embattled Vision of Norman Mailer," in *Doings and Undoings* (New York: Farrar, Straus & Giroux, 1964), p. 187.

and autobiographical reference from the "timeless" literary truths in Mailer's work, but to see instead how they intertwine to form what Irving Howe has called Mailer's "characteristic mixture of professional skill and a refusal of the professional stance." [2] In flight from the embalming fame that America pours over writers who achieve youthful success, Mailer has stepped deliberately into the little death of American letters, where an eager public substitutes the author's personality for his work and explicates the one by the other. "Do not understand me too quickly," Mailer quotes from André Gide in the epigraph to *The Deer Park* (1955). But he has himself contributed to the oversimplification of his work by his constant impulse to polemicize when he might meditate, preferring to remain alive by touching the contradictory ends of his nature instead of staying in the more intelligible middle.

Excessive personal reference is in fact only the most recent of the critical objections to Mailer's work. For many earlier critics, the "betrayal" of *Barbary Shore* involved not self-advertisement but what at the time might have been referred to as an "un-American descent into ideology" that sullied the "purities of the novel." In *Barbary Shore* Mailer was for the first time in his career truly experimenting with the received tradition of the American novel, and his experimentation, to use Richard Foster's apt distinction, was not an experimentation with form, in the manner of modernist novelists like James Joyce, but an experimentation with subject matter, in the tradition of D. H. Lawrence. Begun in Paris, while Mailer was studying at the Sorbonne under the G.I. Bill of Rights, *Barbary Shore,* in content, is an ideological novel more in the European than the American tradition, although its allegorical landscape may be reminiscent of Hawthorne and its amalgam of politics and dream akin to *The Blithedale Romance.* Through an atmosphere of political allusion, *Barbary Shore* implicitly atacks the dogged anti-ideological stance of *The Naked and the Dead,* with its freight of Dos Passos-like distancing devices, such as the "Time Machine" flashbacks and the playlet interludes. But if *Barbary Shore* is a novel concerned with ideology, it is also a novel in flight from ideology, at least from any institutionalized ideology associated with a particular party or any group outside the searching individual. Prophetically charged with the sense of political

2. "Norman Mailer: A Quest for Peril," in *A World More Attractive* (New York: Horizon Press, 1963), p. 124.

romance that becomes so important in America during the 1960s, *Barbary Shore* is Mailer's first attempt to bring together his interests in both politics and psychology. In *Advertisements For Myself* he will describe this imaginative synthesis as an effort to build a bridge between Marx and Freud. In *Barbary Shore* neither politics nor art can exist apart from the individual's engagement with them. Mailer is not pessimistic about the inclusiveness of art that fueled *The Naked and the Dead* as it fueled the work of Dos Passos, Farrell, and Steinbeck; but he does reject the bland assumption that the novelist's vision will triumph.

From *Barbary Shore* onward Mailer attempts to merge his ideological and philosophical interests with the more anti-intellectual tradition of American naturalism, bringing together the meditative European intellectual with the craftless American *naïf*, Malraux's scholar-adventurer with Faulkner's stay-at-home social criticism, Fitzgerald's innocence, and Hemingway's commitment to unmeditated action. In 1951 Mailer said to Harvey Breit, "I don't think of myself as a realist," and he shied comically away from "that terrible word" *naturalism*.[3] Mailer's own interpretation of "naturalism," as it develops through his work, tends to view the novel as social solipsism rather than social panorama, a private vision each of us has of our world (as he later says in *Of a Fire on the Moon*), rather than the aggressively "objective" picture promised by many other American novelists. Instead of narrative detachment and an encyclopedic effort to encompass American life, with *Barbary Shore* Mailer begins to develop his own more subjective mixture of description and metaphysic, social criticism and personal reference, journalism and fantasy. A Marxist analysis of society could stand in the wings behind the naturalistic novel, but Mailer wanted also to include Freud, to emphasize the actor beneath the makeup, the imaginative and psychological effects of ideology. Individual novelists might have political interests and individual novels might spring from a radical or Marxian critique of American society. But until *Barbary Shore* (unless one counts the Hearn–Cummings sections of *The Naked and the Dead*) ideology was one thing in America and literature was something quite different. Mailer authenticates the place of ideological controversy in American literature, not because he is the first to use political themes, but because he fuses these

3. *The Writer's Art* (Cleveland and New York: World, 1956), p. 199.

themes with the psychological preoccupations that had distinguished American romance from the English and European social novel in the nineteenth century. From *Barbary Shore* on, thinking, ruminating, and philosophizing become an essential characteristic of Mailer's work, whether it appears in the form of non-fiction or fiction.

Although *The Naked and the Dead* exhibits naturalistic methods, it contains the seeds of Mailer's later revisions of naturalism. The older optimism in the American novel about the ability of the writer to encompass society has fled with the individual-destroying fatalities of global war. On the Pacific island of Anopopei, in *The Naked and the Dead,* the broad American experience has been funneled into a limited situation that allows little room for the strivings of human will. Mailer remarks in *Advertisements For Myself* that since World War II only three writers have attempted what every American novelist until the war had accepted as his necessity and his birthright—to encompass the variety and complexity of society. The three writers Mailer has in mind are James Jones (*From Here to Eternity, Some Came Running*), Joseph Heller (*Catch-22*), and William Burroughs (*Naked Lunch*). Of these three, writes Mailer, only Jones has made the attempt in the old realistic style; both Heller and Burroughs have chosen or been forced by the cultural climate to choose styles of fantasy and exaggeration. Mailer himself will make a similar decision in *An American Dream* (1964) —the decision that comicbook paranoia and melodramatic excess more clearly mirror the present realities of the American experience than either the careful social explorations of Henry James or the homey, nation-spanning detail of Dos Passos, Farrell, and Steinbeck.

In *An American Dream* Mailer simultaneously explores and parodies the desire of the naturalistic novelist to take the measure of America by nomadically searching for the national experience as a short-order cook in California, a gas station attendant in Alabama, a fire-spotter in Washington, and an advertising copywriter in New York. Literary naturalism often assumed that the sociological make-up of society was a key to problems of self-definition within the individual. The true life of a nation could be found in the interminglings of class and job. But Mailer characterizes almost all of his heroes as men who attempt to fulfill several jobs or social roles, cutting across the conventional divisions of society. Stephen Rojack, in *An American Dream,* prides himself on being the only university professor of existential psychology who is also a television personality as well as an ex-congressman. D.J., the young Texan who is the narrator of *Why Are We In Viet Nam?*, continually brings up the possibility that he is actually the ventriloquist's dummy of a Negro in Harlem. To deepen this sense of variety and apparent contradiction within individuals, Mailer's heroes often have polyglot, polynational backgrounds. O'Shaugnessy is not Sergius's real last name, "but something which sounded close in Slovene." Mailer's long digression in *Of a Fire on the Moon* about the various national backgrounds of his wives and what he has learned from them seems a conscious attempt to supply himself with the varieties of experience he gives to his characters.

In older terms, the pluralistic background and vocation of such characters might make make them paradigmatic Americans. But Mailer emphasizes instead the uncertainty, the lack of coherent identity, involved in having such a nature. After the detached omniscience of *The Naked and the Dead,* in the later works it is Mailer's heroes who have become his narrators. For the easily accessible past of *The Naked and the Dead,* Mailer in *Barbary Shore* substitutes a world in which the past and its meaning are uncertain. To describe this world he creates a narrator, Mikey Lovett, who may have been in the war but has lost his memory and who, like Sergius O'Shaugnessy in *The Deer Park,* Stephen Rojack in *An American Dream,* and D.J. in *Why Are We In Viet Nam?,* must make or remake himself, discovering both his past and his character in the process. Lovett's disjointed situation in the Brooklyn rooming house that furnishes the setting of *Barbary Shore* arises in great part from political disillusionment; the Marxian truth in history has failed to heal the fragmented self by its merely theoretic continuities. Ideology had promised a support outside the self that has turned out to be totally illusory.

Mailer's solution to this dilemma seems to be a recommitment to defining the novelist's task and achieving that task through art. Mikey Lovett is trying to write a novel, which he describes as a mountain, perhaps an allusion to the mountain the patrol must climb in *The Naked and the Dead.* The balm for the pains of political disillusionment will be Lovett's finished novel. When the events of *Barbary Shore* have worked themselves out, Lovett feels not that he can act politically but that he can write again. Ideology therefore seems to pull in one direction while professional craft pulls in the other, the former pointing toward the more encompassing and inclusive continuities that lie in the ideological interpretation of history, the latter discovering a reconciliation of the divergent impulses toward politics and psychology in the creative act itself. But such a reconciliation is possible only for the author *of Barbary Shore* and not for the author *in Barbary Shore*. Mailer's heroes tend to be either frustrated writers, like Lovett or Sergius, or partially successful ones, like Rojack or D.J. More often than not they are also orphans, and frequently impotent. Sam Slovoda, the failed writer who is the central character in the short story "The Man Who Studied Yoga," uses a friend's blue movie to help recharge his own and his wife's sex life. No matter what their small success, Mailer's heroes are essentially bottled up, doomed by their own weaknesses and inadequacies to use their creativity with little effect. But the creative potential does persist in such characters, however repressed it may be. After the overpowering fatality of *The Naked and the Dead,* in which accident seems to dominate human affairs totally, Mailer, in *Barbary Shore,* makes the first of many affirmations of the power of human will. But these affirmations are imaged, paradoxically enough, in this and later novels by a weak and fallible central character and in his so-called journalism by the comic device of a narrator named "Norman Mailer."

The two largest stumbling blocks in the way of deeper appreciation of Mailer's work—personal reference and ideological polemic —are therefore tugged into position by Mailer himself. Typically he is indicted for too much autobiography in his nonfiction and too much ideology in his fiction. But Mailer in fact controls these two important elements in his work by a romantic irony that involves self-consciousness first about the position of the writer and then about the individual created work. Through a fascination with the examples of Fitzgerald and Hemingway, he has expanded this self-consciousness into a preoccupation with the nature of the artistic career reminiscent of Spenser's and Milton's preoccupation with the career of Vergil. Unlike these earlier writers, however, he has not been concerned with the grandeur of the life of the artist but with the failures and evasions, small pleasures and hard-wrung successes, that make up the life of the literary artist in America. In a review of *Advertisements For Myself,* Gore Vidal quotes Stephen Spender on the way England and America treat their writers: "The difference in England is that they *want* us to

be distinguished, to be good." [4] Mailer has made the difficulties of
being a writer in America one of his most powerful themes because
he has seen its inseparable relation to the difficulties of being a
human being in America, filling contradictory roles, being asked
to believe contradictory things. Self-consciousness has always been
Mailer's way of dealing with literary tradition. His decision to
write in what resembles a personal voice expresses a particularly
literary self-consciousness rather than the arch candor of the confessional writer or the mannered innocence of the *naïf* so often
imitated by Hemingway. When Steven Marcus asked Mailer in
1963, "What writers have you learned the most from, technically?"
Mailer answered with seeming perversity, "E. M. Forster, I suppose." Then he explained: ". . . in some funny way Forster gave
my notion of personality a sufficient shock that I could not manage
to write in the third person. Forster after all had a developed view
of the world. I did not. I think I must have felt at the time as if
I would never be able to write in the third person until I developed
a coherent view of life. I don't know that I've been able to altogether." [5]

The moment in Mailer's career that seems to have turned him
toward exploration of the uses of the first person in both fiction
and nonfiction occurred in the middle 1950s, after the comparative
critical failure of *Barbary Shore,* with the editorial clashes over his
revisions of *The Deer Park* and a series of columns he wrote for
the *Village Voice.* Both experiences allowed him to expose and
nurture the varieties of self-awareness as writer and man that would
later appear in *Advertisements For Myself* (1959). Through *The
Deer Park* conflicts he discovered the insubstantiality of his previ-
ous ideas about the life of a writer in America, ever subject to
the commercialism that lay beneath a mask of detached profes-
sionalism. In the *Village Voice* he first explored a journalistic form
that could, as he would say later in *Of a Fire on the Moon,* emphasize the perceptions of an individual confronting events. Thus
at the same time that he was personally upset by what he considered
to be the faithlessness of his publishers, he was able to discover a
kind of strength in exposing the weaknesses that he felt. Under

4. "Norman Mailer: The Angels are White," in *Rocking the Boat* (Boston:
Little, Brown and Company, 1962), pp. 165–66.
5. See below, p. 30.

the pressure of such events, his sense of the role of the writer in America gradually shifted. He discovered that his private problems could also serve as his public themes. In *Advertisements For Myself,* Hemingway and Fitzgerald have become alternative possibilities: Hemingway never achieving any self-consciousness that could be used in his work, finally letting his personality stand as a creation superior to his work; Fitzgerald learning self-consciousness through weakness and failure after early success; both writers either directly or circuitously ending in self-destruction, unable to find in either personality or self-consciousness a renewal of creative energy.

Mailer's choosing to write *Advertisements For Myself,* to put himself at the center of his work, corresponds, therefore, to a crisis in his definition of the direction of his work. In 1957 a "biblio-biographical" study had said of Mailer: "Described as confident but modest in manner, he has a distaste for personal publicity." [6] But in *Advertisements For Myself* autobiography and personal publicity become the means to a meditation on the meaning of his own life that Mailer believes every reader could write for himself: "Let others profit by my unseemly self-absorption, and so look to improve their own characters." *Advertisements For Myself* makes Mailer's own life and career a laboratory for his examination of American life. In it and in his later works he carries on a gradually developing exploration of himself as a paradigmatic American personality (in the same way that every American sees himself to be typical) but with little self-congratulation. The harsh clarity of Mailer's self-examination is mitigated only by the wry humor he pokes at his own pretensions, a rich and mellow wit that receives its fullest expression in *The Armies of the Night.* Lacking such saving self-consciousness, a character like Stephen Rojack in *An American Dream* needs violent action to regain his sense of himself, murdering his wife Deborah, who has been "the armature for [his] ego." Rojack expresses the emptiness that Mailer finds in the Hemingwayesque hero of solitude, for whom action takes the place of understanding. Rojack has never been able to integrate the two. *An American Dream* has been frequently attacked because of its surface similarity to Mailer's personal life (his 1961 stabbing of his wife during a party and his subsequent seventeen-day imprisonment in Bellevue for observation) and its seeming approval of

6. Robin Nelson Downes, "A Biblio-biographical study of Norman Mailer," unpublished Ph.D. dissertation, Tallahassee, Florida State University, 1957, p. 14.

Rojack's murder of Deborah. But, as Leo Bersani points out in the article reprinted below, *An American Dream* is palpably Rojack's version of things.[7] Amid a fantastic urban landscape, *An American Dream* is an allegory of the self adrift in a technological society manipulated by mysterious powers. The extremity of the murder indicates the depth of nonentity Rojack has been reduced to by his frantic urge to fulfill all the most prestigious roles in American society.

The critical attack against the "egotism" of Mailer's work may be in fact the projection of a belief that the self is one of the most trivial topics for literature, inferior especially to the social world that preoccupied the great nineteenth-century novels. But Mailer is fascinated with the dialectic between faceless destiny and individual will, whether destiny be the capricious island world of *The Naked and the Dead* or the interlocking directorate of power in *An American Dream*. Action, for Mailer, is something stolen from necessity, even in the face of human weakness.

In the 1960s Mailer was also developing his ideas of the "existential," discussed by George Schrader in the essay reprinted below.[8] As Mailer writes elsewhere, he wanted to take the first step inside his fear and follow a mystique of action akin to that in Martin Buber's *Tales from the Hasidim*, about which he wrote several articles for *Commentary* in 1961, drawing in one the conclusion that ". . . one only learns from situations in which the end is not known." [9] Similarly, Rojack's extreme actions in *An American Dream* force him to respond in a new way to new situations. From the determinisms of society and the self he attempts to steal a personal freedom defined by its source in the secret parts of the psyche, in magic and the supernatural, and in a vital relation to one's own body. Rojack's early predilection for anal intercourse had exposed the void his personality was built upon. Mailer's iconography replaces the navel with the rectum as a symbol of destructive self-involvement; in his Donnean metaphors the kiss *sub cauda* and traffic with the Devil characterize the self-involvement that leads to social power. As Mailer once said, "One should dig deep within oneself to find out his own nature. But you can't dig down too far

7. See below, pp. 120–26.
8. See below, pp. 82–95.
9. "Responses and Reactions, IV," *The Presidential Papers* (New York: G. P. Putnam's Sons, 1963), p. 197.

or you'll come out your own asshole." True sexuality and true virtue reside in relation. "Rather think of Sex as Time, and Time as the connection of new circuits," says Sergius at the end of *The Deer Park.* At a recent discussion of women's liberation, Diana Trilling accused Mailer of arguing for the unconditioned life in all his works, stopping only at one point, the biological nature of women. Mailer responded that of course he believed in biological necessity, for both men and women, but he also believed that necessity could be fought against, and that anything won from it entailed loss as well as gain.[10]

"Elizabeth and I think you're the best journalist in America," says Robert Lowell to Mailer in *The Armies of the Night,* and that remark mirrors the sigh of relief with which critics in the 1960s turned to Mailer's journalism after they had dismissed his fiction. (In fact, Elizabeth Hardwick, Lowell's wife, had been one of the severest reviewers of *An American Dream.*) Such remarks often implied that there were two Mailers: a terrible novelist and a fine journalist. But the personal journalism that begins with his coverage of the 1960 Democratic convention and the first Patterson-Liston fight—both included in *The Presidential Papers* (1963)—is intricately related to his fiction. In the personal journalism Mailer explores from another angle problems like those posed in *Advertisements for Myself*: how does an American writer follow his craft and grow within it? what is the nature of American character and American society and how can both best be given fictional life? These early assortments of reporting and semi-autobiography, which prepare the way for the subtle perspective on events in *The Armies of the Night,* contain a central character named "Mailer," a writer attempting to create a career and an identity for himself within both the public world of the American present and the American literary tradition. "Existential" difficulties for Mailer's fictional characters lead to journalism for himself because Mailer has returned by a longer route to test once again the possibility, which seemed lost in *Barbary Shore,* that an understanding of history might bring the fragments of the self together. But this new public world is not shaped by Marxian his-

10. For an account of this evening, see "What happened to Mozart's sister?" by Rosalyn Drexler and "Sexism—a better show than sex" by Frederic Morton in *The Village Voice,* May 6, 1971, pp. 28, 70, 72, 75.

tory. It is shaped by a history defined through the sense of time and connection that Sergius celebrates at the end of *The Deer Park*; and Mailer will attack the use of LSD in *The Armies of the Night* because it "tears holes in time."

Mailer chooses journalism because it offers the most satisfying mixture of participation and detachment. He never really "gives the news." His recent essay on the Ali–Frazier fight, "King of the Hill," first published in *Life,* is perhaps the closest to the event of any writing he has done, and perhaps as a result is the least digested and most perfunctorily "philosophical" of his reportage. At its best, and it is frequently on that level, Mailer's journalism is his own reaction, always a little earlier than anyone else's, to the emphasis on the validity of personal experience that in the 1960s brought the Left in America closer to the more libertarian and antigovernmental Right than to the corporate and rational liberal Middle. Mailer's search for an authentic point of view in his journalism, as well as his search for an authentic connection to his past and his traditions, is an attempt to make some relation between the individual and the nation. In the early 1960s John F. Kennedy became a kind of hero for Mailer, despite Kennedy's old-fashioned New Deal politics, because Mailer believed that Kennedy's personal style bridged the American gap between the politician and the movie star. In *The Presidential Papers,* published only a few weeks before Kennedy's assassination, Mailer takes semiseriously the American myth that anyone can become President, and constructs an anthology of advice to the President. But Mailer's presidential advisor is more Falstaff than MacGeorge Bundy or Arthur Schlesinger, Jr. By the time he runs an actual political campaign (to seek the New York Democratic mayoralty nomination in 1969), Mailer's literary sense of always standing to one side, even at the moments of greatest assertiveness, yields the campaign slogan "Power to the Neighborhoods" and the platform promise to make New York City the fifty-first state. After Kennedy's assassination and the loss of hope in any integration between the individual and public history, Mailer turns away from the public centers of power to the local enclaves where private desires may have some hope of being achieved.

Mailer's journalism plays most heavily on the secret enmities in the old naturalistic entente between observer and detail. His factual material, such as the documents of *The Armies of the Night* or the technical information in *Of a Fire on the Moon,* is neither a correlative nor an authentication of his perspective. It becomes instead a base on which he builds his own interpretation of the meaning of the events he describes, not as a congeries of otherwise isolated facts, but as part of both a historical tradition and a personal metaphysic. "Mailer" within events becomes both our surrogate and our scapegoat, taking risks and exposing personal foolishness and fallibility that no reader would dare reveal. Through such self-exposure Mailer comes to understand both the external events themselves as well as the place of the individual consciousness within a society where such events can occur and within a history grown irremediably complex. *The Armies of the Night* gains much of its power from the perfect melding of the public author and the private foolish individual, the public event and the limited individual perspective. All of Mailer's impotent and weak heroes culminate for a moment in this "Norman Mailer," whose double consciousness, as detached author and participating actor, can understand the Pentagon march, both in its immediacy and its history, its moment-to-moment nature and its ultimate meaning.

Ever since *Barbary Shore* Mailer has explored the problem of point of view, which he calls "the strongest lever in all of literature." His fiction explores point of view through the first-person narrator; his journalism attempts the perhaps more complex task of creating for each occasion a new personal voice that yet has distinct ties to earlier perspectives: the Historian and the Beast in *The Armies of the Night,* the Reporter in *Miami and the Siege of Chicago* (1969) Aquarius in *Of a Fire on the Moon* (1970), and, with a self-parodying flourish, the FNPW (False Nobel Prize Winner), the Acolyte, the Prisoner, and the Advocate in *The Prisoner of Sex* (1971). The meaning of events, he implies, is more accessible to one who has known the taint of involvement and partiality than to the detached observer. As he says in *The Armies of the Night,* the best account of an event will come from "an eyewitness who is a participant but not a vested partisan . . . an egotist of the most startling misproportions, outrageously and often unhappily self-aggressive, yet in command of a detachment classic in severity . . . such egotism being two-headed, thrusting itself forward the better to study itself." Georg Lukács, in *The Historical Novel,* argues that in *A Tale of Two Cities* Charles Dickens implies that the only answer to history is a retreat into the isolation of private life rather than an exploration of the connection between individuals that an understanding of history could bring. But in Mailer's work the continuing exploration of the vitality of the private self is a cleansing process that must occur before or even while history is being engaged; an understanding of the prejudices and complacencies of the self can furnish an energy toward history rather than an escape from it.

Mailer's fictional themes influence his journalism through their preoccupation with the split in the American character between public demands and private necessities: in terms of a character like Sergius O'Shaugnessy, to fulfill a role, find a job, or, alternatively, to bring out what is most creative and valuable in one's inner nature. The American character, in Mailer's view, is torn between these two possibilities of self-definition; in literary terms, it might be expressed as a conflict between journalism and romance. But in the twentieth century, Mailer implies, there is no longer any possibility of a Thoreauvian retreat. Stephen Rojack can go to Guatemala and Yucatan only as part of a fantasy solution; Mailer himself must turn to a deeper exploration of the possibilities of the world around him. Each individual, he implies, must steal something from the fear of what lies outside himself. Paradoxically, in the face of its "objective" billing, Mailer's journalism actually serves to develop his sense that the main business of the novel is exploration of the defects and beauties of character. Public and private pressures on individual character move together in Mailer's eye in the same way as many other seemingly opposed concepts.

It is in fact very difficult to discuss Mailer's work without mentioning his fondness for antinomies or simple opposites—for example, the conceptual pairs mentioned above, the Stevensonian linking of such characters as D.J. and his friend "Tex" Hyde in *Why Are We In Viet Nam?*, and, by extension, Mailer's own efforts to merge journalism and fiction in his literary nature. Richard Poirier, in his review of *Of a Fire on the Moon,* reprinted below,[11] argues that many of these antinomies have been overworked by Mailer in his exploration of American "schizophrenia." But it is difficult to deny their frequent power. *The Armies of the Night* marks the first concerted exploration of these themes of doubleness

11. See below, pp. 167–74. See also Richard Gilman's review of *The Armies of the Night* below, pp. 158–66.

in Mailer's work. The book itself falls into two parts: first, the experiences of "Norman Mailer," the reluctant activist and catalytic clown, who is rejected by the very situations he helps create; and then, the flatter and more traditionally reportorial view of the preparations for the Pentagon march, presided over by Dave Dellinger, who must mediate between the various groups on the Left, as well as between the marchers and the government. All three of Mailer's books of reportage—*The Armies of the Night, Miami and the Siege of Chicago,* and *Of a Fire on the Moon*—move between event and background, impression and detail, to work out themes of contradiction or dialectic that are replicated in Mailer's own point of view. *The Prisoner of Sex* acts as a coda to this trilogy because it asserts what has been implicit all through them: the primacy of the writer who attempts, however subjectively, to understand the world around him and convey to his audience some sense of its complexity.

The interplay between Mailer's fictional and nonfictional work satisfied his need for a realistic base while releasing him for more melodramatic and fantastic speculations. To complement his discovery of new creative power in this interplay, he was also building a new style. The first inklings of it come in the final sections of *The Deer Park* and in a few places in *Advertisements for Myself,* where Mailer first explores the themes the style is meant to express. But it appears full-blown only with *The Presidential Papers*. It is long-line, sinuously rippling, filled with reference and allusion, very different from the more clipped and spare manner of his earlier work. Paradoxically enough, as Hemingway begins to fascinate Mailer more and more as one type of the American author, Mailer's own style departs further and further from Hemingway's parataxis. Instead it moves toward a hypotactic style more characteristic of Hawthorne, Faulkner, or the Robert Penn Warren of *All the King's Men,* a style that is unsure of the meaning it searches for, rather than a style, like that of more realistic writers, that contains meaning and dispenses it in tight droplets. Mailer's new style implies that much less is known than the clarity of naturalistic description assumes. Metaphors are picked up, their uses assayed, and then they are discarded for more appropriate ones. Language becomes a medium for meaning rather than merely a convention to be rendered as transparently as possible. In some sense, it is not a new style, but a style that Mailer is creating, a style continually aware of the process that creates it.

Secured by this increasingly metaphysical style, Mailer faces concrete detail with a more balanced perspective. Whereas one learned something about the psyches and interrelations of several characters in *Barbary Shore* and *The Deer Park,* one also learns quite a lot about police operations in *An American Dream,* and guns and bear-hunting in *Why Are We In Viet Nam?* The description of the Republican conventioneers in *Miami and the Siege of Chicago* might easily fit into a "Camera Eye" section from Dos Passos's *U.S.A.* In *Of a Fire on the Moon* the first sections deal primarily with Mailer's philosophic response to the vast technology needed to put the moon rocket into the air; he also examines the possible heroic qualities of the astronauts. The tone here is speculative and metaphoric. In the second, much larger section that retraces the flight Mailer adds the hard ballast of factual information. Both detail and metaphor, observation and meditation, are needed for the final synthesis; each protects against the exaggerations of the other. The final, elegiac section of the book, in which Mailer goes to Provincetown—his marriage falling around him—includes a description of the burial of a car on the beach. The burial party can uneasily represent a victory of humanity over technology. But Mailer's own need to absorb the details of the space flight have put him out of the mood for such Luddite victories. He returns to Houston to look at a piece of moon rock the astronauts have brought back. There he feels a sense of communion with the rock, a communion with the magic of the moon that has in fact been allowed and achieved by technology. Another seeming antinomy has been bridged by the writer's openness to both direct experience and detached meditation.

The heroes of Mailer's novels tend to escape from the conflicts of being American. But in his "own" voice Mailer defines himself within an American context as an "accessible" writer, the novelist and journalist of immediacy, not closeted in some remote literary world, but present to attack and be attacked in his turn. Personal style becomes the vehicle of a literary sensibility that constantly engages events, and the difficulty of these engagements becomes one of the most important subjects the style expresses. After the "comic hero" of *The Armies of the Night,* for example, the narrator of *Miami and the Siege of Chicago* (once again a book cast in two parts) calls himself "the Reporter," to gain some kind of role at the Republican and Democratic conventions of 1968. But this "Reporter" is constantly berating himself for missing the good story, even while he pretends to give journalistic advice. In fact, the theme of the first section of *Miami and the Siege of Chicago* is concealment, spying, and loss of identity. Not sure about his own beliefs, Mailer constantly poses in the theatrical Miami of the convention. He even finds himself liking Richard Nixon, because of Nixon's daughters, and getting tired of Negro rights, because Reverend Ralph Abernathy is late for a press conference. The most compelling image of this confusion is the accident by which Mailer, with a stern expression on his face and hands clasped firmly behind his back, sneaks into a Nixon reception, mistaken, he thinks, for a plainclothesman.

In Chicago Mailer is forced to define his beliefs more sharply because the forces let loose there are nominally those radical impulses he has supported throughout his career. But in his typical penchant for opposites, he is as put off by the radicals as he was attracted by the Republicans. He is filled with the uneasiness of what he calls a "Left Conservative" at the prospect of joining the Chicago radicals in Lincoln Park. He is afraid when the police chase the demonstrators; he makes up elaborate plans to reconcile the demonstrators and the more liberal delegates, but they are never realized. Mailer accepts finally that all his action has served only to salve his own conscience; without at least a moiety of political sense he can accomplish nothing. Instead of having a journalistic control over events, with ready-made meaning yielding easily to his analysis, Mailer defines his point of view through a rendering of the actual confusions of the events. He seems finally to accept the demonstrators as his own people only after they tell him that he need not make excuses for not participating in a march because it's his job to write instead. In its panorama of different kinds of Americans, *Miami and the Siege of Chicago* may come closer than any of Mailer's works since *The Naked and the Dead* to a total vision of society. Mailer's America is inclusive, not exclusive. It has no "real self" encrusted with bad habits or bad heredity. Only the formulaic views of America are wrong. From *The Presidential Papers* on, Mailer indicts American "schizo-

phrenia." But his growing counterassumption and undertheme, as
Michael Cowan argues in the article printed below,[12] is that schizophrenia rightly understood can be health rather than disease, a
dialectic of renewal rather than a deadend of hateful contraries.
A bitter-sweet patriotism scents all of Mailer's journalism; as he
says in *Miami and the Siege of Chicago,* ". . . he loathed the
thought of living anywhere but in America." In his vision of
America, "the Nijinsky of ambivalence," as he calls himself at the
end of *Of a Fire on the Moon,* has half-found and half-created an
arena capacious enough for his imagination.

In parts of *Of a Fire on the Moon,* however, and especially in the
short "King of the Hill," the vitality of journalism for further
defining Mailer's themes seems to have run dry. In many places
the language does not flow; it is wrung out. *The Prisoner of Sex*
shows Mailer's awareness of this deficiency. It furnishes what I have
called a coda to the three journalistic works because it concentrates
on what Mailer believes is worthwhile in his own point of view,
beyond the specific positions he holds—cranky, persuasive, or idi-
otic as they may be. Many critics have wondered why *The Prisoner
of Sex* devotes so much space to an attack on Kate Millett's *Sexual
Politics.* Mailer obviously makes this choice because her literary
attack stings so much more than any ideological attack. He is more
eager to defend his right to create characters who hold specific
beliefs he does not have than he is to defend any particular belief.
Interestingly enough, his strongest defense of his position is not
his defense of himself, but his defense of D. H. Lawrence. Here
Mailer focuses not only on the relation between a writer's life and
his work, but also on the ways ideology and fiction can mix.

Mailer has been overtly interested in the problems of fiction
since his earliest writings, and his remarks about Lawrence in *The
Prisoner of Sex* remind one what a brilliant critic he has frequently
been. But it is precisely this concern for craft that has escaped the
attention of many of his critics. Blinded by his polemical style,
many do not pause to examine what he is polemical about. They
are content to condemn his manner, without perceiving that it
springs from a belief that a novel or a film or any work of art
should have the potential to change the reader's life. Such a commitment to the power of art has impelled his whole career. Follow-

12. See below, pp. 143–57.

ing his sense of what is most appropriate to a particular situation, Mailer has often catered to what is worst in his audience even while he has tried to make them more sensitive to the nuances of his work. The two may be inexorably connected, for his invention of and grappling with his public self have allowed him insight into the cultural movement of America since World War II that few writers have shown and fewer still have expressed with the same style, wit, and grace. This may be a good moment to take a long-range look at his career, for the end of a period seems to have been reached. The large novel Mailer has promised for some many years may finally be gestating. And perhaps, with the journalistic method so richly ransacked now behind him, Norman Mailer will become once again, if he ever could, that young author of *The Naked and the Dead* who told an interviewer in *The New Yorker*:

> I think it's much better when people who read your book don't know anything about you, even what you look like. I have refused to let *Life* photograph me. Getting your mug in the papers is one of the most shameful ways of making a living. But there aren't many ways of making a living that aren't shameful.[13]

This collection of essays makes no final statement about Mailer's achievement as a whole. It merely takes what I believe is a propitious moment in the midst of his career to make a preliminary assessment of what he has accomplished. Because Mailer is a constantly changing writer, whose works have a powerful and complex effect on his readers, many aspects of his work have received little critical attention beyond a few allusions or a few paragraphs. The essays, reviews, and articles that follow represent a substantial opportunity for deeper appreciation. I have chosen them in an effort to give some idea of the total critical response to Mailer, both in immediacy and at long range. Although an essay, and especially a review, will often show the bones of its particular moment of composition, I think such contemporaneity is an essential part of any true picture of Mailer either as writer or as cultural figure. The first selection is a long interview with Mailer, conducted by Steven Marcus, that reveals more clearly than many subsequently published interviews the creative and philosophical impulses behind Mailer's work. Then follows an essay by Diana Trilling that was

13. *New Yorker*, 24, no. 35 (October 23, 1948), 25.

one of the first to bring his work into critical perspective; although it was written more than ten years ago, the Trilling essay is remarkably acute in its delineation of the themes that Mailer would later develop with more complexity.[14] The next two articles, by James Baldwin and George Schrader, form a kind of critical diptych in their focus on Mailer's essay "The White Negro," first printed in *Dissent*, that prompted the critical hostility to Mailer so common in the 1960s before the publication of *The Armies of the Night*. Each of these studies errs in its own way, Baldwin's toward the personal and Schrader's toward the abstract; but together they strengthen each other. Baldwin's final paragraphs deserve to be classic: they are a brief and effective rebuke to those critics liable to confuse literary gossip with criticism.

After these essays I have placed some more immediate responses to Mailer's work. First is a long review of *Advertisements for Myself*, in which F. W. Dupee assesses Mailer within the tradition of American literature. Then I have selected three views of *An American Dream*, which has become a crux for so many of Mailer's critics: Stanley Edgar Hyman expresses some of the disdain verging on critical violence that the novel provoked; Leo Bersani sums up the novel's varied reception and makes some acute comments of his own; and John W. Aldridge uses the novel as a focus for a discussion of Mailer's work in general.

Then follow a group of essays in which the authors attempt to place Mailer's work in the context of other literature: Richard Foster writes a persuasive essay that makes sense of Mailer's many allusions to F. Scott Fitzgerald; Michael Cowan sets Mailer's writing in the context of American romanticism and finely analyzes the uses to which he has put his literary forebears. To preserve the openness that Mailer's work always demands of the reader, I have chosen as the final essays two reviews that show an enriched critical awareness of Mailer's achievement: Richard Gilman on *The Armies of the Night* and Richard Poirier on *Of a Fire on the Moon*.

14. I would like to have paired Diana Trilling's essay with Norman Podhoretz's "The Embattled Vision of Norman Mailer," which places a greater emphasis on Mailer's politics, but space limitations made that impossible. The essay is readily available as the introduction to the Grosset and Dunlap paperback edition of *Barbary Shore* (New York, 1963).

An Interview with Norman Mailer

by Steven Marcus

The interview took place on the afternoon of Saturday, July 6, 1963. The setting was Norman Mailer's Brooklyn Heights apartment, whose living room commands a panoramic view of lower Manhattan, the East River, and the New York harbor. The living room is fitted out with certain nautical or maritime furnishings and decorations, and Mailer, his curls unshorn, seemed at odd moments during the afternoon the novelist-as-ship-captain, though less Ahab than Captain Vere, and less both than Captain Shotover in ripe middle-age. Mailer had recently stopped smoking, and the absence of nicotine had caused him to put on weight, which he carries gracefully and with vigor; the new amplitude of flesh seems to have influenced his spirit in the direction of benignity.

Shortly after the interviewer arrived, Mailer excused himself for a few moments. He wanted to change, he said, into his writer's costume. He emerged wearing faded dungarees and an open-necked sport shirt. His sharp blue eyes sparkled as he suggested that the interviewer keep this fashion note in mind. Lunch was then prepared and served by Mailer in what must be called lordly fashion. In general, he conducts himself without affectation as a kind of secular prince. The interviewer was repeatedly struck during the course of a long afternoon's work by Mailer's manners, which were exquisite. The role of novelist-being-interviewed suits him very well.

INTERVIEWER. Do you need any particular environment in which to write?

MAILER. I like a room with a view, preferably a long view. I dislike looking out on gardens. I prefer looking at the sea, or ships, or anything which has a vista to it. Oddly enough, I've never worked in the mountains.

INTERVIEWER. Do you need seclusion?

MAILER. I don't know if I need seclusion, but I do like to be alone in a room.

INTERVIEWER. When did you first think of becoming a writer?

MAILER. That's hard to answer. I did a lot of writing when I was young.

INTERVIEWER. How young?

MAILER. Seven.

INTERVIEWER. A real novel?

MAILER. Well, it was a science fiction novel about people on Earth taking a rocket ship to Mars. The hero had a name which sounded like Buck Rogers. His assistant was called Dr. Hoor.

INTERVIEWER. Doctor . . . ?

MAILER. Dr. Hoor. WHORE, pronounced H-O-O-R. That's the way we used to pronounce whore in Brooklyn. He was patterned directly after Dr. Huer in Buck Rogers who was then appearing on radio. This novel filled two and a half paper notebooks. You know the type, about 7 × 10. They had soft shiny blue covers and they were, oh, only ten cents in those days, or a nickel. They ran to perhaps 100 pages each, and I used to write on both sides. My writing was remarkable for the way I hyphenated words. I loved hyphenating, so I would hyphenate "the" and make it th-e if it came at the end of the line. Or "they" would become the-y. Then I didn't write again for a long time. I didn't even try out for the high school literary magazine. I had friends who wrote short stories, and their short stories were far better than the ones I would write for assignments in high school English and I felt no desire to write. When I got to college I started again. The jump from Boys' High School in Brooklyn to Harvard came as a shock. I started reading some decent novels for the first time.

INTERVIEWER. You mentioned in *Advertisements For Myself* that reading *Studs Lonigan* made you want to be a writer.

MAILER. Yes. It was the best single literary experience I had had because the background of *Studs* was similar to mine. I grew up in Brooklyn, not Chicago, but the atmosphere had the same flatness of effect. Until then I had never considered my life or the life of the people around me as even remotely worthy of—well, I didn't believe they could be treated as subjects for fiction. It had never occurred to me. Suddenly I realized you could write about your own life.

INTERVIEWER. When did you feel that you were started as a writer?

MAILER. When I first began to write again at Harvard. I wasn't very good. I was doing short stories all the time, but I wasn't good. If there were fifty people in the class, let's say I was somewhere in the top ten. My teachers thought I was fair, but I don't believe they ever thought for a moment that I was really talented. Then in the middle of my sophomore year I started getting better. I got on the *Harvard Advocate,* and that gave me confidence, and about this time I did a couple of fairly good short stories for English A-1, one of which won *Story Magazine's* college contest for that year. I must say that Robert Gorham Davis, who was my instructor then, picked the story to submit for the contest and was confident it would win.

INTERVIEWER. Was that the story about Al Groot?

MAILER. Yes. And when I found out it had won—which was at the beginning of the summer after my sophomore year (1941)—well, that fortified me, and I sat down and wrote a novel. It was a very bad novel. I wrote it in two months. It was called *No Percentage.* It was just terrible. But I never questioned any longer whether I was *started* as a writer.

INTERVIEWER. What do you think were some of the early influences in your life? What reading, as a boy, do you recall as important?

MAILER. *The Amateur Gentleman* and *The Broad Highway* were glorious works. So was *Captain Blood.* I think I read every one of Farnol's books and there must be twenty of them. And every one of Sabatini's.

INTERVIEWER. Did you ever read any of them again?

MAILER. No, now I have no real idea of their merit. But I never enjoyed a novel more than *Captain Blood.* Nor a movie. Do you remember Errol Flynn as Captain Blood? Some years ago I was asked by a magazine what were the ten most important books in my development. The book I listed first was *Captain Blood.* Then came *Das Kapital.* Then *The Amateur Gentleman.*

INTERVIEWER. You wouldn't say that *Das Kapital* was boyhood reading?

MAILER. Oh, no, I read that many years later. But it had its mild influence.

INTERVIEWER. It's been said often that novelists are largely nostalgic for their boyhood, and in fact most novelists draw on their youthful experiences a great deal. In your novels, however, the evocation of scenes from boyhood is rare or almost absent.

MAILER. It's difficult to write about childhood. I never felt I understood it in any novel way. I never felt other authors did either. Not particularly. I think the portrait of childhood which is given by most writers is rarely true to anything more than the logic of their novel. Childhood is so protean.

INTERVIEWER. What about Twain, or Hemingway—who drew on their boyhoods successfully?

MAILER. I must admit they created some of the psychological reality of my own childhood. I wanted, for instance, to be like Tom Sawyer.

INTERVIEWER. Not Huck Finn?

MAILER. The magic of Huck Finn seems to have passed me by, I don't know quite why. *Tom Sawyer* was the book of Twain's I always preferred. I remember when I got to college I was startled to find that *Huckleberry Finn* was the classic. Of course I haven't looked at either novel in thirty years.

INTERVIEWER. Can you say something about your methods of working?

MAILER. They vary with each book. I wrote *The Naked and the Dead* on the typewriter. I used to write four days a week: Mondays, Tuesdays, Thursdays and Fridays.

INTERVIEWER. Definite hours?

MAILER. Yes, very definite hours. I'd get up about 8:00 or 8:30 and I'd be at work by 10:00. And I'd work till 12:30; then I'd have lunch. I'd get back to work about 2:30 or 3:00, and work for another two hours. In the afternoon I usually needed a can of beer to prime me. But I'd write for five hours a day. And I wrote a great deal. The average I tried to keep was seven typewritten pages a day, twenty-eight pages a week. The first draft took seven months, the second draft which really was only half a draft took four months. The part about the platoon went well from the beginning, but the Lieutenant and the General in the first draft were stock characters. If it had been published at that point the book would have been considered an interesting war novel with some good scenes, no more. The second draft was the bonus. Cummings and Hearn were done in the second draft. If you look at the book you can see that the style shifts, that the parts about Cummings and Hearn are written in a somewhat more developed vein. Less forceful but more articulated. And you can see something of the turn my later writing would take in the scenes between Cummings and Hearn.

INTERVIEWER. What methods did you pursue in your next books?

MAILER. Well, with *Barbary Shore*, I began to run into trouble. I started it in Paris about six months after I finished *The Naked and the Dead*, and did about fifty pages. It was then called *Mrs Guinevere* and was influenced by Sally Bowles in Isherwood's *Berlin Stories*. *Mrs Guinevere* never went anywhere. It stopped, just ground down after those first fifty pages. My novelistic tanks ran out of gas. I dropped it completely, thought I'd never pick it up again, and started to work on another novel. Did all the research, went to Indiana to do research.

INTERVIEWER. On what?

MAILER. On a labor novel. There was a union in Evansville with which I had connections. So I stayed for a few days in Indiana, and then went to Jamaica, Vermont, to write the novel. I spent four to six weeks getting ready to begin. I made a great push on the beginning, worked for two weeks, and quit cold. I didn't have the book. I didn't know a damned thing about labor unions. In desperation (I was full of second novel panic) I picked up *Mrs Guinevere* and looked at it. And found something there I could go on with. So I worked on it all through the spring of 1949, and then I moved out to Hollywood for the summer. I finished the second half in Hollywood. *Barbary Shore* is really a Hollywood novel. I think it reflected the impact of Hollywood on me in some subterranean fashion. Certainly the first draft is the wildest draft of the three; it's almost insane, and the most indigestible portions were written in the first couple of months I was in Hollywood. I never knew where the book was going, I had no idea where it was going to move from day to day. I'd wake up and push the typewriter in great dread, in literal terror, wondering when this curious and doubtful inspiration was going to stop. It never quite did. It ground along at the rate of three pages, three difficult pages a day. But I'd get it out. I got a first draft done, and was quite unhappy with it; it was a very bad book at that point. When I rewrote it later, in Provincetown, a summer later, again it went at the rate of three pages a day. This revision was different from the first draft, and I think much better. But working on *Barbary Shore* I always felt as if I were not writing the book myself, but rather as if I were serving as a subject for some intelligence which had decided to use me to write the book. It had nothing to do with whether the work was good or bad. It just had to do with the fact that I had absolutely no conscious control of it; if I hadn't heard about the unconscious I would have had to postulate one to explain this phenomenon. For the first time I became powerfully aware of the fact that I had an unconscious which seemed to have little to do with me.

INTERVIEWER. What about *The Deer Park*?

MAILER. For *The Deer Park* I didn't have much of a method. It was agony; it was far and away the most difficult of my three novels to write. The first and second drafts were written with the idea that they were only the first part of an eight-part novel. I think I used that enormous scheme as a pretext to get into the work. Apparently I just couldn't sit down and write a nice modest Hollywood novel. I had to have something grandiose, in conception, anyway. I started *The Deer Park* with "The Man Who Studied Yoga." That was supposed to be a prologue to all eight novels. It went along nicely and was done in a few weeks. And then I got into *The Deer Park*, and I forget what my methods were exactly; I think they varied. In the revision of *Barbary Shore* I had started working in longhand; as soon as I found myself blocked on the typewriter I'd shift to longhand. By the time I got to *The Deer Park* I was writing in longhand all the time. I'd write in longhand in the morning, and type up what I'd written in the afternoon. I was averaging about four-five pages a day, I think, three days a week; about fifteen pages a week. But I found it an unendurable book to write because I'd finish each day in the most profound depression; as I found out later it was even a physical depression. I was gutting my liver.

INTERVIEWER. It wasn't alcohol?

MAILER. No, I wasn't much of a drinker in those days. The liver, you see, is not unlike a car battery, and I was draining mine. I was writing with such anxiety and such fear and such distaste, and such gloom and such dissatisfaction that . . .

INTERVIEWER. Dissatisfaction with what?

MAILER. Oh, everything. My work, my life, myself. The early draft of *The Deer Park* was terrible. It had a few good things in it, but it was slow to emerge, it took years, and was stubborn. It still emerges. I mean, I could sit down today and rewrite *The Deer Park*. Of course, what was happening was that this work, such as it was, was continuing to move in a direction which was completely against the grain of my intellect—insofar as my intellect was developed, and had standards and tastes and attitudes toward the novel. I was working toward a novel utterly outrageous to my notion of things.

INTERVIEWER. Say it again?

MAILER. Well, I was a socialist after all, and I believed in large literary works which were filled with characters, and were programmatic, and had large theses, and were developed, let's say, like the Tolstoyan novel. It's as if, all proportion naturally being kept, as if Tolstoy had sat down with the intention of writing *Anna Karenina* and instead came out with *Crime and Punishment*. Obviously, it would have been intolerable for him, and he would have disliked *Crime and Punishment* very much. That was what was going on with me at a much lower level.

INTERVIEWER. How does the idea of a novel come to you?

MAILER. I don't know that it comes. A more appropriate image for me might be that I start with the idea of constructing a treehouse and end with a skyscraper made of wood.

INTERVIEWER. Well, how did the idea of *The Naked and the Dead* come to you?

MAILER. I wanted to write a short novel about a long patrol. All during the war I kept thinking about this patrol. I even had the idea before I went overseas. Probably it was stimulated by a few war books I had read: John Hersey's *Into the Valley*, Harry Brown's *A Walk in the Sun*, and a couple of others I no longer remember. Out of these books came the idea to do a novel about a long patrol. And I began to create my characters. All the while I was overseas a part of me was working on this long patrol. I even ended up in a reconnaissance outfit which I had asked to get into. A reconnaissance outfit, after all, tends to take long patrols. Art kept traducing life. At any rate, when I started writing *The Naked and the Dead* I thought it might be a good idea to have a preliminary chapter or two in which to give the reader a chance to meet my characters before they went on patrol. But the next six months and the first 500 pages went into that, and I remember in the early days I was annoyed at how long it was taking me to get to the patrol.

INTERVIEWER. Do you keep notes, or a journal, or diaries, or write scenarios? What's your preparatory material?

MAILER. That also varies with each of the books. For *The Naked and the Dead* I had a file full of notes, and a long dossier on each man. Many of these details never got into the novel, but the added knowledge made me feel more comfortable with each character. Indeed I even had charts to show which characters had not yet had scenes with other characters. For a book which seems spontaneous on its surface, *The Naked and the Dead* was written mechanically. I studied engineering at Harvard, and I suppose it was the book of a young engineer. The structure is sturdy, but there's no fine filigree to the joints. Just spot welding and riveting. And the working plan was very simple. I devised some preliminary actions for the platoon in order to give the reader an opportunity to get to know the men, but this beginning, as I said, took over two-thirds of the book. The patrol itself is also simple, but I did give more thought to working it out ahead of time.

INTERVIEWER. People have commented on the pleasure you seem to take in the military detail of *The Naked and the Dead.*

MAILER. Compared to someone like James Jones, I'm an amateur at military detail. But at that time I did like all those details. I even used to enjoy patrols, or at least I did when I wasn't sick with jungle rot and viruses or atabrine poisoning. I was one of the few men in the platoon who could read a map. I was the only enlisted man I know who really cared about reading a map and once I gave myself away. We used to have classes after a campaign was over; we'd come back to garrison—one of those tent cities out in a rice paddy—and they would teach us all over again how to read maps and read compasses, or they would drill us on the nomenclature of the machine gun for the eighth time. One day very bored, I was daydreaming, and the instructor pointed to a part of the map and said, "Mailer, what are these co-ordinates?" If I had had a moment to think I would never have answered, it was bad form to be bright in my outfit, but I didn't think: he caught me in a daze, and I looked up and said, "320.017 dash

146.814" and everyone's mouth dropped. It was the first time anybody
ever answered such a question thus briskly in the history of infantry
map reading. At any rate, that was the fun for me, the part about the
patrol. I suppose it had something to do with *Captain Blood* and *The
Amateur Gentleman* . . .

INTERVIEWER. How much of a plan did you have for *Barbary Shore?*

MAILER. None. As I indicated earlier, *Barbary Shore* just birthed itself
slowly. The book came out sentence by sentence. I literally never knew
where the next day's work was coming from.

INTERVIEWER. You don't mention (in your description of writing *Barbary
Shore*) anything about politics. Wasn't your *engagement* at the time a
considerable part of the plan?

MAILER. I think it was the unspoken drama in the working-up of the
book. I started *Barbary Shore* as some sort of fellow-traveler, and
finished with a political position which was a far-flung mutation of
Trotskyism. And the drafts of the book reflected these ideological
changes so drastically that the last draft of *Barbary Shore* is a different
novel altogether and has almost nothing in common with the first draft
but the names.

INTERVIEWER. Did Jean Malaquais (to whom the book is dedicated) have
much to do with this?

MAILER. Yes. He had an enormous influence on me. He's the only man
I know who can combine a powerfully dogmatic mind with the keenest
sense of nuance, and he has a formidable culture which seems to live
in his veins and capillaries. Since he also had a most detailed vision
of the Russian Revolution—he was steeped in it the way certain American families are imbued with the records of their clan—I spent a
year living more closely in the history of Russia from 1917 to 1937
than in the events of my own life. I doubt if I would even have gone
back to rewrite *Barbary Shore* if I didn't know Malaquais. Certainly
I could never have conceived McLeod. Malaquais, of course, bears no
superficial resemblance whatsoever to McLeod—indeed Malaquais was
never even a communist, he started as an anti-Stalinist, but he had a
quality when I first met him which was pure Old Bolshevik. One knew
that if he had been born in Russia, a contemporary of Lenin's, he
would have been one of the leaders of the Revolution and would
doubtless have been executed in the trials. So his personality—as it
filtered through the contradictory themes of my unconscious—inhabits
Barbary Shore.

INTERVIEWER. Would you care to discuss what you mean by the "contradictory themes" of your unconscious? Is that related to what you
said a little while ago about becoming aware of your unconscious while
writing *Barbary Shore?*

MAILER. *Barbary Shore* was built on the division which existed then in my mind. My conscious intelligence, as I've indicated, became obsessed by the Russian Revolution. But my unconscious was much more interested in other matters: murder, suicide, orgy, psychosis, all the themes I discuss in *Advertisements*. Since the gulf between these conscious and unconscious themes was vast and quite resistant to any quick literary coupling, the tension to get a bridge across resulted in the peculiar feverish hothouse atmosphere of the book. My unconscious felt one kind of dread, my conscious mind another, and *Barbary Shore* lives somewhere between. That's why its focus is so unearthly. And of course this difficulty kept haunting me from then on in all the work I did afterward. But it was a book written without any plan.

INTERVIEWER. And *The Deer Park?*

MAILER. That was different. There I had an idea of what I was going to do. I knew it was going to be a story about a most unhappy love. The problem was getting to the affair: I could hardly wait to reach it, especially because the early parts of the novel were so difficult to write. It is truly difficult to trap Hollywood in a novel. Only in the last draft did I finally get the setting the way I wanted it. I think now the setting is probably the best part. In fact I would judge that the first fifty pages of *The Deer Park* are the best writing I have ever done in fiction. But they were the hardest fifty pages of the book to write and certainly took the longest time.

INTERVIEWER. Do you have any superstitions about your methods of work?

MAILER. I wouldn't call them superstitions exactly. I just think it's bad to talk about one's present work, for it spoils something at the root of the creative act. It discharges the tension.

INTERVIEWER. What writers have you learned the most from, technically?

MAILER. E. M. Forster, I suppose. I wouldn't say he is necessarily one of the novelists I admire most. But I have learned a lot from him. You remember in *The Longest Journey* somewhere about the fourth chapter, you turn the page and read, "Gerald was killed that day. He was beaten to death in a football game." It was quite extraordinary. Gerald had been very important through the beginning of the book. But now that he was suddenly and abruptly dead, everyone else's character began to shift. It taught me that personality was more fluid, more dramatic and startling, more inexact than I had thought. I was brought up on the idea that when you wrote a novel you tried to build a character who could be handled and walked around like a piece of sculpture. Suddenly character seemed related more closely to the paintings of the new realists. For instance I saw one recently which had a painted girl reclining on a painted bed, and there was a television set next to her in the canvas, a real one which you could turn on. Turning on the literal factual set changes the girl and the painting both. Well, Forster gives you something of that sensation in his novels. I played with such a concept a great deal in *Barbary Shore* and I began to play with it in *The Deer Park* in an altogether different way. I suppose the concept was parallel to the 'Alexandria Quartet' in its preoccupations. When you tell the same story through the eyes of different characters, you have not only a different novel but a different reality. I think I could sit down today and write *The Deer Park* through Charles Francis Eitel's eyes, and if I changed the names and the place, no one might know the new book had anything to do with *The Deer Park*. I suppose what I realized, after reading Forster, was that a novel written in the third person was now impossible for me for many years.

INTERVIEWER. Forster has never written a novel in the first person.

MAILER. I know he hasn't, but in some funny way Forster gave my notion of personality a sufficient shock that I could not manage to write in the third person. Forster after all had a developed view of the world. I did not. I think I must have felt at that time as if I would never be able to write in the third person until I developed a coherent view of life. I don't know that I've been able to altogether.

INTERVIEWER. You know, Thackeray says at one point, that the novelist knows everything. He is like God, and this may be why he could write in the third person.

MAILER. God can write in the third person only so long as He understands His world. But if the world becomes contradictory or incomprehensible to Him, then God begins to grow concerned with his own nature. It's either that, or borrow notions from other Gods.

INTERVIEWER. Have you ever cribbed anything from other writers?

MAILER. Oh, you know, I have such a—what shall I say?—such a stuffy view of myself that I could never *conceive* of cribbing. But I have been *influenced* by—well, Farrell to begin with. Dos Passos, Steinbeck (I am trying to do it chronologically), Hemingway, and later Fitzgerald —much, much later. And Thomas Wolfe of course.

INTERVIEWER. But back to cribbing. Shakespeare cribs, for example. He never invented a plot.

MAILER. No, but my plots are always rudimentary. Whatever I've accomplished certainly does not depend on my virtuosity with plot. Generally I don't even have a plot. What happens is that my characters engage in an action, and out of that action little bits of plot sometimes adhere to the narrative. I never have to worry about lifting a plot, because I don't conceive of a book that way.

INTERVIEWER. In connection with plot, when did the idea of using a hornet's nest to thwart the climbers in *The Naked and the Dead* come to you?

MAILER. That idea was there before I wrote the first sentence of the book. Actually that incident happened to my reconnaissance platoon on the most ambitious patrol I ever took with them. They sent out thirty of us to locate and destroy one hundred Japanese marines who had gotten behind our lines. Well, we never found the marines, but we did get stuck climbing one hell of an enormous hill with a mean slimy trail, and when we were almost up to the ridge, somebody kicked over a hornet's nest. Half the platoon went tearing up the hill, and the machine gun squad went flying down to the valley. We never did find each other again that day. We just slunk back to our bivouac.

INTERVIEWER. Putting aside the fact that it happened, do you think in fact it was a satisfactory device? It seems to have bothered some people.

MAILER. I think I'd do it the same way again. War is disproportions, and the hornet's nest seemed a perfect disproportion to me. We were ready to lose our lives but we weren't up to getting stung by a hornet.

INTERVIEWER. Would you say something about style, prose style, in relation to the novel?

MAILER. A really good style comes only when a man has become as good as he can be. Style is character. A good style cannot come from a bad undisciplined character. Now a man may be evil, but I believe that people can be evil in their essential natures and still have good characters. Good in the sense of being well-tuned. They can have characters which are flexible, supple, adaptable, principled in relation to their own good or their own evil—even an evil man can have principles— he can be true to his own evil, which is not always so easy, either. I think good style is a matter of rendering out of oneself all the cupidities, all the cripplings, all the velleities. And then I think one has to develop one's physical grace. Writers who are possessed of some physical grace may tend to write better than writers who are physically clumsy. It's my impression this is so. I don't know that I'd care to attempt to prove it.

INTERVIEWER. Well, how would you describe your own style? I ask this question because certain critics have pointed to deficiencies in it, or what they think of as deficiencies. Didn't Diana Trilling, for instance, criticize certain flatnesses in your style?

MAILER. I think that flatness comes out of certain flatnesses in me. And in trying to overcome that flatness I may push too hard in the other direction. Alfred Kazin once said something very funny about the way I write: "Mailer is as fond of his style as an Italian tenor is of his vocal cords."

INTERVIEWER. Have you ever written to merely improve your writing, practiced your writing as an athlete would work out?

MAILER. No. I don't think it's a proper activity. That's too much like doing a setting-up exercise; any workout which does not involve a certain minimum of danger or responsibility does not improve the body—it just wears it out.

INTERVIEWER. In writing your novels, has any particular formal problem given you trouble—let's say a problem of joining two parts of a narrative together, getting people from point A to point B.

MAILER. You mean like getting them out of a room? I think formal problems exist in inverse proportion to one's honesty. You get to the problem of getting someone out of the room when there's something false about the scene.

INTERVIEWER. Do you do any research or special reading to prepare for writing a novel, or while you're writing a novel?

MAILER. Occasionally I have to look something up. But I'm always unhappy about that and mistrust the writing which comes out of it. I feel in a way that one's ignorance is part of one's creation, too. I don't know quite how to put it, but for instance if I, as a Jew, am writing about other Jews, and if my knowledge of Jewish culture is exceptionally spotty, as indeed it is, I am not so sure that that isn't an advantage in creating a modern American Jew. Because *his* knowledge of Jewish culture is also extremely spotty, and the way in which his personality is composed may be more in accordance with my ignorance than with a cultivated Jew's immersion in the culture. So in certain limited ways one's ignorance can help to buttress the validity of a novel.

INTERVIEWER. Have you ever written about a situation of which you have had no personal experience or knowledge?

MAILER. I don't know. Let's see . . . *Barbary Shore,* for example, is the most imaginative of my novels. But I did live in a rooming house for a short period while I was writing *The Naked and the Dead.* I certainly didn't live in it the way Lovett lived in it. I never met an F.B.I. agent, at least I had no sense of having met one at the time I was writing *Barbary Shore.* I am sure I have met a great many since. They didn't necessarily introduce themselves to me. I had never met an Old Bolshevik, either, although ironically, writing about F.B.I. agents and Old Bolsheviks in *Barbary Shore,* the greatest single difficulty with the book was that my common sense thought it was impossible to have all these agents and impossible heroes congregating in a rooming house in Brooklyn Heights. Yet a couple of years later I was working in a studio on Fulton Street at the end of Brooklyn Heights, a studio I have had for some years. It was a fine old studio building and they're tearing it down now to make room for a twenty-story building which will look like a Kleenex box. At any rate, on the floor below me, worked one Colonel Rudolph Abel who was the most important spy for the Russians in this country for a period of about eight or ten years, and I am sure we used to be in the elevator together many times. I think he literally had the room beneath me. I have always been overcome with that. It made me decide there's no clear boundary between experience and imagination. Who knows what glimpses of reality we pick up unconsciously, telepathically.

INTERVIEWER. To what extent are your characters modelled on real people?

MAILER. I think half of them might have a point of departure from somebody real. Up to now I've not liked writing about people who are close to me, because they're too difficult to do. Their private reality obviously interferes with the reality one is trying to create. They become alive not as creatures in your imagination but as actors in your life. And so they seem real while you work but you're not working *their* reality into your book. For example it's not a good idea to try to put your wife into a novel. Not your latest wife, anyway. In practice I prefer to draw a character from someone I hardly know. Hollingsworth came from someone I met in Paris, a vapid young American who inveigled me to have a cup of coffee with him in a cafe, and asked a lot of dull questions. *The Naked and the Dead* had just come out and I think he was impressed with that. Yet, there was something sinister about him. I had met him at the Sorbonne a week or two before and I saw him again just for this afternoon for no more than an hour, but he stayed in my memory and became Leroy Hollingsworth in *Barbary Shore*.

INTERVIEWER. How do you name your characters?

MAILER. I try to let the name emerge, because I've found out that the names of my characters usually have roots in the book. I try to avoid quick or cheap symbolisms. Although, I contradict myself, for much is made in *The Deer Park* of the way the name Eitel is pronounced Eye-tell.

INTERVIEWER. I-tell?

MAILER. Eye-tell. But I became aware of that, believe it or not, only when the book was half done. The original title of *The Deer Park* was *The Idol and the Octopus*. The book was going to be about Charles Francis Eitel, the Director, and Herman Teppis, the Producer, and the underlying theme was the war between those who wished to make an idol out of art, the artists, and the patron who used art for power, the octopus.

INTERVIEWER. You also called him "Idell."

MAILER. Frankie Idell in "The Man Who Studied Yoga," yes, but there again, I was obviously getting ready for some—shall we say, hanky-panky, in the eight novels.

INTERVIEWER. Can you describe how you turn a real person into a fictional one?

MAILER. I try to put the model in situations which have very little to do with his real situations in life. Very quickly the model disappears. His private reality can't hold up. For instance, I might take somebody who is a professional football player, a man let's say whom I know slightly, and make him a movie star. In a transposition of this sort, everything which relates particularly to the professional football player quickly disappears, and what is left, curiously, is what is *exportable* in his character. But this process while interesting in the early stages is not as exciting as the more creative act of allowing your characters to grow once they're separated from the model. It's when they become almost as complex as one's own personality that the fine excitement begins. Because then they are not really characters any longer—they're beings, which is a distinction I like to make. A character is someone you can grasp as a whole, you can have a clear idea of him, but a being is someone whose nature keeps shifting. Like a character of Forster's. In *The Deer Park* Lulu Myers is a being rather than a character. If you study her closely you will see that she is a different person in every scene. Just a little different. I don't know whether initially I did this by accident or purposefully, but at a certain point I made the conscious decision *not* to try to straighten her out, she seemed right in her changeableness.

INTERVIEWER. Is Marion Faye a character or a . . .

MAILER. No, he's a being. Everybody in *The Deer Park* is a being except the minor characters like Herman Teppis.

INTERVIEWER. Do specific characters reappear in different guises as the novels appear?

MAILER. To a mild degree. Actually it's easier for me to create a new character than to drag along one of the old ones. No, I think it's more that certain themes reappear in my novels, but I'd rather not get into this just yet.

INTERVIEWER. How did Marion Faye emerge?

MAILER. The book needed something which wasn't in the first draft, some sort of evil genius. One felt a dark pressure there in the inner horizon of the book. But even as I say this I know it's not true to the grain of my writing experience. I violate that experience by talking in these terms. I am not sure it's possible to describe the experience of novel-writing authentically. It may be that it is not an experience.

INTERVIEWER. What is it, then?

MAILER. It may be more like a relation, if you will—a continuing relation between a man and his wife. You can't necessarily speak of that as an experience because it may consist of several experiences which are braided together; or it may consist of many experiences which are all more or less similar, or indeed it may consist of two kinds of experiences which are antagonistic to one another. Throughout all of this I've spoken of characters *emerging*. Quite often they don't emerge; they fail to emerge. And what one's left with is the dull compromise which derives from two kinds of experiences warring with one another within oneself. A character who should have been brilliant is dull. Or even if a character does prove to be first-rate, it's possible you should have done twice as much with him, three times as much.

INTERVIEWER. You speak of character as emerging, and I gather by that that you mean emerging from yourself and emerging from your idea?

MAILER. They are also emerging from the book. A book takes on its own life in the writing. It has its laws, it becomes a creature to you after a while. One feels a bit like a master who's got a fine animal. Very often I'll feel a certain shame for what I've done with a novel. I won't say it's the novel that's bad; I'll say it's I who was bad. Almost as if the novel did not really belong to me, as if it was something raised by me like a child. I know what's potentially beautiful in my novel, you see. Very often after I've done the novel I realize that that beauty which I recognize in it is not going to be recognized by the reader. I didn't succeed in bringing it out. It's very odd—it's as though I had let the novel down, owed it a duty which I didn't fulfill.

INTERVIEWER. Would you say that there was any secret or hidden pattern being worked out in your novels?

MAILER. I'd rather leave that to others. If I answer the question badly, nothing is accomplished. If I answer too well, it's going to discourage critics. I can imagine nothing more distressing to a critic than to have a writer see accurately into his own work. But I will say one thing, which is that I have some obsession with how God exists. Is He an essential god or an existential god; is He all-powerful or is He, too, an embattled existential creature who may succeed or fail in His vision? I think this theme may become more apparent as the novels go on.

INTERVIEWER. When did this obsession begin?

MAILER. I think it began to show itself while I was doing the last draft of *The Deer Park*. Then it continued to grow as a private theme during all the years I was smoking marijuana.

INTERVIEWER. You have spoken so often of the existential view. What reading or individuals brought you to this?

MAILER. The experience came first. One's condition on marijuana is always existential. One can feel the importance of each moment and how it is changing one. One feels one's being, one becomes aware of the enormous apparatus of nothingness—the hum of a hi-fi set, the

emptiness of a pointless interruption, one becomes aware of the war
between each of us, how the nothingness in each of us seeks to attack
the being of others, how our being in turn is attacked by the nothingness in others. I'm not speaking now of violence or the active conflict
between one being and another. That still belongs to drama. But the
war between being and nothingness is the underlying illness of the
twentieth century. Boredom slays more of existence than war.

INTERVIEWER. Then you didn't come to existentialism as a result of some
literary influence?

MAILER. No. I'd hardly read anything by Sartre at this time, and nothing
by Heidegger. I've read a bit since, and have to admire their formidable powers, but I suspect they are no closer to the buried continent
of existentialism than were medieval cartographers near to a useful
map of the world. The new continent which shows on our psychic
maps as intimations of eternity is still to be discovered.

INTERVIEWER. What do you feel about the other kinds of writing you
have done and are doing. How do they stand in relation to your work
as a novelist?

MAILER. The essays?

INTERVIEWER. Yes: journalism, essays.

MAILER. Well, you know, there was a time when I wanted very much to
belong to the literary world. I wanted to be respected the way someone
like Katherine Anne Porter used to be respected.

INTERVIEWER. How do you think she was respected?

MAILER. The way a cardinal is respected—weak people get to their knees
when the cardinal goes by.

INTERVIEWER. As a master of the craft, do you mean?

MAILER. As a master of the craft, yes. Her name is invoked in an argument. "Well, Katherine **Anne** Porter would not do it *that* way." But
by now I'm a bit cynical about craft. I think there's a natural mystique
in the novel which is more important than craft. One is trying, after
all, to capture reality, and that is extraordinarily and exceptionally
difficult. I think craft is merely a series of way-stations. I think of
craft as being like a St. Bernard dog with that little bottle of brandy
under his neck. Whenever you get into *real* trouble the thing that can
save you as a novelist is to have enough craft to be able to keep warm
long enough to be rescued. Of course this is exactly what keeps good
novelists from becoming great novelists. Robert Penn Warren might
have written a major novel if he hadn't had just that little extra bit
of craft to get him out of all the trouble in *All The King's Men*. If
Penn Warren hadn't known anything about Elizabethan literature,
the true Elizabethan in him might have emerged. I mean, he might

have written a fantastic novel. As it was, he knew enough about craft to . . .

INTERVIEWER. To use it as an escape hatch?

MAILER. Yes. And his plot degenerated into a slambang of exits and entrances, confrontations, tragedies, quick wails and woe. But he was really forcing an escape from the problem.

INTERVIEWER. Which was?

MAILER. Oh, the terror of confronting a reality which might open into more and more anxiety and so present a deeper and deeper view of the abyss. Craft protects one from facing those endless expanding realities of deterioration and responsibility.

INTERVIEWER. Deterioration in what sense?

MAILER. The terror, let's say, of being reborn as something much less noble or something much more ignoble. I think this sort of terror depresses us profoundly. Which may be why we throw up our enormous evasions—such as craft. Indeed, I think this adoration of craft, this specific respect for craft makes a church of literature for that vast number of writers who are somewhere on the spectrum between mediocrity and talent. But I think it's fatal for somebody who has a large ambition and a chance of becoming a great writer. I know for myself, if I am going to make this attempt—that the only way to do it is to keep in shape in a peculiar way.

INTERVIEWER. Can you explain what you mean by that?

MAILER. It's hard to talk about. Harry Greb, for example, was a fighter who used to keep in shape. He was completely a fighter, the way one might wish to be completely a writer. He always did the things which were necessary to him as a fighter. Now, some of these things were extremely irrational, that is, extremely irrational from a prize-fight manager's point of view. That is, before he had a fight he would go to a brothel, and he would have two prostitutes, not one, taking the two of them into the same bed. And this apparently left him feeling like a wild animal. Don't ask me why. Perhaps he picked the two meanest whores in the joint and so absorbed into his system all the small, nasty, concentrated evils which had accumulated from carloads of men. Greb was known as the dirtiest fighter of his time. He didn't have much of a punch but he could spoil other fighters and punish them, he knew more dirty tricks than anyone around. This was one of his training methods and he did it over and over again until he died at a relatively early age of a heart attack, on an operating table. I think he died before he was thirty-eight, or so. They operated on him, and bang, he went. Nothing could be done. But the point I make is that he stayed in training by the way he lived his life. The element which was paramount in it was to keep in shape. If he were drinking, you see, the point was to keep in shape *while* drinking. I'm being a touch imprecise about this . . .

INTERVIEWER. Well . . . what?

MAILER. He would not drink just to release his tension. Rather, what went on was that there was tension in him which was insupportable, so he had to drink. But reasoning as a professional he felt that if he had to drink, he might as well use that too. In the sense that the actor uses everything which happens to him, so Greb as a fighter used everything which happened to him. As he drank he would notice the way his body moved. One of the best reasons one drinks is to become aware of the way your mind and body move.

INTERVIEWER. Well, how do you keep in shape?

MAILER. Look, before we go on, I want to say a little more about craft. It is a grab-bag of procedures, tricks, lore, formal gymnastics, symbolic superstructures, methodology in short. It's the compendium of what you've acquired from others. And since great writers communicate a vision of existence, one can't usually borrow their methods. The method is married to the vision. No, one acquires craft more from good writers and mediocre writers with a flair. Craft after all is what you can take out whole from their work. But keeping in shape is something else. For example, you can do journalism, and it can be terrible for your style. Or it can temper your style . . . in other words you can become a *better* writer by doing a lot of different kinds of writing. Or you can deteriorate. There's a book came out a few years ago which was a sociological study of some Princeton men—I forget the name of it. One of them said something which I thought was extraordinary. He said he wanted to perform the sexual act under every variety of condition, emotion, and mood available to him. I was struck with this not because I ever wanted necessarily to have that kind of sexual life, but because it seemed to me that was what I was trying to do with my writing. I try to go over my work in every conceivable mood. I edit on a spectrum which runs from the high clear manic impressions of a drunk which has made one electrically alert all the way down to the soberest reaches of depression where I can hardly bear my words. By the time I'm done with writing I care about, I usually have worked on it through the full gamut of my consciousness. If you keep yourself in this peculiar kind of shape, the craft will take care of itself. Craft is very little finally. But if you're continually worrying about whether you're growing or deteriorating as a man, whether your integrity is turning soft or firming itself, why then it's in that slow war, that slow rearguard battle you fight against diminishing talent that you stay in shape as a writer and have a consciousness. You develop a consciousness as you grow older which enables you to write about anything, in effect, and write about it well. That is, provided you keep your consciousness in shape and don't relax into the flabby styles of thought which surround one everywhere. The moment you borrow other writers' styles of thought, you need craft to shore up the walls. But if what you write is a reflection of your own consciousness, then even journalism can become interesting. One wouldn't want to spend one's life at it and I wouldn't want ever to be caught justifying journalism as a major activity (it's obviously less interesting than to write a novel), but it's better, I think, to see journalism as a venture of one's ability to keep in shape than to see it as an essential betrayal of the chalice of your literary art. Temples are for women.

INTERVIEWER. Temples are for women?

MAILER. Temples are for women.

INTERVIEWER. Well, Faulkner once said that nothing can injure a man's writing if he's a first-rate writer.

MAILER. Faulkner said more asinine things than any other major American writer. I can't remember a single interesting remark Faulkner ever made.

INTERVIEWER. He once called Henry James a "nice old lady."

MAILER. Faulkner had a mean small Southern streak in him, and most of his pronunciamentoes reflect that meanness. He's a great writer, but he's not at all interesting in most of his passing remarks.

INTERVIEWER. Well, then, what can ruin a first-rate writer?

MAILER. Booze, pot, too much sex, too much failure in one's private life, too much attrition, too much recognition, too little recognition, frustration. Nearly everything in the scheme of things works to dull a first-rate talent. But the worst probably is cowardice—as one gets older, one becomes aware of one's cowardice, the desire to be bold which once was a joy gets heavy with caution and duty. And finally there's apathy. About the time it doesn't seem too important any more to be a great writer, you know you've slipped far enough to be doing your work now on the comeback trail.

INTERVIEWER. Would you say that is where you are now?

MAILER. Let others say it. I don't know that I choose to. The hardest thing for a writer to decide is whether he's burned out or merely lying fallow. I was ready to think I was burned out before I even started *The Naked and the Dead.*

INTERVIEWER. What kind of an audience do you keep in mind when you write?

MAILER. I suppose it's that audience which has no tradition by which to measure their experience but the intensity and clarity of their inner lives. That's the audience I'd like to be good enough to write for.

INTERVIEWER. Do you feel under any obligation to them?

MAILER. Yes. I have a consciousness now which I think is of use to them. I've got to be able to get it out and do it well, to transmit it in such a way that their experience can rise to a higher level. It's exactly . . . I mean, one doesn't want one's children to make one's own mistakes. Let them make better mistakes, more exceptional mistakes.

INTERVIEWER. What projects do you have for the future?

MAILER. I've got a very long novel I want to do. And beyond that I haven't looked. Some time ahead I'd like to be free of responsibilities so I could spend a year just taking on interesting assignments—cover the World Series, go to report a war. I can't do that now. I have a feeling I've got to come to grips with myself, with my talent, with what I've made of it and what I've spoiled of it. I've got to find out whether I really can write a large novel or not.

INTERVIEWER. What have you spoiled?

MAILER. All sorts of potentialities. I've burned them out—squandered them, wasted them. I think everybody does. It's a question of whether I've spoiled more than my share.

INTERVIEWER. You once said that you wished to become consecutively more disruptive, more dangerous, and more powerful, and you felt this sentence was a description of your function as a novelist. I wonder if you still think that?

MAILER. I might take out "disruptive." It's an unhappy word to use. It implies a love of disruption for the sake of disruption. Actually, I have a fondness for order.

INTERVIEWER. Do you enjoy writing, or is such a term irrelevant to your experience?

MAILER. Oh no. No, no. You set me thinking of something Jean Malaquais once said. He always has a terrible time writing. He once complained with great anguish about the unspeakable difficulties he was having with a novel. And I asked him, "Why do you do it? You can do many other things well. Why do you bother with it?" I really meant this. Because he suffered when writing like no one I know. He looked up in surprise and said, "Oh, but this is the only way one can ever find the truth. The only time I know that something is true is at the moment I discover it in the act of writing." I think it's that. I think it's this moment when one knows it's true. One may not have written it well enough for others to know, but you're in love with the truth when you discover it at the point of a pencil. That in and by itself is one of the few rare pleasures in life.

INTERVIEWER. How do you feel when you aren't working?

MAILER. Edgy. I get into trouble. I would say I'm wasting my substance completely when I'm not writing.

INTERVIEWER. And to be writing . . . to be a writer?

MAILER. Well, at best you affect the consciousness of your time, and so indirectly you affect the history of the time which succeeds you. Of course, you need patience. It takes a long time for sentiments to collect into an action and often they never do. Which is why I was once so ready to conceive of running for Mayor of New York. I wanted to make actions rather than effect sentiments. But I've come to the middle-aged conclusion that I'm probably better as a writer than a man of action. Too bad. Still it's no little matter to be a writer. There's that godawful Time Magazine world out there, and one can make raids on it. There are palaces, and prisons to attack. One can even succeed now and again in blowing holes in the line of the world's communications. Sometimes I feel as if here's a vast guerrilla war going on for the mind of man, communist against communist, capitalist against capitalist, artist against artist. And the stakes are huge. Will we spoil the best secrets of life or will we help to free a new kind of man? It's intoxicating to think of that. There's something rich waiting if one of us is brave enough and good enough to get there.

The Radical Moralism of Norman Mailer

by Diana Trilling

In 1959, at the not very advanced age of thirty-six, Norman Mailer published what amounted to a grand view of his literary lifetime. In a single big volume, *Advertisements for Myself*, he not only reprinted virtually everything he had written except his three novels—and there are even excerpts from these—but also prefaced, or connected, his stories, essays, and journalism with an extended commentary in which he reported on his states of mind at various stages of his development as an author and public figure, on the reception given his work in the press and by his publishers, and on his present estimate of his earlier performances. A retrospective enterprise of such proportions is bound to tax the generosity of the public. It assumes, for one thing, that its audience shares the writer's own sense of his importance in the record of his period—which indeed it may, but no public likes to have this certification demanded of it. It also presents its author as if in the absolving perspective of history. And it requires of its readers enough grace to forgive, if they cannot welcome, the persistent self-reference inevitable in such a sustained task of self-evaluation. For someone of Mailer's age and present uncertain place in the American literary scene, the undertaking was perhaps ill-advised. By most of its reviewers, *Advertisements* was received reservedly, or with condescension, or irony. The compelling force of the volume, its demonstration of the courage and complexity of Mailer's talent, was slighted in the apparent desire of its critics to separate themselves from his recent questionable, even distressing, moral positions.

This is unfortunate, and it perhaps constitutes one of those occasions when criticism has failed to live up to its responsibility of open-mindedness and has not met its claim of being able to adjudicate between the valuable and the inconsequent, or shoddy, or even out-and-out wrong in a man's work. But one cannot overlook Mailer's share in confounding criticism, even before the publication of *Advertisements*. We live, of course, in a period in which precocity is no longer regarded as it was in, say, Dickens' time, as the sign of a genius so deep-rooted and natural that it must surely augur long years of fulfillment. Instead, we take it as the portent of imminent extinction. While Mailer has neither stopped writing nor succumbed to the temptations of Hollywood, he has had his own gifted way of co-operating in our more cynical expectations for him as a novelist and of obstructing the development that might once have followed upon the early flowering of so much talent. After the extraordinary triumph of *The Naked and the Dead*, he not only deserted the "naturalism" of his first novel but more and more moved from fiction to nonfiction, and of a polemical sort. And increasingly he has offered the public the myth of the man rather than the work of the writer. When we add to this the nature of his present doctrine and the degree to which he has met the challenge of modernity by disavowing that considerable part of his sense of life which is traditional in favor of the more subversive aspects of his thought, it is scarcely surprising that his career is now shadowed in dubiety.

And yet, whatever Mailer's truancy from the novel, or his self-mythologizing impulse, or the violence he does to our traditional moral values, perhaps it is none of these but only the paradoxical character of his talent that finally creates his present equivocal situation. Where a writer exists in this much contradiction, the realization of his possibilities is always chancier than it would be in a more unitary talent, and it would be hard to name a writer of our or any time whose work reveals a more abundant or urgent endowment which is yet so little consistent with itself—so much moral affirmation coupled with so much moral anarchism; so much innocence yet so much guile; so much defensive caution but such headlong recklessness; so much despair together with so imperious a demand for salvation; so strong a charismatic charge but also so much that offends or even repels; so much intellection but such a frequency of unsound thinking; such a grand and manly impulse to heroism but so inadequate a capacity for self-discipline; so much sensitiveness and so little sensibility; so much imagination and such insufficient art. Contradictions like these no doubt contribute to Mailer's appeal; but they also make for his limitations. And they describe a talent which necessarily lives on the sharp edge of uncertainty.

Yet to trace the paradoxes in Mailer is not to figure an unknown constellation. It is to experience the shock of recognition, for in the sum of his contradictions he bears a striking resemblance to present-day America. What distinguishes him, however, from other contemporary American writers who also express their culture even while they reject it is the depth to which he is shaken by the crash of modernity against the poor bulwarks of Western tradition and, even more, his driving need to turn this experience to social use.

For the advanced writer of our time, the self is his supreme, even sole, referrant. Society has no texture or business worth bothering about; it exists because it weighs upon us and because it conditions us so absolutely. The diverse social scene is homogenized into a force we feel only grossly, as a source of our horror or terror or emptiness. The job of literature in our period is thus more poetical than novelistic—our advanced fiction neither anatomizes the society that is nor conceives the society that might be; it deals merely with the massive brute social fact in its impress upon the individual consciousness. Where the novelist of an earlier day helped us to understand and master a mysterious or recalcitrant environment, the present-day novelist undertakes only to help us define the self in relation to the world that surrounds and threatens to overwhelm it. And this search for self-definition proceeds by sensibility, by the choice of a personal style or stance which will differentiate the self from, or within, its undifferentiated social context.

Mailer is no Balzac of the twentieth century. And he is engrossed in his own grim effort of self-validation. But he conceives society as being quite as actual as the self, and as much to be addressed. It is not so much that he thinks of the modern world as a world of negotiable particulars. But he believes the social totality generates a dialectic between itself and the individual; it is therefore not merely to be endured in self-pity, it can be faced up to and changed. For instance, in his fine story, "The Man Who Studied Yoga"—it is, I think, one of the best stories of our time and aesthetically Mailer's best-integrated piece of fiction—he has a would-be novelist protest to a friend that he "does not want to write a realistic novel, because reality is no longer realistic"; but Mailer's immediate riposte to this familiar statement is a description of the boring "petulance of their small voices" as the two young men luxuriate in their dreariness. Or, typically, he remarks of Beckett's *Waiting for Godot*:

> I doubt if I will like it, because finally not everyone is impotent, nor is our final fate, our human condition, necessarily doomed to impotence, as old Joyce knew, and Beckett I suspect does not. . . .

And in *The Deer Park*, where he momentarily borrows Hemingway's symbol of sexual impotence for his narrator, Sergius O'Shaugnessy, he has this predate the opening of the story; once the novel begins, O'Shaugnessy is active enough.

Mailer's temperament, in other words, is adversary not fugitive, hortatory not seismographic. Even his Hipsterism, concerned as it is with styles of personal being, rejects the premise of a self at the mercy of society, and refuses the sanctuary of sensibility. And no doubt this has much to do with the striking fact that, big as Mailer looms as a personality of the literary left, one can name only a single serious critic of his general cultural persuasion, Norman Podhoretz in *Partisan Review* (Summer, 1959), who has written about him without embarrassment, as an author of stature. While he outrages conservative opinion by the ultimateness of his judgment upon modern life, he equally alienates radical literary opinion by his offense against the reality it is most disposed to acknowledge—that of our helplessness before Conditions.

"Hip is not totally negative," Mailer declares, "and has a view of life which is predicated on growth." And in the figure of the cool cat he projects an image of man as someone who, far from being inert before danger, is precisely poised for action against the enemy—it is a posture without great appeal to the contemporary distaste for "hostility." And despite Hipsterism's emphasis upon the self, it places on the self the largest possible responsibility for the "collective creation" (as Mailer calls it) which is our culture. "If society was so murderous," he asks, "then who could ignore the most hideous of questions about his own nature?" There is, of course, menace in so primary an inquiry, and Mailer has himself been badly scarred in its pursuit. The question nevertheless carries us a salutary distance beyond our modern view of the individual as victim of a world he never made and cannot remake.

Mailer's adversary disposition recalls D. H. Lawrence, his prede-cessor in the line of literary minds dedicated to the renovation of society by means of a revolution in the individual consciousness. But of the two, Lawrence is actually closer to our present literary spirit, for he is not only the more subjective writer but also the more abstract. Society exists in his novels only as an aggregate of unspecified destructive conditions. The most poetical of social revo-lutionaries, he scorned politics in their troublesome concreteness. But Mailer has always carried the burden of social actuality of the intellectual thirties. He has engaged in politics—the politics of literary intellectuals—through his career, even in years when it has not been the literary fashion. At the time of the publication of his first novel, he was a Communist sympathizer and campaigned vigorously for Henry Wallace in that same year. Then, when Stalin-ism failed him, he turned to Trotskyism and even today he still professes a modified allegiance to Marxism. For instance, in an interview with Mr. Richard Wollheim in England as recently as September 1961, Mailer describes the Socialist preference which has remained to him from his old Communist commitment as now only a choice made *faute de mieux,* certainly with no passion or confidence. Of Marxism, however, he speaks like a man of honor who would not disavow a once-precious love. By and large, his criti-cism of Socialism is much the same as his criticism of modern civilization: just as it is the ugliness and minimalism of modern life that make him dissent from civilization and wish to prod it into a more conscious barbarism from which he can hope there will arise a revitalized way of personal being, just so he dissents from the ungenerosity, the uncourageousness, the lack of elegance and wit and charm, the personally minimal quality which he finds in Socialism. Yet despite his belief that the Marxist economic emphasis is not adequate to the present crisis in world affairs, he still calls himself a Marxist, albeit in the tone of someone sub-mitting to a rather tedious test of his integrity. What Mailer im-plies is that in a world as ripe for reaction as he thinks ours is, a man sticks to his guns even though they are obsolete.

This is a far cry from Mailer's younger Marxism. In fact, the single live line of connection between the monolithic doctrine of a book like *Barbary Shore,* which came out in 1951, three years after *The Naked and the Dead,* and his present merely vestigial

Marxism is Mailer's continuing fear of political reaction in the democracies. For Mailer, as for so many Western intellectuals, political probity rests essentially in demonstrating one's anxiety about the threat from the right; the abrogation of human rights under the dictatorship of the left is allowed to disappear in a generalized disapprobation of Communism; or another way to put it is that the threat of armed conflict between the democracies and the Soviet Union overrides the principled opposition to Communist totalitarianism which, for the sake of convenience, as it were, is presumed to exist in a different moral context from any totalitarianism which might appear in the West. Even before the height of McCarthyism, as far back as his first novels, Mailer had arrived at this conviction that fascism is not merely a potential in America as in any modern capitalism but, what is quite another order of political hypothesis, that it is the most coherent and dominant force in American society. And this fear is apparently no less compelling in Mailer today than it ever was: as late as the spring of 1961, he published an open letter to Fidel Castro in which he addressed the Cuban dictator as "Brother" and elevated him to the rank of a born Hipster in order to sanctify his role as savior of the Cuban workers and peasants from American fascism. But then we must remember, of course, that John F. Kennedy also figures in Mailer's pantheon as a natural Hipster; at least he did at the time of his nomination.

Whatever our evaluation of Mailer's political predictions for America, the important point is that his work is not properly to be understood apart from his profound preoccupation with the idea that modern democratic man is about to yield his dignity, his freedom, his very manhood before the onslaught of political reaction. Second only to his religious zeal, it is Mailer's sense of himself as the heroic antagonist of a malevolent reactionary authority that has powered his fictional imagination.

The Naked and the Dead (1948), published when Mailer was twenty-five, two years after his separation from the Army in which he served with credit in Leyte, Luzon and Japan, was everywhere acclaimed as the best novel of World War II. And even as we read it today, knowing what the war brought as its aftermath of futility and desperation, it remains a remarkable document of the defeat inherent in any modern victory in war. Technically, his first novel advances no farther than Dos Passos, whose influence Mailer acknowledges in *Advertisements*. And in the main it relies on fictional materials which were well-exploited in the first war. But it brings to a familiar subject the informing view of a new and radically altered generation. Our present-day belief that we stand outside the ordinary movements of historical evolution, our loss of faith in both the orderly and the revolutionary processes of social development, our always increasing social fragmentation and our always diminishing trust in our individual possibility—it is these changes in consciousness that separate Mailer's war novel from the novels that followed World War I, as does, too, its drastically accelerated sense of time. Time is always running out on a soldier, in the midst of the inexorable tedium of his days, but this fact of experience is raised to a principle for Mailer's G.I.s. The hot breath of the future—one might better say, the hot breath of our own expiring day—broods over the pages of *The Naked and the Dead* as foul and stifling as the surrounding jungle air.

Although even before Tolstoy, literature had of course represented the common soldier as the victim of a force he could neither understand nor control, it is only in our time that the Army has become identified with the irrational and destructive authority of society itself. *The Naked and the Dead* incorporates this death-dealing power in two characters, General Cummings and Sergeant Croft. Cummings is a man of the rising middle classes whose overweening personal ambition, bolstered by great gifts for organization and by an imagination which knows no restraints of human feeling, leads him, for private reasons, to order a reconnaissance platoon on a tour of duty which must inevitably end in catastrophe. Croft is an illiterate Army regular, brave, skillful and cunning, for whom the hieratical sanctions of war provide a nice measure of satisfaction of an unquenchable lust for conquest and blood. Cummings is sufficiently educated to bring the historical process and his own ambitions into working conjunction with each other; he has announced himself on the side of the future. He thinks of his men as the instruments of history and his own will—the two are synonymous. In Mailer's political scheme he is, simply, fascism, and Croft is his eager though unconscious collaborator. The suffering men in Croft's platoon, who endure unspeakable torments as they struggle through swamp and jungle on Cummings' order and who, without voice in their fate, stumble mindlessly in their Sergeant's footsteps as he pits himself against the unscalable heights of Mt.

Anaka, are the masses of mankind who lack the individual or collective will to resist being propelled to annihilation. This Army which, in the name of historical necessity, captures, rules and destroys the common life of humanity, is modern society as Mailer sees it, and the presentiment of worse to come. And his introduction of Lieutenant Hearn, the intelligent, decent liberal whom Cummings cannot quite seduce and must therefore kill, completes his political indictment and prophecy.

The influence of Dos Passos' *U.S.A.* is obvious in Mailer's management of his fictional forces in *The Naked and the Dead*—his crowded canvas of G.I.s together with their officers, and behind them their families, their wives, their girl friends. Where his own young genius announces itself is in his dramatic inventiveness and, even more, in his feeling—unmatched in our time, even by Hemingway in *For Whom the Bell Tolls*—for topography, for the look of the natural scene. As a matter of fact, the two gifts are associated: the most dramatic moments in *The Naked and the Dead* are precipitated by intensities in nature. Indeed, this loyal delight in physical truth is what gives *The Naked and the Dead* its extraordinary distinction. It is therefore of some interest that Mailer's first novel is, so far, his last to be set outdoors—it would seem that his fiction must now be enclosed in walls in order to reproduce the strangling effects of modern life.

The bald schematic structure of Mailer's novels, starting with the first of them, suggests a paraphrase of T. S. Eliot's comment on Henry James, that James had a mind so pure that no idea could violate it: of Mailer we can say that his novelist's mind is peculiarly violable by idea, even by ideology. In *The Naked and the Dead* there is at least the battle of man against nature to excite the artist in Mailer; but even here the contest between man and society has already begun to make him its ideological prisoner. Despite its brilliant evocation of atmosphere, and its integrity as a story of war, *The Naked and the Dead* takes its ultimate stand, not in art, but in doctrine. As much as it is a drama of human motives, Mailer's first novel is a political document—the testimony of a young Marxist, or proto-Marxist, whose experience of war confirms his worst reading of history. If, however, *The Naked and the Dead* is to be understood as Mailer's forecast of the dreaded victory of fascism, we are bound to balk at the moral as well as political ascendancy of Croft at the end of the book. In Mailer's reading of the future, Croft is clearly the coadjutor of ruthless reactionary assertion. And yet, as the novel draws to its conclusion, Croft ceases to be one of its villains and usurps the place in his author's sympathies which we had thought was Hearn's. This curious shift in the moral focus of *The Naked and the Dead* perhaps adds to its fictional interest, but it remains unexplained in Mailer's system of thought until we meet Marion Faye, the Hipster hero of Mailer's third novel, *The Deer Park,* in whose resemblance to Croft we discover the ominous political implications of Mailer's criteria for heroism.

Mailer's disillusionment with Communism followed rapidly on the publication of *The Naked and the Dead* but it was a break only with Stalinism, from which he moved to the Trotskyite Marxism of his second novel. In *Barbary Shore* (1951) Mailer attempted a new literary manner, and he paid dearly in popular success for disappointing a public eager for more of the seen and felt life of his first book. But as doctrine his second novel took up virtually where its predecessor left off—with liberalism dead and with the confusion and despair of the working classes sounding their dull prelude to the victory of the right; the fact that, between 1948 and 1951, Mailer had himself lost faith in the Communism of Soviet Russia simply reinforced his earlier perception of the hopelessness of the American proletariat rescuing itself from its bad situation. What had happened to Mailer's politics in the three years between his first and second novels shows itself, in fact, chiefly in the changed perspective of the two books. Whereas in *The Naked and the Dead* the historical process is viewed in terms of its effect upon the general run of mankind, in *Barbary Shore* Mailer writes out of the dilemma of the defeated radical intellectual. The great battle of history is now fought out, not on the wide "proletarian" front where his first novel had located it, but on the intellectual left flank where Mailer had been isolated by his inability to maintain his trust in Stalin's revolution.

In Mailer's second novel, fascism again trumpets its advance, but now it is personified in an FBI agent named Hollingsworth—the collocation is not absurd to Mailer nor, presumably, to his putative readers. As befits the representative of a social force that is already licensed to execute the political dreams of a Cummings, Hollingsworth has none of the human attributes of a mere novice in tyranny like Mailer's General; for all his shrewdness and sharp-wittedness, Hollingsworth moves through *Barbary Shore* robot-like, directed by a power remote from the scene of his activities. His assignment in the novel is to track down a "little object" stolen from the State Department by a man named McLeod, who had come to work for the Government after a considerable period as a Communist leader and then as a member of the Communist Opposition. When we meet McLeod in the surrealist Brooklyn boardinghouse which is the setting of *Barbary Shore*, even this recourse has failed him; he has nothing to which to dedicate himself except an intensive study of Marxism and the preservation of the Communist ideal which, detached from the Soviet reality which has betrayed it, persists in the form of the stolen token he has stashed away for use in an improbable future. As Mailer's highly allegorical story progresses, it turns out that this secret of our future rehabilitation is never recaptured by Hollingsworth, but the dark powers of reaction are nonetheless triumphant—the novel ends with Hollingsworth stealing, if not McLeod's key to the salvation of mankind, then at least his wife, who, in *Barbary Shore*, stands for pretty much what Mailer's G.I.s did in *The Naked and the Dead*: the common life of humanity but grown distinctly less human and more sinister with the passage of the years. McLeod commits suicide—we are reminded of Hearn's suicidal conspiracy with his murderers in Mailer's first novel—and the young narrator of the book, an amnesiac who has wandered by historical "accident" into this epochal war and been cast as McLeod's confidant and disciple, is left the guardian of our small unpromising legacy of political hope.

In spite of its many funny passages, most of which center around McLeod's mad wife, Guinevere, *Barbary Shore* is a web of fine-spun phantasies, as obscure as they are frightening, allowing us no connection with any recognizable world of feeling. Even Guinevere is drawn so outrageously and abstrusely that we can never be certain of the meaning Mailer attaches to this sharp, slobby lady who is always bartering or withholding her fly-blown sexuality in some strange, awful enterprise of personal advantage. It is only at the last, when McLeod's wife chooses to run off with Hollingsworth, that we begin to understand her place in the ideological scheme of the novel. Greed, cupidity, sloth, a sporadic and wildly misdirected energy, spiritless lust, stupidity, and mean ambition—these, Mailer is telling us, are what today define democratic man, or woman; and in a society in which the masculine principle is reduced to an automaton like Hollingsworth, a woman perhaps best symbolizes our deteriorated situation. Guinevere is the civilization—or, if you will, the American masses—with whom the revolutionary idealist has perforce had to align himself, and to whose partnership with fascism his death must be witness.

McLeod dead, it is to a writer and intellectual—or Mailer's rather shadowy version of one—who has lost his memory except for vagrant recollections of having once been close to the radical movement, that our decent social values are bequeathed. Lovett, the amnesiac narrator of *Barbary Shore,* is of course the precursor of the orphaned Sergius O'Shaugnessy, Mailer's spokesman in *The Deer Park* and again in his most recent story, "Time of Her Time." Both men are without tie to the past; both inhabit a universe without historical precedent or direction. Both of them announce, that is, Mailer's own thoroughly democratic stance of the self-made man, and his detachment from cultural tradition—Harvard to the contrary notwithstanding. Certainly in view of Mailer's obsessive interest in history, it is remarkable how little reference there is in his work to anything—political, philosophical, or literary—that happened day before yesterday; there is only now and tomorrow. Even when Mailer alludes to such towering figures as Hemingway or Faulkner in the generation before his own, they are introduced like parents into a gathering of contemporaries and friends. It is only when he writes about his literary siblings—Bellow, Styron, Jones, Capote, Vidal, Baldwin—that we feel the direct fire of his personal and literary judgment. Mailer's concern with history, in other words, is a concern with history-in-the-making. It is the Marxist's preoccupation with present-day action in the light of future necessity.

Implicit in Marxism as a method of historical analysis there is always this assumption that if we correctly track the movements of history we can foretell future developments and put ourselves in accord with them; we can then aid prophecy in fulfilling itself. But in Mailer there is an unusual collaboration between the higher and lower arts of prognostication: the Marxist's prophetic faculty can regularly call upon the assistance of irrational intuition and even downright superstition. For example, in the early pages of *The Naked and the Dead,* when we first meet Sergeant Croft, he is playing poker and has had a run of bad hands, but firm in his belief that "whatever made things happen was on his side," he awaits the better luck that he is certain is in store for him, and soon he is the winner. Then, later the same day, Croft correctly predicts that before nightfall a boy named Hennessey will be dead, and Mailer tells us of this accurate prevision that it fills the Sergeant with a sense "of such omnipotence" and "such portents of power" that his life is as if magically altered. What happens, obviously, is that, by imagining himself in alliance with fate, Croft marshals a will he otherwise lacks, which does indeed alter his fate. General Cummings, too, exemplifies Mailer's providential view of the relation between destiny and perspicuity: "The fact that you're holding the gun and the other man is not," he explains to Hearn, "is no accident. . . . If you're aware enough, you have the gun when you need it." Thus the rationalistic Marxist, the wily General, and the ignorant superstitious Sergeant are all blood-brothers in their ability to envision and foster what anyway lies ahead. The Marxist determinist who charts the inevitable course of events so that we can put ourselves on the side of history is of the same family with the military tactician or the gambler whose correct hunch puts him on the winning side of fate.

The fate Mailer's Marxism foretold with the completion of *Barbary Shore* was of a society whose determining forces produced only its dissolution, never its reconstruction along the hoped-for revolutionary lines, and the publication of his second book therefore marked a turning-point in Mailer's career. If the alternative to a fascist triumph was so remote from political actuality that it could be represented in an unnamed little lost object, then clearly the political solution had failed. From this point forward, Mailer has sought salvation elsewhere than in politics—in Hipsterism, a mode of being that will re-energize a worn and perverted civilization irresistibly drawn toward reaction.

Hipsterism—or Hip, as Mailer sometimes calls it in a discrimination whose meaning is uncertain—is, we are told, an American Existentialism designed to return man to the center of the universe and to bring the individual into direct and vital communication with the self and its needs. It is the doctrine which, enshrined in the place that Marxism once had in his system of thought, allows Mailer to probe modern society on a level deeper than that of political and economic determinism. Since it is manifestly man's destiny in our century to live with death and destruction, then the only life-giving answer is to accept the terms of death, to live with death as immediate danger, to divorce oneself from society, to exist without roots, to set out on that uncharted journey into the rebellious imperatives of the self.

God is in danger of dying—this, in fact, is the "single burning pinpoint of the vision in Hip." Because God is no longer all-powerful, man must take His place at the center of the universe and become the embodiment of His embattled vision.

The original settler in this terrain which lies beyond the demands of society, the guide Mailer offers us in our unmapped journey of self-exploration, is not the dark primitive of Lawrence, but he is similarly alien to a white Protestant middle-class culture. He is the Negro; and Mailer makes his most complete statement of the meaning of Hipsterism in his essay, "The White Negro." The Negro, says Mailer,

> has the simplest of alternatives: live a life of constant humility or ever-threatening danger. In such a pass where paranoia is as vital to survival as blood, the Negro has stayed alive and begun to grow by following the need of his body where he could.

So we, too, must know our impulse as it speaks to us of a true need of the self. "One must know one's desires, one's rages, one's anguish, one must be aware of the character of one's frustrations." And we must be prepared to act on the mandate of the self:

> Whether the life is criminal or not, the decision is to encourage the psychopath in oneself, to explore that domain of experience where society is boredom and therefore sickness, and one exists in the present. . . . One is Hip or one is Square. . . . One is a rebel or one conforms.

Although "The White Negro" appeared in 1957, two years after *The Deer Park*, Mailer's third novel already contained in embryo the chief ideas Mailer would develop in his celebrated essay. Among the rebellious imperatives of the self, none is more exigent than sex, and surely the novelist who would treat this aspect of the modern consciousness not, like Lawrence, as a sacred lost essence but as existential fact cannot do better than to turn to Hollywood. But Mailer would seem to have come to the sexual theme of *The Deer Park* only secondarily, or even incidentally, while embarked upon a political novel along familiar simplistic lines, about a liberal movie director, Charles Eitel, who is blacklisted in the studios for his refusal to talk before a Congressional investigating committee but who then capitulates to the joint pressure of authoritarian government and ruthless finance and is reinstated in his job. It would appear, that is, that the sexual life of the movie colony originally served somewhat the same function as the tropical setting of *The Naked and the Dead,* of providing the context for a political drama, but that by the time Mailer was fully launched in his story, he realized that politics was failing him as the material of fiction, as it had failed him as a means of saving the world; Eitel's crisis of political conscience had turned out to be but a dim counterpoint to the larger crises of personal feeling in which he and the people around him were involved. The sexuality of Hollywood, once intended as merely the ambiance in which political hope is defeated, became then the drama itself—the account of a last-ditch fight on behalf of a personal destiny that could no longer be sought in politics.

Considering his sensational material, Mailer is notably neutral in his report of the Hollywood sexual scene. This neutrality of voice must be understood, however, as an aspect of his aesthetic procedure rather than of his moral judgment. Although nothing could be less conventionally censorious than Mailer's investigation of the diverse sexual tastes and deportment of his stars and their hangers-on, of his movie moguls and their call-girls, *The Deer Park* is finally as charged with morality as *Lady Chatterley's Lover.* For Mailer, as for Lawrence, sexual activity is never its own justification; its good is measured by the quality of the emotions it produces or expresses. The moral platform of Mailer's Hollywood novel reveals itself from behind the apparent irony of its epigraph—a quotation from a shocked description of the sexual life in the Deer Park of Louis XV —and is clearly argued in every line of Mailer's portrait of a society which manufactures the American mass sexual dream. Here is truly our jungle within walls, a miasma of desire fulfilled and yet always unfulfilled, as torturing as the burning, tangled, insect-infested jungle of *The Naked and the Dead.* The inhabitants of Mailer's Hollywood are wracked by a fever without cure; in their freedom from conventional sexual restraint there sounds the rattling of the chains of a bondage as awful as that of the Army. Only love and tenderness, only the terrible self-denying imperatives of feeling can release these victims from the tyranny of their unimpeded sexual compulsions—and their search for feeling is their futile struggle toward the unattainable heights of an emotional Mt. Anaka.

"The only revolution which will be meaningful and natural for the 20th century," Mailer has said, "is the sexual revolution one senses everywhere." And as one reads his account of the free sexual life of Hollywood, one might perhaps be misled into thinking that this is the revolution to which he is referring. But Mailer is more complex than this. While he recognizes that the Hollywood life of free sexual impulse does indeed constitute a major rebellion against conventional sexual morality, his novelist's eye for truth has searched out the frenzy and emptiness in the lives of his sexual free-booters. Mailer has a predilection for last-minute heroes; just as Croft's sudden triumph at the end of *The Naked and the Dead* suggests the changes in feeling that Mailer was experiencing in the course of composing his first novel, so the replacement of Eitel by Faye as the most significant figure in *The Deer Park* indicates the dramatic evolution of Mailer's thought while writing his Hollywood novel. In Marion Faye we discover the distinction Mailer makes between a sexuality which, like that of the movie colony, appears to be free but is really an enslavement, and the sexuality of Hipsterism which expresses a new, radical principle of selfhood. The difference is not one of behavior but of consciousness. Whereas all the other characters in the novel, whether in their political decisions or their sexual conduct, follow the worn paths of consciousness laid out for them by an exhausted civilization, Mailer's incipient Hipster hero has settled the new direction the world must take to save itself: it is the direction of purposeful, as opposed to purposeless, death. Faye is not God the Father, but he is unmistakably in training to be God the Son. Dying for us, the Hipster becomes our savior; he is the resurrection and the life in a society of Eitels and call-girls who, will-lessly submitting to their poor destinies, can promise us nothing but further desperation and enervation.

Faye is a young, elaborately sadistic pimp who closely conforms to Mailer's anatomy of the white Negro several years later. He is totally bored by society, paranoically alert to danger, and he lives in an acute intimacy with the criminal and the psychopath in himself. This intimacy has, in fact, the charge of a mystical fulfillment: it is when Faye is most wholly possessed by his psychopathic needs that he achieves his strongest sense of spiritual exaltation. As jealous of his freedom of will as Dostoevsky's Underground Man, he finds the assurance of his autonomy in a strenuous rationalism—his re-iterative reminder to himself that he is master of his fate, uncondi-tioned by the moral values of his culture. And the question seems never to enter his or his author's mind whether a man is any the less a victim for being at the mercy of his own psychopathology rather than that of his society.

In Faye, then, we are introduced to the new hero of Hip. And yet he is of course not a wholly new figure in Mailer's work: he has made a premonitory appearance as Sergeant Croft in *The Naked and the Dead*. The single indispensable ingredient Mailer has added to Croft in creating Faye is the consciousness that his program of cruelty and self-imposition has a large social and spiritual meaning. The passage of nearly a decade, in other words, has brought Mailer full circle to the exposure of the unresolved conflict which already existed in his first novel—between his overriding fear, in politics, of an authority which makes its law in defiance of the decent social values and his powerful attraction to the same authority in the personal or spiritual realm.

The conflict is not without literary precedent: the modern imagi-nation apparently takes the heroic leap only at some cost in moral logic. But writers like Lawrence or Yeats had the advantage, we now see, of living in a time when they were not required to give public account of their political preferences, and we can suppose that had Mailer been of their period instead of ours, he would have similarly avoided the predicament of presenting us with a hero not easily distinguishable from his named political enemy. He would have been able to evade the political consequences of consigning the future of civilization to a personal authority morally identical with the dark reaction from which it is supposed to rescue us. Or, to put the matter in even cruder terms, he would not have exposed himself to our ridicule for offering us a God who is a fascist.

But the situation has changed: today Mailer is guilty of a mortal fallacy in his moral-political thought. And yet, even as we trap him, we realize that our whole "enlightened" culture is caught in the same inconsistency. No less than Mailer, we all of us who accede in the moral implications of modern literature but continue to make our political choices on the basis of traditional moral values exist in ambiguity. It is quite a long time now since Conrad asked us to choose between his Kurtz and his "Pilgrims," between a heroic prin-ciple of evil and a seedy, hypocritical bourgeoisie that lacks the courage of its inherent malevolence. And once we received such an alternative as really our only option, we accepted the premise of a civilization intolerable to itself; we concurred in the negation of the moral values on which we had established our enlightened political ideals. The very notion of a hero of liberalism, or a hero of anti-dictatorship, or a hero of social justice becomes absurd, even unimaginable, in a literature whose moral habitude it is to assign personal grandeur to the demonic and destructive. If Mailer's dual wish—to preserve us from the malign forces of political reaction but also to give civilization another push toward the extinction to which it seems inexorably drawn—leads him into moral and political self-contradiction, he is not alone in this dilemma. It is the dilemma of anyone of high political seriousness who also identifies himself with the characteristic moral tendency of our literature.

And the moral tendency of contemporary art is not isolated in our culture. Everywhere in Western society there is an erosion, if not an entire sweeping-away, of assumptions once thought secure, which takes place not at the behest of reason but by an undirected tide of feeling, by what almost seems to be a psychological mutation. The psychologists may not be noting the change but the novelists record it even when they are not always aware of the significance in what they so circumstantially bear witness to. Where do we, where shall we, where can we derive our moral sanctions—from a failing tradition or from the wild free impulses of our racial infancy, from the Ego or the Id? This is the ultimate pressing question of our time, separating our historical period from any that came before it. And because Mailer not only knows the full force of the question but passionately dedicates himself to its answer, he transcends the follies and excesses which attend Hipsterism and claims his place in the forefront of modern writers.

Obviously in Mailer's application to this ultimate issue, far more than in his politics, we discover his radicalism just as it is in their deep involvement with this large moral-cultural tendency of our period rather than in their newly fervid Socialism or their disenchantment with the democracies that we locate the radicalism of his literary contemporaries. For Mailer, as for the whole of a new literary generation, politics is today the least revolutionary aspect of social protest.

That, despite the political struggles which fed his moral imagination, Mailer's present moral radicalism came to him only gradually and from such emotional sources as have always nourished the traditional novelist is plainly indicated in his story, "The Man Who Studied Yoga," written in 1952, shortly after the political dis-illusionment of *Barbary Shore* but well before the appearance of Marion Faye. Product of a moment of suspension between ideo-logical engagements, this superb long story is singularly free of the restrictions imposed upon Mailer's fiction by his usual sys-tematic thought. And it is also the warmest and most domestic of his fictional works, his sole exclursion into the middle-class "nor-mality" in which he, too, like the characters in his story, might have entrenched himself against the dangerous next steps in his development. In Mailer's brilliant description of Sam and Eleanor Slovoda we can examine the supposedly "mature" alternative our civilization offers those of us who scorn "regression" to the bar-barism of infancy. Sam, an ex-radical and novelist *manqué,* earns his living writing continuities for comics; Eleanor, a painter *manqué,* is a suburban housewife and the dutiful jargon-driven mother of two fine modern-reared children. The course of their lives of quiet-desperation-cum-psycho-analysis is interrupted (but only for a day while the children visit their grandmother) by the showing of a pornographic film at a party. After ten years of mar-riage, the Slovodas and their friends are responsible citizens and parents, responsible matrimonial partners, responsible and tender, even humorous social companions. But they ache with the sexual longings that are never to be satisfied, and with the frustration of their dreams of themselves. They are the human counterparts of the charmless rational housing development their culture has pro-vided for them. If this is what it means—and who can argue the flawless truth of what Mailer shows us?—to take our due place in society without violating the established decencies, then Mailer is surely right that conformity is purposeless death. But at this point in his career Mailer has no taste for pressing the polemical issue. The story delivers its message without preachment and this is its triumph.

Sam Slovoda has turned to psychoanalysis for the deliverance that will never come, and from Mailer's satiric references we can take it that the therapy is orthodox, therefore, to him, especially suspect. In later essays, Mailer goes on to make Freudianism the target of some of his sharpest attacks on the modern dispensation; expectedly enough, he by and large lines up with the Reichians. Jung, Fromm, Reich: it is among these analytical dissidents that protest now regularly seeks the psychology with which to replace the Freudian psychology which it believes lives too comfortably with the traditional attitudes of our society. Like Reich, Mailer rejects the idea of a self obedient to social law, and from Reich he takes his measure of instinctual gratification, the orgasm: it is in his orgasmic potency that the Hipster finds the best test of his capacity for self-realization. As a matter of fact, Mailer's most recent story, "Time of Her Time," carries this criterion of personal release to the amusing point where, notwithstanding the ingenious twists Mailer makes on his sexual theme, the orgasm plays the same tyrannous role in assessing psychic well-being that sexual "adjustment" does in the mental-health culture that has sprung from Freudianism.

In "Time of Her Time," O'Shaugnessy is returned to New York from Hollywood and Mexico. By day he teaches bull-fighting; his nights are for love-making with an endless series of Village girls who prey upon his swaggering maleness. The epitome of these predators is a graceless, tight-knit, Jewish college student who defies him to give her the sexual satisfaction she has not yet experienced. Challenged, O'Shaugnessy finally accomplishes his grim mission by fiercely forcing upon her a reversion to a more primitive zone of feeling than the female genital; stripped of her defenses, the girl attains to womanliness—and she is not grateful. She must hit back at her despised savior, or master, with her own bleak, ugly attempt to rob him of his masculine pride. The story ends with both partners in this loveless battle worn and battered, both equally the victims of their excoriated egotism—and with the girl bound again for the Freudian couch where, so Mailer has it, she has learned the tactics of assault which are her civilized protection.

"Time of Her Time" is the crudest of Mailer's attacks upon Freudianism, and it is peculiarly anomalous that Mailer should deal with Freud this unworthily. For, although he is himself not aware of it, the fortitude which is implicit in the demand he makes upon the self is much closer to the Freudian than the Reichian temperament. Mailer's heroic assertion and his insistence upon the controlling power of man's consciousness have their antecedents not in the psychoanalysis that has diverged from Freud but in Freud himself; the Reichian psychology proposes a character considerably less valorous and self-contained. The heroism of Freud, however, was the heroism of endurance; he knew better than most the price that civilization exacts in denied instinct, and tragically, resentfully, he was prepared to pay it. Mailer's is the courage of non-acceptance; he refuses to sacrifice instinct to a civilization which is itself so little removed from savagery. But perhaps because of Freud's readiness to face into the issue as between civilization and instinct, Mailer does, in fact, direct his criticism not so much to Freud himself as to his disciples today, where he stands on firmer territory. The unwillingness of contemporary orthodox analysis to take account of the actualities of a culture in significant transition, its unacknowledged acquiescence in a moribund middle-class morality, its reluctance to treat with the human personality apart from the limitations of social imperatives—these are the grounds of Mailer's adverse judgment upon present-day Freudianism. One could fairly put it that what Mailer atttacks in Freud's followers is their passive or neutral assent in a choice which, as Freud made it, had such harsh resonances.

Naturally enough, of the various excesses into which Mailer is led by his own option against civilization, the most disturbing is his expressed tolerance of, even his partisanship with, extreme personal violence. And he is not speaking metaphorically; here, as elsewhere, he is announcing a program of action. What is worse, he speaks of violence in a language of love learned in the moral culture he undertakes to dismiss in its entirety. For example, in a statement which he made in the course of an interview in *Mademoiselle* (February 1961), he has this to say about a brutal gratuitous murder:

> Let's use our imaginations. It means that one human being has determined to extinguish the life of another human being. It means that two people are engaging in a dialogue with eternity. Now if the brute does it and at the last moment likes the man he is extinguishing then perhaps the victim did not die in vain. If there is an eternity with souls in that eternity, if one is able to be born again, the victim may get his reward. At least it seems possible that the quality of one being passes into the other, and this altogether hate-filled human, grinding his boot into the face of someone . . .

in the act of killing, in this terribly private moment, the brute feels a moment of tenderness, for the first time perhaps in all of his experience. What has happened is that the killer is becoming a little more possible, a little bit more ready to love someone.

This is of course monstrous and intolerable. We recall, however, that the statement was made at a time of great personal stress, and we are relieved to counter to its enormity the modified terms in which Mailer, but a few months later, discussed the violence of Hipsterism with Richard Wollheim in England:

> I don't see the real choice as one between violence and non-violence. It's rather between the violence of the individual and collective violence. . . . [Whether or not protest needs to take such a total form as that of Hipsterism] depends on whether one thinks a society can solve its problems rationally. If one thinks it can, then hip will go nowhere. But if one thinks it can't, and that barbarism is closer, and that violence is in the seed, then at least hip introduces the notion of art into barbary.

We might reply to a formulation like this that barbary is precisely where art is not and never can be; that art and civilization are genetically inseparable. But no one who admits into the record of contemporary civilization the savagery of Nazism, or the spiraling success of Communist totalitarianism or, at a perhaps absurd extreme, even the gruesome spectacle of professional wrestling, can evade the validity of the problem Mailer poses for us when he asks that we look at the collective violence we call our moral order and, in the light of what we see, decide whether we can exempt the individual of responsibility for our degradation, and continue, as a culture, to feel morally superior to our collective conduct. While Hipsterism's conspiracy with the vicious in man's nature suggests a "cure" which certainly is little better than the disease for which it is prescribed, Mailer at least presses upon us an effort of honesty without which we live in moral delusion.

And yet is it not enough that he tell us what we must learn instead of telling us what we must do?

Clearly, this is the chief pitfall Mailer has contrived for himself as a writer—his neglect of the metaphoric character of the literary endeavor. For it is here that his espousal of violence ceases to be a strategy by which we are shorn of the hypocrisies and self-delusions with which we surround our participation in a violent civilization and becomes so gross an offense against the decency we still cherish both in our personal and in our collective lives. But if Mailer's actualization, even in his own conduct, of ideas that, for another writer, would remain simply figures of speech, has had its inevitable effect of nullifying some of the difficult truth with which he is dealing, it may also in the long run protect his radical insights from being so quickly and easily absorbed that we make no use of them. "The world doesn't fear a new idea. It can pigeon-hole any idea. But it can't pigeon-hole a real new experience." This is D. H. Lawrence speaking, who produced a body of work which is entirely metaphoric. And Lawrence left the world, certainly not untouched by his urgent insights, but sadly unaltered in its main course.

But Mailer's impulse to break the metaphor-barrier and himself act out, or ask that we act out, his ideas would now appear to have another, much deeper source than his impatience with the ability of art to achieve its tangible miracle of renovation. Intense as his literary dedication unquestionably is, his religious mission is now infintely more compelling. Just as he writes in order to preach the word of God, he acts in order to attain to God, by whatever thorny path. And when he invites us to follow his example he literally means us to join a religious crusade.

Even as a young writer and young Marxist, Mailer's vision carried him beyond a world of simply defined or materially determined notions of good and evil. We look back upon his first novel from our present vantage to see that Sergeant Croft's ascent of Mt. Anaka must be interpreted as the ascent of the Cross, and that Croft's triumph at the end of *The Naked and the Dead* represents a transcendence not merely over his own poor character, as we would judge it, but over an inglorious mankind which presumes to pass moral judgment and which fails to realize that God may appear to us in the strangest of disguises. And similarly with Marion Faye: while so far we see only the stigmata, we can suppose that in the long novel on which Mailer is working, in which Faye is said to have a leading part, Mailer's Hipster will come into the fullness of his spiritual blessedness. Nor is Mailer's invitation to sin so that we may find grace an unfamiliar heresy. If there has always been missing from Mailer's writing any true perception of the mysterious circuitous paths by which literature accomplishes its improving work, undoubtedly this is because he has always been

occupied with the mysterious circuitous ways in which God performs His work. His moral imagination is the imagination not of
art but of theology, theology in action.

This defect in Mailer's artistic imagination has many corollaries,
of which the most obvious are his small fictional concern with the
complexity and variety of human responses and, even more dis-
abling, the absence of a prose adequate to the larger intentions
of literature. If we were to conceive of Hemingway offering us his
heroic choice and his disenchantment with the hollow idealisms
of modern life in a language which was sufficient to propagate a
doctrine but no more than that; which failed to be its own quintes-
sential comment on the modern world and which exposed us to
the crude manipulations of ideology, without those areas of retire-
ment and indecision and even discordance which are so perfectly
re-created for us in the subtle tones and rhythms of Hemingway's
best writing—this would approximate Mailer's situation as a
novelist. For the life-giving subtleties of style, Mailer substitutes
a generosity of words. Like Thomas Wolfe before him, like Saul
Bellow in his own generation, he has a giant energy of vocabulary
with which he undertakes to make his discriminations of meaning.
But his taut strings of noun upon noun, adjective upon adjective,
intended to sharpen our response to reality, in fact sharpen only
his own act of assertion.

Of some (superficial) aspects of his stylistic problem, Mailer
is himself aware. Often in *Advertisements* he refers to his continuing effort to achieve a prose which will support his vision of
modernity and forbid us our easy evasions and falsifications. But
if, so far, his endeavor has largely missed its goal and indeed has
had the perverse effect of reinforcing Mailer's rhetoric of will, this
is by no means an inappropriate outcome. To a greater extent
than he perhaps recognizes, Mailer is an anti-artist, deeply dis-
trustful of art if only because it puts a shield between the perception and the act. His writer's role, as he conceives it, is much more
messianic than creative. While it was in the very nature of Hemingway's literary vocation that even in the moment of his most urgent
masculine assertion he was able to keep in abeyance the imposi-
tions of the merely personal masculine will, it is in the nature of
Mailer's social and spiritual vocation that he should wish to challenge, even personally dominate, his reader.

But if we listen closely, we perhaps hear his insistence as less the expression of personal authority than a call to a time when religion was still a masculine discipline—a call, that is, to a Hebraic world, still molded in the image of the stern father, Moses. From Moses to Marion Faye, with a stopover at Marx: Mailer's religious route is surely a strange one. But the braver efforts of culture are not always straightaway and simple.

The Black Boy Looks at the White Boy

by *James Baldwin*

> I walked and I walked
> Till I wore out my shoes.
> I can't walk so far, but
> Yonder come the blues.
> —*Ma Rainey*

I

I first met Norman about four years ago, in Paris, at the home of Jean Malaquais. Let me bring in at once the theme that will repeat itself over and over throughout this love letter: I was then (and I have not changed much) a very tight, tense, lean, abnormally ambitious, abnormally intelligent, and hungry black cat. It is important that I admit that, at the time I met Norman, I was extremely worried about my career; and a writer who is worried about his career is also fighting for his life. I was approaching the end of a love affair, and I was not taking it very well. Norman and I are alike in this, that we both tend to suspect others of putting us down, and we strike before we're struck. Only, our styles are very different: I am a black boy from the Harlem streets, and Norman is a middle-class Jew. I am not dragging my personal history into this gratuitously, and I hope I do not need to say that no sneer is implied in the above description of Norman. But these are the facts and in my own relationship to Norman they are crucial facts.

Also, I have no right to talk about Norman without risking a distinctly chilling self-exposure. I take him very seriously; he is

"The Black Boy Looks at the White Boy" by James Baldwin. From *Esquire* 55, no. 5 (May, 1961), 102–6. Copyright © 1961 by Esquire, Inc. Reprinted by permission of the publisher. This essay has also appeared in *Nobody Knows My Name* (New York: Dial Press, 1961), pp. 216–41.

very dear to me. And I think I know something about his journey from my black boy's point of view because my own journey is not really so very different, and also because I have spent most of my life, after all, watching and outwitting white people. I think that I know something about the American masculinity which most men of my generation do not know because they have not been menaced by it in the way that I have been. It is still true, alas, that to be an American Negro male is also to be a kind of walking phallic symbol: which means that one pays, in one's own personality, for the sexual insecurity of others. The relationship, therefore, of a black boy to a white boy is a very complex thing.

There is a difference, though, between Norman and myself in that I think he still imagines that he has something to save, whereas I have never had anything to lose. Or perhaps I ought to put it another way: the things that most people seem to imagine that they can salvage from the storm of life are really, in sum, their innocence. It was this commodity precisely which I had to get rid of at once, literally, on pain of death. I am afraid that most of the white people I have ever known impressed me as being in the grip of a weird nostalgia, dreaming of a vanished state of security and order, against which dream, unfailingly and unconsciously, they tested and very often lost their lives. It is a terrible thing to say, but I am afraid that for a very long time the troubles of white people failed to impress me as being real trouble. They put me in mind of children crying because the breast has been taken away. Time and love have modified my tough-boy lack of charity, but the attitude sketched above was my first attitude and I am sure that there is a great deal of it left.

To proceed: two lean cats, one white and one black, met in a French living room. I had heard of him, he had heard of me. And here we were, suddenly, circling around each other. We liked each other at once, but each was frightened that the other would pull rank. He could have pulled rank on me because he was more famous and had more money and also because he was white; but I could have pulled rank on him precisely because I was black and knew more about that periphery he so helplessly maligns in *The White Negro* than he could ever hope to know. Already, you see, we were trapped in our roles and our attitudes: the toughest kid on the block was meeting the toughest kid on the block. I think that both of us were pretty weary of this grueling and thankless role; I know that I am; but the roles that we construct are constructed because we feel that they will help us to survive and also, of course, because they fulfill something in our personalities; and one does not, therefore, cease playing a role simply because one has begun to understand it. All roles are dangerous. The world tends to trap and immobilize you in the role you play; and it is not always easy—in fact, it is always extremely hard—to maintain a kind of watchful, mocking distance between oneself as one appears to be and oneself as one actually is.

I think that Norman was working on *The Deer Park* at that time, or had just finished it, and Malaquais, who had translated *The Naked and the Dead* into French, did not like *The Deer Park*. I had not, then, read the book; if I had, I would have been astonished that Norman could have expected Malaquais to like it. What Norman was trying to do in *The Deer Park,* and quite apart, now, from whether or not he succeeded, could only—it seems to me—baffle and annoy a French intellectual who seemed to me essentially rationalistic. Norman has many qualities and faults, but I have never heard anyone accuse him of possessing this particular one. But Malaquais' opinion seemed to mean a great deal to him; this astonished me, too; and there was a running, good-natured but astringent argument between them, with Malaquais playing the role of the old lion and Norman playing the role of the powerful but clumsy cub. And, I must say, I think that each of them got a great deal of pleasure out of the other's performance. The night we met, we stayed up very late, and did a great deal of drinking and shouting. But beneath all the shouting and the posing and the mutual showing-off, something very wonderful was happening. I was aware of a new and warm presence in my life, for I had met someone I wanted to know, who wanted to know me.

Norman and his wife Adele, along with a Negro jazz-musician friend and myself, met fairly often during the few weeks that found us all in the same city. I think that Norman had come in from Spain, and he was shortly to return to the States; and it was not long after Norman's departure that I left Paris for Corsica. My memory of that time is both blurred and sharp, and, oddly enough, is principally of Norman—confident, boastful, exuberant, and loving—striding through the soft Paris nights like a gladiator. And I think, alas, that I envied him: his success, and his youth, and his love. And this meant that, though Norman really wanted to know

me, and though I really wanted to know him, I hung back, held
fire, danced, and lied. I was not going to come crawling out of my
ruined house, all bloody, no, baby, sing no sad songs for *me*. And
the great gap between Norman's state and my own had a terrible
effect on our relationship, for it inevitably connected, not to say
collided, with that myth of the sexuality of Negroes which Norman,
like so many others, refuses to give up. The sexual battleground,
if I may call it that, is really the same for everyone; and I, at this
point, was just about to be carried off the battleground on my
shield, if anyone could find it; so how could I play, in any way
whatever, the noble savage?

At the same time, my temperament and my experience in this
country had led me to expect very little from most American
whites, especially, horribly enough, my friends; so it did not seem
worthwhile to challenge, in any real way, Norman's views of life
on the periphery, or to put him down for them. I was weary, to
tell the truth. I had tried, in the States, to convey something of
what it felt like to be a Negro and no one had been able to listen:
they wanted their romance. And, anyway, the really ghastly thing
about trying to convey to a white man the reality of the Negro
experience has nothing whatever to do with the fact of color, but
has to do with this man's relationship to his own life. He will face
in your life only what he is willing to face in his. Well, this means
that one finds oneself tampering with the insides of a stranger, to
no purpose, which one probably has no right to do, and I chickened
out. And matters were not helped at all by the fact that the Negro
jazz musicians, among whom we sometimes found ourselves, who
really liked Norman, did not for an instant consider him as being
even remotely "hip" and Norman did not know this and I could
not tell him. He never broke through to them, at least not as far
as I know; and they were far too "hip," if that is the word I want,
even to consider breaking through to him. They thought he was
a real sweet ofay cat, but a little frantic.

But we were far more cheerful than anything I've said might
indicate and none of the above seemed to matter very much at the
time. Other things mattered, like walking and talking and drinking
and eating, and the way Adele laughed, and the way Norman
argued. He argued like a young man, he argued to win; and while
I found him charming, he may have found me exasperating, for
I kept moving back before that short, prodding forefinger. I

couldn't submit my arguments, or my real questions, for I had too much to hide. Or so it seemed to me then. I submit, though I may be wrong, that I was then at the beginning of a terrifying adventure, not too unlike the conundrum which seems to menace Norman now.

"I had done a few things and earned a few pence"; but the things I had written were behind me, could not be written again, could not be repeated. I was also realizing that all that the world could give me as an artist, it had, in effect, already given. In the years that stretched before me, all that I could look forward to, in that way, were a few more prizes, or a lot more, and a little more, or a lot more money. And my private life had failed, had failed, had failed. One of the reasons I had fought so hard, after all, was to wrest from the world fame and money and love. And here I was, at thirty-two, finding my notoriety hard to bear, since its principal effect was to make me more lonely; money, it turned out, was exactly like sex, you thought of nothing else if you didn't have it and thought of other things if you did; and love, as far as I could see, was over. Love seemed to be over not merely because an affair was ending; it would have seemed to be over under any circumstances; for it was the dream of love which was ending, I was beginning to realize, most unwillingly, all the things love could not do. It could not make me over, for example. It could not undo the journey which had made of me such a strange man and brought me to such a strange place.

But at that time it seemed only too clear that love had gone out of the world; and not, as I had thought once, because I was poor and ugly and obscure, but precisely because I was no longer any of these things. What point, then, was there in working if the best I could hope for now was the Nobel Prize? And *how,* indeed, would I be able to keep on working if I could never be released from the prison of my egocentricity? By what act could I escape this horror? For horror it was, let us make no mistake about that.

And beneath all this, which simplified nothing, was that sense, that suspicion—which is the glory and torment of every writer— that what was happening to me might be turned to good account, that I was trembling on the edge of great revelations, was being prepared for a very long journey, and might now begin, having survived my apprenticeship (but had I survived it?), a great work. I might really become a great writer. But in order to do this I would have to sit down at the typewriter again, alone—I would have to accept my despair: and I could not do it. It really does not help to be a strong-willed person, or, anyway, I think it is a great error to misunderstand the nature of the will. In the most important areas of anybody's life, the will usually operates as a traitor. My own will was busily pointing out to me the most fantastically unreal alternatives to my pain, all of which I tried, all of which—luckily—failed. When, late in the evening or early in the morning, Norman and Adele returned to their hotel on the Quai Voltaire, I wandered through Paris, the underside of Paris, drinking, screwing, fighting—it's a wonder I wasn't killed. And then it was morning, I would somehow be home—usually, anyway —and the typewriter would be there, staring at me; and the manuscript of the new novel, which it seemed I would never be able to achieve, and from which clearly I was never going to be released, was scattered all over the floor.

That's the way it is. I think it is the most dangerous point in the life of any artist, his longest, most hideous turning; and especially for a man, an American man, whose principle is action and whose jewel is optimism, who must now accept what certainly then seems to be a grey passivity and an endless despair. It is the point at which many artists lose their minds, or commit suicide, or throw themselves into good works, or try to enter politics. For all of this is happening not only in the wilderness of the soul, but in the real world which accomplishes its seduction not by offering you opportunities to be wicked, but by offering opportunities to be good, to be active and effective, to be admired and central and apparently loved.

Norman came on to America, and I went to Corsica. We wrote each other a few times. I confided to Norman that I was very apprehensive about the reception of *Giovanni's Room,* and he was good enough to write some very encouraging things about it when it came out. The critics had jumped on him with both their left feet when he published *The Deer Park*—which I still had not read— and this created a kind of bond or strengthened the bond already existing between us. About a year and several overflowing wastebaskets later, I, too, returned to America, not vastly improved by having been out of it, but not knowing where else to go; and one day, while I was sitting dully in my house, Norman called me from

Connecticut. A few people were going to be there—for the week end—and he wanted me to come, too. We had not seen each other since Paris.

Well, I wanted to go; that is, I wanted to see Norman; but I did not want to see any people, and so the tone of my acceptance was not very enthusiastic. I realized that he felt this, but I did not know what to do about it. He gave me train schedules and hung up.

Getting to Connecticut would have been no hassle if I could have pulled myself together to get to the train. And I was sorry, as I meandered around my house and time flew and trains left, that I had not been more honest with Norman and told him exactly how I felt. But I had not known how to do this, or it had not really occurred to me to do it, especially not over the phone.

So there was another phone call, I forget who called whom, which went something like this:

N: Don't feel you have to. I'm not trying to bug you.

J: It's not that. It's just—

N: You don't really want to come, do you?

J: I don't really feel up to it.

N: I understand. I guess you just don't like the Connecticut gentry.

J: Well—don't you ever come to the city?

N: Sure. We'll see each other.

J: I hope so. I'd like to see you.

N: Okay; till then.

And he hung up. I thought, I ought to write him a letter—but of course I did nothing of the sort. It was around this time I went South, I think; anyway, we did not see each other for a long time.

But I thought about him a great deal. The grapevine keeps all of us advised of the others' movements, so I knew when Norman left Connecticut for New York, heard that he had been present at this or that party and what he had said: usually something rude, often something penetrating, sometimes something so hilariously silly that it was difficult to believe he had been serious. (This was my reaction when I first heard his famous remark about running for mayor of New York. I dismissed it. I was wrong.) Or he had been seen in this or that Village spot, in which unfailingly there would be someone—out of spite, idleness, envy, exasperation, out of the bottomless, eerie, aimless hostility which characterizes almost every bar in New York, to speak only of bars—to put him down. I heard of a couple of fist fights, and, of course, I was always encountering people who hated his guts. These people always mildly surprised me, and so did the news of his fights: it was hard for me to imagine that anyone could really dislike Norman, anyone, that is, who had encountered him personally. I knew of one fight he had had, forced on him apparently by a blow-hard Village type whom I considered rather pathetic. I didn't blame Norman for this fight, but I couldn't help wondering why he bothered to rise to such a shapeless challenge. It seemed simpler, as I was always telling myself, just to stay out of Village bars.

And people talked about Norman with a kind of avid glee, which I found very ugly. Pleasure made their saliva flow, they sprayed and all but drooled, and their eyes shone with that blood lust which is the only real tribute the mediocre are capable of bringing to the extraordinary. Many of the people who claimed to be seeing Norman all the time impressed me as being, to tell the truth, pitifully far beneath him. But this is also true, alas, of much of my own entourage. The people who are in one's life or merely continually in one's presence reveal a great deal about one's needs and terrors. Also one's hopes.

I was not, however, on the scene. I was on the road—not quite, I trust, in the sense that Kerouac's boys are; but I presented, certainly, a moving target. And I was reading Norman Mailer. Before I had met him, I had read only *The Naked and the Dead, The White Negro,* and *Barbary Shore;* I think this is right, though it may be that I only read *The White Negro* later and confuse my reading of that piece with some of my discussions with Norman. Anyway, I could not, with the best will in the world, make any sense out of *The White Negro* and, in fact, it was hard for me to imagine that this essay had been written by the same man who wrote the novels. Both *The Naked and the Dead* and (for the most part) *Barbary Shore* are written in a lean, spare, muscular prose which accomplishes almost exactly what it sets out to do. Even *Barbary Shore,* which loses itself in its last half (and which deserves, by the way, far more serious treatment than it has received) never becomes as downright impenetrable as *The White Negro* does.

Now, much of this, I told myself, had to do with my resistance to the title, and with a kind of fury that so antique a vision of the blacks should, at this late hour and in so many borrowed heirlooms, be stepping off the A train. But I was also baffled by the passion

with which Norman appeared to be imitating so many people less
talented than himself, i.e., Kerouac, and all the other Suzuki
rhythm boys. From them, indeed, I expected nothing more than
their Pablum-clogged cries of *Kicks!* and *Holy!* It seemed very clear
to me that their glorification of the orgasm was but a way of avoid-
ing all of the terrors of life and love. But Norman knew better,
had to know better. *The Naked and the Dead, Barbary Shore,* and
The Deer Park proved it. In each of these novels, there is a tough-
ness and subtlety of conception and a sense of the danger and complexity of human relationships which one will search for in vain,
not only in the work produced by the aforementioned coterie, but
in most of the novels produced by Norman's contemporaries. What
in the world, then, was he doing, slumming so outrageously, in such
a dreary crowd?

For, exactly because he knew better and in exactly the same way
that no one can become more lewdly vicious than an imitation
libertine, Norman felt compelled to carry their *mystique* further
than they had, to be more "hip," or more "beat," to dominate, in
fact, their dreaming field; and since this *mystique* depended on a
total rejection of life, and insisted on the fulfillment of an infantile
dream of love, the *mystique* could only be extended into violence.
No one is more dangerous than he who imagines himself pure in
heart; for his purity, by definition, is unassailable.

But *why* should it be necessary to borrow the Depression language of deprived Negroes, which eventually evolved into jive and
bop talk, in order to justify such a grim system of delusions? Why
malign the sorely menaced sexuality of Negroes in order to justify
the white man's own sexual panic? Especially as, in Norman's case,
and as indicated by his work, he has a very real sense of sexual
responsibility, and even, odd as it may sound to some, of sexual
morality, and a genuine commitment to life. None of his people,
I beg you to notice, spend their lives on the road. They really become entangled with each other, and with life. They really suffer,
they spill real blood, they have real lives to lose. This is no small
achievement; in fact it is absolutely rare. No matter how uneven
one judges Norman's work to be, all of it is genuine work. No
matter how harshly one judges it, it is the work of a genuine novelist, and an absolutely first-rate talent.

Which makes the questions I have tried to raise—or, rather, the
questions which Norman Mailer irresistibly represents—all the

more troubling and terrible. I certainly do not know the answers and, even if I did, this is probably not the place to state them.

But I have a few ideas. Here is Kerouac, ruminating on what I take to be the loss of the garden of Eden:

"At lilac evening I walked with every muscle aching among the lights of 27th and Welton in the Denver colored section, wishing I were a Negro, feeling that the best the white world had offered was not enough ecstasy for me, not enough life, joy, kicks, darkness, music, not enough night. I wished I were a Denver Mexican, or even a poor overworked Jap, anything but what I so drearily was, a 'white man' disillusioned. All my life I'd had white ambitions. —I passed the dark porches of Mexican and Negro homes; soft voices were there, occasionally the dusky knee of some mysterious, sensuous gal; and dark faces of the men behind rose arbors. Little children sat like sages in ancient rocking chairs."

Now, this is absolute nonsense, of course, objectively considered, and offensive nonsense at that; I would hate to be in Kerouac's shoes if he should ever be mad enough to read this aloud from the stage of Harlem's Apollo Theatre.

And yet there is real pain in it, and real loss, however thin; and it *is* thin, like soup too long diluted; thin because it does not refer to reality, but to a dream. Compare it, at random, with any old blues:

> Backwater blues done caused me
> To pack my things and go
> 'Cause my house fell down
> And I can't live there no mo'.

"Man," said a Negro musician to me once, talking about Norman, "the only trouble with that cat is that he's white." This does not mean exactly what it says—or, rather, it *does* mean exactly what it says, and not what it might be taken to mean—and it is a very shrewd observation. What my friend meant was that to become a Negro man, let alone a Negro artist, one had to make oneself up as one went along. This had to be done in the not-at-all-metaphorical teeth of the world's determination to destroy you. The world had prepared no place for you, and if the world had its way, no place would ever exist. Now, this is true for everyone, but, in the case of a Negro, this truth is absolutely naked: if he deludes himself about it, he will die. This is not the way this truth presents itself to white men, who believe the world is theirs and who, albeit unconsciously, expect the world to help them in the achievement of their identity. But the world does not do this—for anyone; the world is not interested in anyone's identity. And, therefore, the anguish which can overtake a white man comes in the middle of his life, when he must make the almost inconceivable effort to divest himself of everything he has ever expected or believed, when he must take himself apart and put himself together again, walking out of the world, into limbo, or into what certainly looks like limbo. This cannot yet happen to any Negro of Norman's age, for the reason that his delusions and defenses are either absolutely impenetrable by this time, or he has failed to survive them. "I want to know how power works," Norman once said to me, "how it really works, in detail." Well, I know how power works, it has worked on me, and if I didn't know how power worked, I would be dead. And it goes without saying, perhaps, that I have simply never been able to afford myself any illusions concerning the manipulation of that power. My revenge, I decided very early, would be to achieve a power which outlasts kingdoms.

II

When I finally saw Norman again, I was beginning to suspect daylight at the end of my long tunnel; it was a summer day, I was on my way back to Paris, and I was very cheerful. We were at an afternoon party, Norman was standing in the kitchen, a drink in his hand, holding forth for the benefit of a small group of people. There seemed something different about him: it was the belligerence of his stance, and the really rather pontifical tone of his voice. I had only seen him, remember, in Malaquais' living room, which Malaquais indefatigably dominates, and on various terraces, and in various dives, in Paris. I do not mean that there was anything unfriendly about him. On the contrary, he was smiling and having a ball. And yet—he was leaning against the refrigerator, rather as though he had his back to the wall, ready to take on all comers.

Norman has a trick, at least with me, of watching, somewhat ironically, as you stand on the edge of the crowd around him, waiting for his attention. I suppose this ought to be exasperating, but in fact I find it rather endearing, because it is so transparent and because he gets such a bang out of being the center of attention. So do I, of course, at least some of the time.

We talked, bantered, a little tensely, made the usual, doomed effort to bring each other up-to-date on what we had been doing. I did not want to talk about my novel, which was only just beginning to seem to take shape, and, therefore, did not dare ask him if he were working on a novel. He seemed very pleased to see me, and I was pleased to see him, but I also had the feeling that he had made up his mind about me, adversely, in some way. It was as though he were saying, "Okay, so now I know who *you* are, baby."

I was taking a boat in a few days, and I asked him to call me.

"Oh, no," he said, grinning, and thrusting that forefinger at me, *"you* call *me."*

"That's fair enough," I said, and I left the party and went on back to Paris. While I was out of the country, Norman published *Advertisements for Myself,* which presently crossed the ocean to the apartment of James Jones. Bill Styron was also in Paris at that time, and one evening the three of us sat in Jim's living room, reading aloud, in a kind of drunken, masochistic fascination, Norman's judgment of our personalities and our work. Actually, I came off best, I suppose; there was less about me, and it was less venomous. But the condescension infuriated me; also, to tell the truth, my feelings were hurt. I felt that if that was the way Norman felt about me, he should have told me so. He had said that I was incapable of saying "F— you to the reader." My first temptation was to send him a cablegram which would disabuse him of that notion, at least insofar as one reader was concerned. But then I thought, no, I would be cool about it, and fail to react as he so clearly wanted me to. Also, I must say, his judgment of myself seemed so wide of the mark and so childish that it was hard to stay angry.

I wondered what in the world was going on in his mind.

Did he really suppose that he had now become the builder and destroyer of reputations?

And of *my* reputation?

We met in the Actors Studio one afternoon, after a performance of *The Deer Park*—which I deliberately arrived too late to see, since I really did not know how I was going to react to Norman, and didn't want to betray myself by clobbering his play. When the discussion ended, I stood, again on the edge of the crowd around him, waiting. Over someone's shoulder, our eyes met, and Norman smiled.

"We've got something to talk about," I told him.

"I figured that," he said, smiling.

We went to a bar, and sat opposite each other. I was relieved to discover that I was not angry, not even (as far as I could tell) at the bottom of my heart. But: "Why did you write those things about me?"

"Well, I'll tell you about that," he said (Norman has several accents, and I think this was his Texas one). "I sort of figured you had it coming to you."

"Why?"

"Well, I think there's some truth in it."

"Well, if you felt that way," I said, "why didn't you ever say so—to me?"

"Well, I figured if this was going to break up our friendship, something else would come along to break it up just as fast."

I couldn't disagree with that.

"You're the only one I kind of regret hitting so hard," he said, with a grin. "I think that I—probably—wouldn't say it quite that way now."

With this, I had to be content. We sat for perhaps an hour, talking of other things, and, again, I was struck by his stance: leaning on the table, shoulders hunched, seeming, really, to roll like a boxer's, and his hands moving as though he were dealing with a sparring partner. And we were talking of physical courage, and the necessity of never letting another guy get the better of you.

I laughed. "Norman, I can't go through the world the way you do because I haven't got your shoulders."

He grinned, as though I were his pupil. "But you're a pretty tough little mother, too," he said, and referred to one of the grimmer of my Village misadventures, a misadventure which certainly proved that I had a dangerously sharp tongue, but which didn't really prove anything about my courage. Which, anyway, I had long ago given up trying to prove.

I did not see Norman again until Provincetown, just after his celebrated brush with the police there, which resulted, according to Norman, in making the climate of Provincetown as "mellow as Jello."

The climate didn't seem very different to me—dull natives, dull tourists, malevolent policemen; I certainly, in any case, would never have dreamed of testing Norman's sanguine conclusion. But we had a great time, lying around the beach, and driving about, and we began to be closer than we had been for a long time.

It was during this Provincetown visit that for the first time I realized, during a long exchange Norman and I had, in a kitchen, at someone else's party, that Norman was really fascinated by the nature of political power. But, though he said so, I did not really believe that he was fascinated by it as a possibility for himself. He was then doing the great piece on the Democratic convention which was published in these pages, and I put his fascination down to that. I tend not to worry about writers as long as they are working —which is not as romantic as it may sound—and he seemed quite happy, with his wife, his family, himself. I declined, naturally, to rise at dawn, as he apparently often did, to go running or swimming or boxing, but Norman seemed to get a great charge out of these admirable pursuits and didn't put me down too hard for my comparative decadence.

He and Adele and the two children took me to the plane one afternoon, the tiny plane which shuttles from Provincetown to Boston. It was a great day, clear and sunny, and that was the way I felt; for it seemed to me that we had all, at last, re-established our old connection.

And then I heard that Norman was running for mayor, which I dismissed as a joke and refused to believe until it became hideously clear that it was not a joke at all. I was furious. I thought, You son-of-a-bitch, you're copping out. You're one of the very few writers around who might really become a great writer, who might help to excavate the buried consciousness of this country, and you want to settle for being the lousy mayor of New York. *It's not your job.* And I don't at all mean to suggest that writers are not responsible to and for—in any case always for—the social order. I don't, for that matter, even mean to suggest that Norman would have made a particularly bad mayor, although I confess that I simply cannot see him in this role. And there is probably some truth in the suggestion, put forward by Norman and others, that the shock value of having such a man in such an office, or merely running for such an office, would have had a salutary effect on the life of this city—particularly, I must say, as relates to our young people, who are certainly in desperate need of adults who love them and take them seriously, and whom they can respect. (Serious citizens may not respect Norman, but young people do, and do not respect the serious citizens; and their instincts here could not possibly be more sound.)

But I do not feel that a writer's responsibility can be discharged in this way. I do not think, if one is a writer, that one escapes it by trying to become something else. One does not become something else: one becomes nothing. And what is crucial here is that the writer, however unwillingly, always, somewhere, knows this. There is no structure he can build strong enough to keep out this self-knowledge. What *has* happened, however, time and again, is that the fantasy structure the writer builds in order to escape his central responsibility operates not as his fortress, but his prison, and he perishes within it. Or: the structure he has built becomes so stifling, so lonely, so false, and acquires such a violent and dangerous life of its own that he can break out of it only by bringing the entire structure down. With a great crash, inevitably, and on his own head, and on the heads of those closest to him. It is like smashing the windows one second before one asphyxiates, it is like burning down the house in order, at last, to be free of it. We do not, in this country now, have much taste for, or any real sense of, the extremes human beings can reach; time will improve us in this regard; but in the meantime the general fear of experience is one of the reasons that the American writer has so peculiarly difficult and dangerous a time.

One can never really see into the heart, the mind, the soul of another. Norman is my very good friend, but perhaps I do not really understand him at all, and perhaps everything I have tried to suggest in the foregoing is false. I do not think so, but it may be. One thing, however, I am certain is *not* false, and that is simply the fact of his being a writer, and the incalculable potential he, as a writer, contains. His work, after all, is all that will be left when the newspapers are yellowed, all the gossip columnists silenced, and all the cocktail parties over, and when Norman and you and I are dead. I know that this point of view is not terribly fashionable these days, but I think we *do* have a responsibility, not only to ourselves and to our own time, but to those who are coming after us. (I refuse to believe that no one is coming after us.) And I suppose that this responsibility can only be discharged by dealing as truthfully as we know how with our present fortunes, these present days. So that my concern with Norman, finally, has to do with how deeply he has understood these last sad and stormy events. If he has understood them, then he is richer and we are richer, too; if he has not understood them, we are all much poorer. For, though it clearly needs to be brought into focus, he has a real vision of ourselves as we are, and it cannot be repeated too often in this country now, that: *Where there is no vision, the people perish.*

Norman Mailer and the Despair of Defiance

by George Alfred Schrader

Norman Mailer, who first attracted attention by his novels, has been attracting attention more recently by his personal exploits. One of the more recent and, perhaps, the most dramatic of these exploits was the reported stabbing of his wife. The strange thing about this action, if we may rely upon the newspaper accounts, was the apparent lack of plausible motive. It was performed from neither jealousy nor anger, nor, if we accept the testimony both of Mr. Mailer and the psychiatrists who examined him by order of the court, out of any unconscious compulsive motivation. He was, he insisted, perfectly sane and aware of what he was doing in assaulting his wife. How, then, are we to understand the behavior of a man who is conscious and sane and yet performs a *motiveless* destructive act? I haven't the slightest doubt that Mailer not only knew what he was doing but performed the action only because he was aware of it—all too much aware of it, perhaps. Though in no way *necessitated* by the life-plan on which Mailer was apparently operating—and hence not compulsive—it fits all too neatly into that plan. If we are inclined to dismiss Mailer's action as "mad," it is only because we have too limited a view of human possibility. Soren Kierkegaard has, as I hope to show, provided us with an exquisitely precise description of the kind of program which Mailer has adopted for himself. Mailer calls it the "philosophy of Hip" and "good orgasm"; Kierkegaard terms it "the despair of defiance." They come to much the same thing.

Speaking of the task of the writer, Mailer asserts that ". . . the novelist who begins by addressing the world with some part of the world as his subject, becomes truly interesting only if he can present some solitary human possibility of choice which goes a

"Norman Mailer and the Despair of Defiance" by George Alfred Schrader. From *The Yale Review* 51, no. 2 (December, 1961), 267–80. Copyright © Yale University Press. Reprinted by permission of *The Yale Review*.

little further, a little deeper, into the mysteries of the self than the last writer before him." It is not, however, simply in his art that Mailer has sought "to present some solitary human possibility that goes a little further, a little deeper, into the mysteries of the self" but in his personal life as well. Mailer seems clearly to believe that in order to present such a radical possibility in the form of art one must first have experienced it oneself. The artist as writer and the artist as an existing human being are not to be separated. To write about courage adequately one must have courage and live by it. It is for this reason, perhaps, that Mailer claims to have written the first existentialist novel in America. (He recognizes that Faulkner might be considered an existentialist writer.) Whether consciously or not, Mailer subscribes to Kierkegaard's dictum that one should "exist in one's thought."

In his remarkably candid description of his state of mind during the period immediately following the success of *The Naked and the Dead*, Mailer informs us that he had suddenly been thrust into the center of things. "I had been moved from the audience to the stage—I was, on the instant, a man—I could arouse more emotion in others than they could arouse in me; if I had once been a cool observer because some part of me knew that I had more emotion than most and so must protect myself with a cold eye, now I had to guard against arousing the emotions of others, particularly since I had a strong conscience, and a strong desire to do just that—exhaust the emotions of others." He is speaking here not primarily of the effects of his novel but of himself as a successful novelist upon other people. Living in what Mailer terms "a psychic landscape of assassins and victims" he found that he had been suddenly lifted from obscurity into the most direct and threatening encounter with other men. "I was obviously a slave to anxiety, a slave to the fear that I could measure my death with every evening on the town, for the town was filled with people who were wired with shocks for the small electrocution of oneself." His success as a novelist had not only brought him prominently into the consciousness of others but delivered him into a dramatically new *self-consciousness* with which he is still attempting to come to terms. "This was experience unlike the experience I had learned from books, and from the war—this was experience without a name —at the time I used to complain that everything was unreal."

Actually this experience, which Mailer has described in considerable detail, is not without a name. It was not only named but thoroughly analyzed over a hundred years ago by Soren Kierkegaard in a work entitled *The Concept of Dread*. And it was further explored in three subsequent works, *Either/Or, Fear and Trembling,* and *The Sickness unto Death*. Dread, as Kierkegaard interprets it, is a constitutive feature of the human spirit. It is operative in every stage of human development from immediacy to the most highly developed self-consciousness. In innocence, where the spirit is dreaming, it takes the form of a vague melancholy, a malaise or "quiet perturbation." "In this state there is peace and repose; but at the same time there is something different, which is not dissension and strife, for there is nothing to strive with. What is it then? Nothing. But what effect does nothing produce? It begets dread. Dreamingly the spirit projects its own reality, but this reality is nothing, but this nothing constantly sees innocence outside of it." Dread is, in other words, that fundamental and pervasive mood in which one experiences his own freedom as the nothingness of possibility. "Thus dread is the dizziness of freedom which occurs when the spirit would posit the synthesis, and freedom then gazes down into its own possibility, grasping at finiteness to sustain itself. In this dizziness freedom succumbs." It is through his response to dread that the individual posits himself as spirit and either wills to be or not to be himself. Dread is, as it were, always one step ahead of the individual, enticing him on with undetermined possibilities. Because of its intrinsic ambiguity it both fascinates and repels, and thus makes possble both despair (anxious dread) and faith. "In dread there is the egoistic infinity of possibility, which does not tempt like a definite choice, but alarms (*Aengster*) and fascinates with its sweet anxiety (*Beaengstelse*)." A "sympathetic antipathy and an antipathetic sympathy," dread is the name of the uncanny experience to which Mailer refers as "unreal."

This is not to suggest that the writer of *The Naked and the Dead* was innocent. Only an ambitious and highly self-conscious individual could have written so powerful a novel. But if dread had been a factor in Mailer's earlier experience, it was now first erupting into the center of his consciousness. For what has Mailer discovered in this experience which he describes as "overheated, brilliant, anxious, gauche, grim—even, I suspect—killing" if not the presence of dread? He describes the situation with greater accuracy than he may have realized in saying that "willy nilly I had existentialism forced upon me." He did, indeed, if by "existentialism" is meant the disclosure of oneself and one's situation through self-conscious dread. Kierkegaard described dread as "the dizziness of freedom" that results when "freedom gazes down into its own possibility, grasping at finiteness to sustain itself." Mailer uses different terms, but characterizes his own predicament in essentially the same way. "I was free, or at least whatever was still ready to change in my character had escaped from the social obligations which suffocate others. I could seek to become what I chose to be, and if I failed—there was the ice pick of fear! I would have nothing to excuse failure. I would fail because I had not been brave enough to succeed. So I was much too free. Success had been a lobotomy to my past, there seemed no power from the past which could help me in the present, and I had no choice but to force myself to step into the war of the enormous present, to accept the private heat and fatigue of setting out by myself to cut a track through a new wild." As often happens, success brought with it a sense of anguished freedom, the power to try again for something more—and to succeed or fail without excuse! The future looms before him as "a new wild," as threatening as it is seductive. Mailer describes this ambivalence in himself as the possession of "two more than average passions going in opposed directions." He is at one and the same time fearful both of success and failure, a "slave to anxiety" and free "to become what I chose to be." Whether or not this experience made Mailer an existentialist on the spot, it certainly provided him with an existential awareness of the phenomenon of dread.

But Mailer is no existentialist—unless we are to consider his brand of self-styled "American existentialism" as an existentialist heresy. Whereas Mailer claims to be a confirmed *romantic* who hopes to find his destiny through Hip and "good orgasm," the European existentialists have been consistently opposed to all varieties of romanticism. Kierkegaard expressed the antiromantic orientation of existentialism pungently and succinctly in his assertion that "there is no immediate health of the spirit." Yet, it is just such an "immediate health of the spirit" which Mailer professes as the fundamental doctrine of his "existentialism." Although he is referring specifically to the psychopath rather than the hipster, what Mailer says about orgasm expresses the basic tenet of "the philosophy of Hip": "At bottom, the drama of the psychopath is that he seeks love. Not love as the search for a mate, but love as the search for an orgasm more apocalyptic than the one which preceded it. Orgasm is his therapy—he knows at the seed of his being that good orgasm opens his possibilities and bad orgasm imprisons him." The very notion of "orgasm," which might be construed as a self-chosen caricature of romantic imagery, is typical of the language and point of view of romanticism. Through the deliberate and repeated use of what is ordinarily considered to be obscene language, Mailer seeks to give his version of romanticism a more virile expression. He fails to recognize, however, that in obliterating the distinction between the sacred and the profane, he deprives obscene language of its shock value. When the language of the soldier becomes the language of the schoolboy—and even of female novelists—obscenity is transmuted into a pale vulgarity. Mailer is, if he only knew it, the worst enemy of Hip. As in so many instances, Mailer must depend upon the "squares" to preserve the purity of the distinction for him.

Whereas the existentialists have been sharply critical of romanticism, charging it with naiveté, "bad faith," or both at once, Mailer wants to recover the primeval vitality of romantic passion and reestablish it in a new power and glory. His quarrel is never with romanticism as such, but with those forms of romanticism which have become effete through social domestication. The chief difference between Mailer and earlier romantic reformers is that he is more violent in his attack upon social decadence and more desperate in his advocacy of the return to primitivism. Moreover, primitive freedom, as Mailer conceives of it, is far from the serene and idyllic affair envisioned by Rousseau. Mailer's faith, he tells us, is in the essential goodness of the uncorrupted (which means socially untrammeled) vitality of man's libidinal energies. Like Nietzsche, he represents himself as an antinihilistic nihilist who is summoning us to rebellion against a society which threatens to emasculate us. ". . . It [*Barbary Shore*] has an air which for me is the air of our time, authority and nihilism stalking one another in the orgiastic hollow of this century."

In his search for the *interesting*, for unexplored possibilities of human choice, Mailer has become fascinated with antisocial and psychopathic behavior. "For I wish to attempt an entrance into the mysteries of murder, suicide, incest, orgy, orgasm, and Time. These themes now fill my head and make me think I have a fair chance to become the first philosopher of Hip." But it is not as a *spectator* that Mailer sought to understand Hip; he was experiencing something of a psychic rebellion (liberation?) in himself. He reports that after his unhappy experience with the publication of *Deer Park* something broke in him and he was "finally open to my anger." "I turned within my psyche I can almost believe, for I felt something shift to murder in me." "All I felt then was that I was an outlaw, a psychic outlaw, and I liked it, I liked it a good sight better than trying to be a gentleman, and mined down deep into the murderous message of marijuana, the smoke of the assassins, and for the first time in my life I knew what it was to make your kicks." This anger, for which Mailer had become "open," was no ordinary anger, but the defiant rage of what Kierkegaard termed "demonic despair." "Now my will was a dictator; like all tyrants it felt the urgency of the present as unendurable."

"Hip," Mailer tells us, "is an exploration into the nature of man, and its emphasis is on the Self rather than Society." Whereas to the square "a rapist is a rapist" to be punished or imprisoned, to the hipster "rape is a part of life." The hipster knows that "even in the most brutal and unforgivable rape, there is artistry or the lack of it, real desire or cold compulsion, and so no two rapists nor no two rapes are ever the same." It is not, however, simply the fact that the hipster knows this—for many squares know it and have said as much, but the *way* in which he knows it that intrigues Mailer. To the hipster, rape is not a mere *theoretical* possibility pertaining indifferently to all men but a *real* possibility which he relates to himself through dread. It is one thing for me to know that all men are capable of committing rape and another to know that *I* can commit rape. The difference is that between an objective but *detached* possibility which applies to me as a member of a universal class, and an *existential* possibility which is real enough to evoke dread and anguish. The hipster knows that he could commit an act of rape—and might very well do it!

But there is an even more significant difference between the hipster and the square. Given the anguished knowledge of the possibility of rape, the hipster adopts a determinate attitude toward it. Unlike French existentialism (the only variety with which Mailer appears to be acquainted), "Hip is based on a mysticism of the flesh, and its origins can be traced back into all the undercurrents and underworlds of American life, back into the instinctive apprehension and appreciation of existence which one finds in the Negro and the soldier, in the criminal psychopath and the dope addict and the jazz musician, in the prostitute, in the actor, in the—if one can visualize such a possibility—in the marriage of the call girl and the psychoanalyst." Mailer is surely correct in calling attention to this difference—*so great a difference, in fact, as to differentiate it completely from all other forms of "existentialism."* Hip, as Mailer portrays it, is, indeed, a "mysticism of the flesh," a romantic glorification of the primordially instinctual. The trouble is that, like most nostalgia for the primitive, Mailer's advocacy of Hip is *phony.* Rape, murder, suicide, orgy, and even orgasm are anything but primitive "instincts." They are in their very nature culturally determined modes of behavior and highly sophisticated forms at that. And, what is more important, they depend for their meaning in Hip on their *negative* quality as rebellious acts against a predominantly square society. There are and could be no hipsters in a primitive African society, nor could hipsterism ever become a prevalent mode of conduct. If enough people became hipsters they would of necessity all turn out to be squares. Were the revolt which Mailer advocates to succeed, all would be lost. The Hip ideal is all too typical of romantic programs which have an essential term outside themselves and are, thus, negatively determined. Even as the romantic novel is over and, perhaps, ruined when the obstacles are finally removed, so it must be, also, with Hip as a program. It can succeed only in failure and be advocated only in "bad faith."

In spite of the fact that he is much concerned about *courage* and has some intimation of the ethical life—at least as it is represented by "squares," Mailer has persistently refused to break out of what Kierkegaard termed "esthetic immediacy." The esthetically determined life is founded upon natural impulses and desire and, hence, remains always within the context of sensuous immediacy. Although passion, which is so prominent in Mailer's consciousness, may be developed within the esthetic life, it represents the modification of natural desire through the infusion of spirit. In the esthetic program, however, spirit essays to be nothing but the *vehicle* through which instinctual power is expressed. Spirit strives for "a mysticism of the flesh" from which it must exclude itself. Herein lies the contradiction within the esthetic life and the seed of despair.

Because of the internal opposition on which it feeds, the esthetic life moves between the extremes of primitive emotion and poetic phantasy. Mailer seems to recognize this fact in the emphasis he places on being able "to swing" and "be with it" in Hip. *The capacity to float gracefully on the surface of desire seems to be the very essence of the Hip view of life.* "But to be with it is to have grace, is to be closer to the secrets of that inner unconscious life, which will nourish you if you can hear it." "So the language of Hip is the language of energy, how it is found, how it is lost." Without class or position the hipster depends entirely upon energy; impotence for him is equivalent to death. Mailer recognizes that the more highly the life founded upon desire is developed, the more it tends to lose its vitality. Primitive warfare gives way to mock combat and the lust for battle to chivalry. The individual discovers that he must preserve his enemy for the sake of the combat—and, if need be, provide him with horse and shield. On Mailer's view this attenuation of the libido is virtually equivalent to castration. What he fails to see is that the dissipation of natural power is not the result of a conspiracy by the "squares," but the inevitable result of a developed sensuousness. Mailer wants to have orgasm over and over again, each time more intense than the last and with no development. He seeks to live only in the *instant* which is unchanged in being repeated. Unfortunately, this view ignores the fact that natural energy is intrinsically and incorrigibly temporal. To affirm the natural and reject *development* is practically absurd. Incurably a romantic, Mailer cannot tolerate the fruits of the romanticism which he embraces. His rage is not so much against the world or anything within the world as against the impossibility of finding ultimate satisfaction within the sensuous while refusing to give up the attempt. He wants to sweep aside the refinements of civilization in order to begin once more at the beginning with an upsurge of primitive vitality. But can the result be any different? Isn't Kierkegaard perfectly correct in maintaining that as the erotic is developed the *rapist* becomes a *seducer*? It is strange indeed for an artist to set himself in violent opposition to the life of art.

The fact is that Mailer, in his new self-consciousness, has come to the point of what Kierkegaard termed "despair over the worldly." The refined world, with the delicate tissues of its artificiality, derives its meaning, esthetically viewed, solely from the natural desire on which it is founded. When the self-consciousness of an individual transcends the world of culture to the point where he can no longer find adequate meaning for himself within it, the bubble of immediacy is broken and he is open for despair over himself. Mailer has discovered what countless men before him have known, namely that the world offers us no self-sustained meaning, no ultimate satisfaction. And he is enraged, blaming everything on the "squares" who have spoiled everything for him. He sees himself now as in the position of having to "make his own kicks."

But even though it is in some respects the rage of a man who has come to consciousness of himself, Mailer's rage is, also, like that of the small boy who has discovered that there is no Santa Claus. Disappointed as we all are at this discovery, Mailer is enraged and refuses to accept the fact. Mailer wants courage, the courage to rebel against the society which has betrayed him. But this is an esthetically determined courage, the courage of rage and defiance. What he needs is the *ethically* determined courage to face up to the fact that the world is inevitably and hopelessly square, and that we must either decide how we are to live with it or set ourselves in futile and childish rebellion against it. It is a metaphysical rage that animates Mailer, a rage not just at this or that institution, but at the world itself.

That Mailer's own personal rebellion is futile could not be more eloquently revealed than in the stabbing of his wife. Mailer not only loved his wife, but it was probably for that reason that he stabbed her.

If Mailer is an existentialist he is an odd one, for he clearly cannot tolerate existence. He is enraged at his own freedom because it is finite. He will settle for nothing short of an omnipotence which would enable him to actualize every possibility. Failing that, he yearns to become fate itself in the hope that it might extinguish his miserable finitude. A mystic of the bottom, he seeks to be consumed by the "spirit of the flesh," not only "nearer to" but *identical* with "that God which every hipster believes is located in the senses of the body." Rape, murder, and suicide are not merely antisocial acts; they are *defiant* acts which seek to annihilate existence. Although the murderer ordinarily seeks to destroy only a single person, the *quality* of his passion is infinite. It is not so much his action as the *infinity* of the murderer's passion which intrigues Mailer. As he half-knows, he is obsessed not simply with violence, but with *death*. "Man's nature, man's dignity, is that he acts, lives, loves, and finally destroys himself seeking to penetrate the mystery of existence."

Mailer's hero, the hipster, corresponds nicely to Kierkegaard's esthetic hero, the "sensuous-erotic genius." Although Mailer chooses a primitive rather than a poetic expression of the erotic, the categories are essentially the same. The esthetic man, Kierkegaard argues, bases his life upon sensuous desire, lives only in the *instant*, and has no reality either for himself or others. The paradox of the esthetic life is that as the individual develops his own sensuousness he develops, also, his capacities as spirit and, hence, transcends immediacy. It is the inescapable fact of transcendence within immediacy which leads the sensuous-erotic genius more and more deeply into despair. For he is ultimately confronted with the choice: either to surrender the attempt to live within natural immediacy and go on to the ethical mode, or to hold himself defiantly within immediacy. To have discovered that an immediate fulfillment of the human spirit is *impossible* and, yet, to refuse to abandon the attempt to achieve it, is to be in *conscious* despair. This is, I would argue, essentially Mailer's predicament as set forth in *The White Negro*.

The sensuous-erotic, Kierkegaard maintained, can be adequately expressed only in *music*. "In its mediacy and as reflected in something other than itself, it comes under language, and becomes subject to ethical categories. In its immediacy, however, it can only be expressed in music." For his representation of the "sensuous-erotic genius" Kierkegaard selected Mozart's Don Juan. "Don Juan is, then, if I dare say so, flesh incarnate, or the inspiration of the flesh by the spirit of the flesh." Referring to the kingdom of the sensuous Kierkegaard observed that "in this kingdom language has no place, nor sober-minded thought, nor the toilsome business of reflection. There sound only the voice of elemental passion, the play of appetites, the wild shouts of intoxication; it exists solely for pleasure in eternal tumult. The first-born of this kingdom is Don Juan." This description could, with a few modifications, serve equally well to characterize the hipster, for he, too, knows only the "voice of elemental passion" and his language is *jazz*. "To be an existentialist (hipster or 'White Negro'), one must know one's desires, one's rages, one's anguish, one must be aware of the character of one's frustration and know what would satisfy it." One must learn to "divorce oneself from society, to exist without roots, to set out on that uncharted journey into the rebellious imperatives of the self." He must, in short, cultivate the psychopathic possibilities in himself. "It may be fruitful to consider the hipster a philosophical psychopath," philosophical because the hipster, unlike the psychopath, "possesses the narcissistic detachment of the philosopher." Hip represents "a dark, romantic, and yet undeniably dynamic view of existence for it sees every man and woman as moving individually through each moment of life forward into growth or backward into death."

Kierkegaard describes the sensuous-erotic in similar terms as "the despairing defiance which in impotence protests, but which can find no consistency, not even in sounds [jazz?]. When sensuousness appears as that which must be excluded, as that which the spirit can have nothing to do with, yet without passing judgment upon it or condemning it, the sensuous assumes the form of the demonic in esthetic indifference." Hip is the incarnation of the flesh from which spirit has been excluded and in which rape and murder are as significant as love and self-sacrifice. This is precisely what Kierkegaard means by "esthetic indifference." There are no genuine contradictions, no irreconcilable oppositions, within esthetic immediacy—whether it be Don Juan or the hipster. It is, however, *spirit* which posits the flesh as the "spirit of the flesh" and endows it with passion and dynamism. It is this feature of the sensuous that gives it a demonic quality—as *the defiant affirmation of the spirit as flesh incarnate.* Hip is, as Mailer states, "a dialectical conception of existence." The question is whether Mailer recognizes the true character of the dialectic. To posit spirit as spirit is to posit the square and, yet, only if one posits the square can he define the hipster.

The comparison between Kierkegaard's erotic genius and Mailer's White Negro is even more striking in view of the stress which Mailer puts upon jazz as the language of Hip. "But the presence of Hip as a working philosophy in the subworlds of American life is probably due to jazz, and its knifelike entrance into culture, its subtle but so penetrating influence on an avant-garde generation." It is through his music alone that the hipster has been able to express and communicate his sensuous eroticism to the culture at large. Because he "could not afford the inhibitions of civilization" the Negro "kept for his survival the art of the primitive, he lived in the enormous present, he subsisted for his Saturday night kicks, relinquishing the pleasures of the mind for the more obligatory pleasures of the body, and in his music he

gave voice to the character and quality of his existence, to his rage
and the infinite variations of joy, lust, languor, growl, crap, pinch,
scream and despair of his orgasm. For jazz is orgasm, it is the
music of orgasm, good orgasm and bad, and so it spoke across a
nation."

In analogous fashion Kierkegaard says of the sensuousness of
Don Juan that "it exists only in the moment." "Everything for him
is a matter of the moment only." Like the hipster, Don Juan exists
in the margin between nature and spirit. "In this generality, in
this floating between being an individual and being a force of
nature, lies Don Juan." The hipster is distinguished from the
square in that he can "swing at the right time." "What dominates
both character and context is the energy available at the moment
of intense context." The hipster "perceives his experience" in "that
dialectic of the instantaneous differentials of existence in which
one is forever moving forward into more or retreating into less."

Mailer's advocacy of Hip represents a curious blending of
nihilism (demonic defiance) and a pagan faith in the essential
goodness of elemental power. He identifies with the hipster both
because the White Negro is in full-scale rebellion against civilization (defiant) and unleashes the life-giving force of primitive emotion. The very notion of the White Negro symbolizes the opposition between civilization (White) and instinctual passion (Negro).
It is not only a *dialectical* but a *contradictory* idea in that rage and
rebellion derive their force and meaning from civilized passion and
can by no act of violence gain reentry into the innocence of immediacy. Mailer refuses to accept original sin as a fact of human
life and would undo the Fall of mankind. He will, if need be,
carry the human race back to the Garden of Eden on his own
shoulders—even if he must tread upon all the edifices of civilization to do it. The courage he wants is heroic, epic, Promethean,
but, also, futile.

Like all romantics, Mailer is overcome with pathos. He would be
omnipotent—and stabs his wife! His action would be comical if it
were not so pathetic. Must he not be aware of the fact that he
cannot remake the world, cannot attain the infinite power for
which he lusts? *Can his action be construed in any other way
than as a confession of despair?* He might equally well have *demon-
strated* his omnipotence by puncturing a balloon. It would have
been equally sound as a "proof" and with the advantages of sub-

stituting humor for pathos. Mailer might well have adopted for himself those words which Kierkegaard assigns to the defiant man: "Would that, along with the tiresome traits which all moral persons have, it possessed this good trait, that it had one head upon a single neck. . . . like Caligula I know what I would do." And Kierkegaard's rejoinder would apply equally well to Mailer: "You surely know the story of the crazy man who had the fixed idea that the room in which he lived was full of flies, so that he was in danger of being suffocated by them. With desperate fear and with desperate fury he fought for his existence. So you seem to be fighting for your life against just such an imaginary swarm of flies, against what you call 'the congregation.' " The esthetically determined man lives in an illusory world and contends with an imaginary enemy—the flies or the squares. The one thing he cannot accept is reality.

Although far advanced, Mailer's despair and defiance have not yet been developed to their highest point. Although he sees the human lot as on the whole miserable and contemptible, he still has hope of an *apocalypse*. He has not as yet experienced an even deeper despair over the primeval forces which lie at the foundation of human existence. What justifies his confidence in the essential goodness of primitive emotion, in the eventual rejuvenation of mankind through Hip? Could he will to be Hip even if it offered no hope of purgation, redemption, or apocalyptic orgasm? Suppose that in the infinity of his passion man were a sheer destructive power? What then? To will oneself as a purely demonic power would require a greater courage than Mailer has contemplated. Sometimes Mailer appears to have reached that point, to have an intimation of the defiant futility that must lie ahead. Kierkegaard says of the demonic man that "in spite of or in defiance of the whole of existence he wills to be himself with it, to take it along, almost defying his torment." "And as for seeking help from any other—no, that he will not do for all the world; rather than seek help he would prefer to be himself—with all the tortures of hell, if so it must be." Such a despair is unsupported by a pagan faith in the goodness of the flesh, is without the hope of a saving remnant at the bottom of society. It is to will oneself without hope and "with hatred for existence." In the case of potentiated despair "it is . . . as if an author were to make a slip of the pen, and that this clerical error became conscious of being such—it is then as if this clerical error would revolt against the author, out of hatred for him were to forbid him to correct it, and were to say, 'No, I will not be erased, I will stand as a witness against thee, that thou art a very poor writer.' " Such despair, which wills its own hopelessness, represents the ultimate in defiant courage.

The point of my remarks and of the comparison of the hipster with Don Juan is to suggest that Mailer has fixed himself in the esthetic mode of defiant despair. It is the *demonic* which he affirms as the heroic courage of Hip. The hope for redemption, as he sees it, lies in our capacity to surrender ourselves to a "dark and mysterious unconscious power" in which we must trust *blindly*. If we are fortunate, it will carry us along to a freeing and purging release in "good orgasm." But such a project cannot arrest despair, for it is based upon an illusory view of the natural. It evades the recognition that it is *spirit* which posits the flesh as flesh and that, once developed, spirit cannot be reabsorbed into the flesh. It only postpones the problem of ethical and religious choice. It is the dread of being responsible for himself that Mailer is as yet unwilling to confront. Either he must go on to an ethical-religious courage in which he affirms existence with all its finite blemishes—or remain in pathos. And, whether personally or as a novelist, for him the pathetic has only a limited scope. If he can free himself of his self-established bondage to the esthetic, he may yet be the outstanding novelist he so desperately wants but does not yet will to be.

The American Norman Mailer

by F. W. Dupee

Some future literary historian will doubtless be able to name the precise moment at which the big change in American literature occurred, and to give the reasons why it occurred at all. When, and from what combination of causes, did ambitious young men cease trying to write the Great American Novel and set about trying to *re*-write the Great American Novel? To the 20's generation, *The Scarlet Letter, Moby Dick, Walden,* James's novels, *The Red Badge of Courage* were all inspirations of one or another kind and degree of intensity. By what historical process did the same works and writers become what they so often are to writers today: sacred ancestral presences, established rituals to be gone through again and again, challenges to greatness, often veritable models?

The tendency began, I suspect, among certain surviving members of the 20's generation itself—writers who had lived to see the closing of European horizons by fascism and war, to be affected at home by the nostalgic spirit of *The Flowering of New England* and the vast body of criticism and scholarship stemming from it. Faulkner was perhaps the chief of these. In "The Old Man" and "The Bear" such ancestral themes as the big hunt, the open boat, the River God, the primitive initiation assumed a ritualistic air, although there was enough of the original Faulkner in those tales to make them masterpieces of a kind. Similarly with Hemingway's belated contribution to the same tendency, *The Old Man and the Sea,* of which a French critic has observed that it is *"classique, trop classique,"* while maintaining, as I do, that the story has enough of the *"vrai* Hemingway" in it to keep it alive. Indeed, such narratives represented a genuine mutation in the works of Faulkner and

"The American Norman Mailer" by F. W. Dupee (review of *Advertisements for Myself*). From *Commentary* 29, no. 2 (February, 1960), 128–32. Copyright © 1960 by the American Jewish Committee. Reprinted by permission of the author and *Commentary*.

Hemingway, and they have become, in turn, an influence on the younger writers.

Norman Mailer is among the more intrepid and protean of these younger writers. He would not be caught dead, I imagine, in the act of venerating the past or anything else. By his own testimony, the contemporary he most admires and envies is not "the most perfect writer" among them, namely Truman Capote; nor is it Gore Vidal, who has the best "formal mind" and most highly developed critical capacities. It is that rank original, who conceivably has never read a classic, James Jones. In fact the book in which Mailer offers these and other evaluations, many of them less generous, of his contemporaries, is rank with his own passion for new experience and his ambition to write the great novel of the future. A big unruly book, bearing a title that stuffs the mouth with consonants, and containing materials that in their variety defy definition, *Advertisements for Myself* (Putnam, 532 pp., $5.00) is partly an anthology of Mailer's shorter writings (though with specimens of some of his novels), partly a series of commentaries on them and his career in general.

As his career so far has been somewhat spotty, and he knows it, the book is rich in evidence bearing on his disappointments. There is blame for the several publishers who, out of prudery or prejudice, refused to accept the moderately daring *The Deer Park*: for the reviewers who, when the book was finally brought out, failed to appreciate its merits, as other reviewers had slighted *Barbary Shore,* his earlier novel; for the public whose taste has been corrupted by prosperity, television, and other recent phenomena. There is also blame, candid and often penetrating, for Mailer's own part in the process: his sometimes aimless malingering; his giving of himself on occasion to large febrile projects which came to nothing; his repeated misjudgments of people, situations, and his own abilities. *Advertisements for Myself* is chaotic; its tone is uncertainly pitched between defiance and apology. So much is this the case that anyone can easily lay hands on its jugular, and many reviewers have done so and thought they severed it. But the condition of Norman Mailer's life and art is that his jugular remains exposed. With all its faults in view, *Advertisements for Myself* is a confessional document of considerable interest and an engrossing chronicle of the postwar literary life. It is also an extremely funny book, for Mailer's gifts as a humorist are among his most reliable gifts. The one thing that his candor and wit leave unmolested is his own heavy dependence on the literary past, on *what has been done*.

He once embarked, he tells us, on "an enormous eight-part novel" and still proposes to complete it in some fashion and at some length—"Will it be a thousand pages?" he asks himself. This projected work he describes as "a descendant of *Moby Dick*." But is American literature so familial an affair that a novelist must conceive of his books in this genealogical way? Professions of piety apart, how is the projected novel really related to Melville's novel? Mailer remarks that *The Deer Park* was an outgrowth of his original project for a novel in eight parts—a black sheep of the white whale family, perhaps. Yet neither *The Deer Park* nor the fragments of the original project included in *Advertisements* shows any connection whatever with *Moby Dick* except one which seems to me unfortunate. "Call me Ishmael," *Moby Dick* begins, as no one needs to be reminded. And Mailer's "The Man Who Studied Yoga," which he says was to have served as "prologue to the early scheme," begins: "I would introduce myself if it were not useless. The name I had last night will not be the same as the name I have tonight. For the moment, then, let me say that I am thinking of Sam Slovoda."

This seems to me one of those conscious echoes which merely succeed in being wordier and shriller than the original. For the rest, the attraction of *Moby Dick* to Mailer, as a writer of future novels, seems to consist largely in its bulk, profundity, and prestige. It is to him, I should imagine, an image of literary power rather than a work to be admired, learned from perhaps, and then returned to its place of honor. And to judge by *Advertisements*, the literary past is all the weightier for him because it includes the achievements of Hemingway, Faulkner, Dos Passos, Fitzgerald, and others of their vintage, all of them together representing to him a massed accumulation of potency. How did he come to write his first published book, *The Naked and the Dead*, a novel of army life in the late war? ". . . I may as well confess I had gone into the army with the idea that when I came out I would write the war novel of World War II." With this idea in mind he did serve in the army (proudly, as a rifleman) and he did produce, punctually, efficiently, and as if on demand, *The Naked and the Dead*.

But what an idea, and what a phrase, "the war novel of World War II"! *The* war novel? To be sure, Hemingway, Dos Passos, and others of their time had used their varied experiences of World War I in the writing of a lot of enormously varied books. Not they, but later journalists and sociologists, lumped those books together in the misleading, the unreal, category of "war novels." And when the second war arrived, the same crowd created that demand for "the novel of World War II" which Mailer determined to meet.

Advertisements for Myself testifies to his constant preoccupation with those 20's writers, in their capacity not merely as war novelists but as symbols of literary prestige in general. Hemingway represents a special example and challenge to Mailer throughout *Advertisements*. He tells one story which, trivial as it looks, is actually significant of his relation to the muscular master. He once mailed to Hemingway, personally a stranger to him, an unsolicited copy of *The Deer Park* and presently got the package back from Havana unopened. As it happened, he was not too sorry to have the book returned, for he had written in it certain words which he now regretted. After some manful sparring in Hemingway's own vein, he had said that he was "deeply curious" to learn Hemingway's reaction to the book. That "deeply curious" had come to seem to him a false note.

Now, Mailer admits that the Cuban postal system, rather than Hemingway, may inadvertently have administered the seeming snub. Yet he includes the episode in *Advertisements*. And one can readily see why he does, just as one can see the point of other apparent irrelevancies and absurdities memorialized in the same volume; these contribute much to its truth and humor. The significance was that the Hemingway whom Mailer addressed was the wrong Hemingway. He was not the young Ernest who conscientiously created the Hemingway art and who, if he had survived, might have shown interest in a young artist like Norman Mailer. The Hemingway he addressed was the swaggering Papa of the later legend, who naturally wouldn't "know" Mailer.

No Olympians can ever have looked more Olympian to an outsider than Hemingway and the others have looked to Mailer. Faulkner, he tells us, recognized his existence only by ridiculing his extravagant claims for Negro sexuality. And Mailer, coming of literary age in the 40's when the older writers were already established, already moneyed, be-prized, widely translated and imitated, acquired a mixed feeling for them. His genuine appreciation of their work was laced with a strong sense of their material stature —their reputation, influence, position in the literary market place. One sees, too, that his disposition to regard them, and the literary past in general, in this light, arose not only from the fact of his coming of age at this formidable phase of their careers. He also came of age at a moment of rapidly growing prosperity and expanding culture in America, when similar rewards seemed to be within reach of himself and other aspiring young writers.

Hence, probably, the dreams of worldly power which, in the pages of *Advertisements,* give unmistakable signs of being conjoined to his legitimate literary ambitions. Unmistakable? He has been "running for President for years," he says, and applies the same phrase to James Jones. Such truculent admissions are evidently supposed to induce in the reader a state of amused shock. To me they represent a rather depressing confusion of purposes. Why, with a thousand-page novel to finish, does anyone *want* to be President, unless he fears that he will never finish the novel?

In his three novels to date, as in *Advertisements for Myself,* Mailer is often a formidably good writer. He also gives, beneath the bluster of *Advertisements,* an appealing account of himself as a person. Scattered throughout that book are wry tales of the predicaments in which he has landed while trying to sustain the life of a free spirit in an unfavorable age. No doubt he sees himself, in Norman Podhoretz's phrase, as "a battleground of history." *Advertisements* may, as Alfred Kazin affirms, resemble Fitzgerald's *The Crackup* in showing "how exciting, yet tragic, America can be for a gifted writer." But Mailer's battleground has at least these resemblances to a city playground: it is strenuous, competitive, gang-conscious, cruel, sporting, amusing. And though America is unquestionably exciting to Mailer, it is wonderful how little he ever allows it to become tragic. Indeed, his response to the excitement of it is intense enough to preclude his feeling "deeply" any tragedy in it. One of the advantages of *Advertisements* over his novels is that the sense of excitement and the laughter get full play here, unembarrassed by any need to write, or rewrite, the Great American Novel. America represents wonderful sport and adventure to Mailer; and they get better as America itself seems to him to grow more corrupt and menacing. Tom Sawyer scarcely relishes his grim games of life and death more thoroughly than Mailer does his experiences as soldier, revolutionary, Hipster, junkie, and associate of pimps and call-girls. And like a far more mature and engaging Tom Sawyer, he relishes "evil" in proportion as he himself is incorrigibly moral.

Or, at least, in proportion as he is preoccupied with "morale," a slightly different matter, I admit. In his well-known and brilliant essay "The White Negro" he formulates the cult and discipline of the Hipster, a charming but probably doomed phenomenon of recent years. He quite possibly *over*-formulates Hip, schematizes it, makes its ways and words merely antithetical to those of its enemy the Square, reduces it to a kind of cross between a game and a form of hygiene. Hip makes for a livelier vocabulary, a more stylish way of carrying oneself, more and better orgasms. Thanks to Hip, a bi-sexual Negro Mailer knows gets as much of a charge out of a certain chick as out of a battalion of Marines. *There's* a testimonial to Hip as conducting to fair play and a well-rounded life. Hip is *good for you.*

Something of this same two-way attitude toward experience seems to me to enter into Mailer's novels, helping to account for both their virtues and their shortcomings. On one of his sides he rejoices in that "appetite for life" which he admires in James Jones. Sheer experience, experience for its own sake, leads him on. And just as this makes him a comparative rarity among younger writers today, so it constitutes his living relation to the older American writers —his living one, that is, as distinguished from the relation by way of familial piety and emulation. But on another side he has an equal hunger for ideas, a hunger that is not so well satisfied by what he can produce in the way of intellectual nourishment. The various forms of enlightenment which the older writers brought to bear on their experience seem to have crystallized, for Mailer, into a vague, self-conscious sort of wisdom. This has sought to express itself in appropriate ideas, Marxist or Nietzschean (Hip has Nietzschean roots, as Norman Podhoretz implies) or Freudian. Of these the Freudian is Mailer's most pervasive source of ideas and images. It is astonishing how often in his novels an authoritative older person is engaged in trying to assist some younger, more amorphous person to maturity. (Eitel, the movie director of *The Deer Park,* is eager to help his mistress "grow up," and Marion

Faye, the glorified pimp of the same book, has a similar relation to his call-girls and junkie acquaintances.) But the Freudian ideas, like those of other derivation, often operate not to reinforce and clarify his experience but to embarrass and devitalize it. The author himself seems frequently to approach his material as the learner, the disciple, the patient, eager to grow up.

The result in his novels is, as I say, a sort of tug of war between his passion for experience and his felt need of enlightening ideas. And it is in *The Deer Park,* that survivor of what was to be his eight-part colossus, that Mailer's contradictions reach their maximum intensity. When Alfred Kazin calls *The Deer Park* a "somehow sick book," "peculiarly airless and closed," I feel obliged to assent even while rebelling against the J. Donald Adams-like adjectives. (*The Deer Park* brings out the old Adams in us all.) For this novel about the sex life, the political, social, and business problems of Hollywood personages gathered in a resort resembling (I gather) Palm Springs, is frequently paralyzed by its opposing intentions. The manners prevailing in this unpleasant pleasure resort are superbly observed. The conversation of Hollywood magnates is admirably comic. The routines of the call-girls form a weird dance-like pattern within the slowly moving narrative. In the rendering of such things Mailer's passion for experience is matched by his expert knowledge of what he writes about. How does it happen, then, that this panorama of iniquity is constantly threatening to turn into a waxworks display? For one thing, Mailer's trio of heroes, Eitel, Faye, and O'Shaugnessy, are too sententious and loquacious and self-conscious. In their frequent colloquies they constitute a sort of committee interminably "chewing on" (in committee jargon) the agenda of the day. And with much help from the author, by way of his often intrusive comments on the action, they just about chew the hell out of it. Literally, they all but convert the experience of modern corruption into something inert, dry, and abstract. Here is an encounter between Marion Faye the super-pimp and a young Mexican delinquent:

> Marion had not seen him in a long time. Paco had been picked up in a robbery and had lived a term in state prison. The fact he dropped in like this after an absence of two years did not startle Faye. Such things were always happening to him.
>
> "I hear you're peddling gash," said Paco, "you got some gash for me?"

It was weird. Paco was neurotic, Faye thought, a pimply dreamy kid, begging for dough. In his family his mother hounded Paco, he used to call her dirty names; in the clubhouse he would lie around for hours reading comic books; once he announced he wanted to go to the South Seas. Even at the age of seventeen, tears came into his eyes at a harsh word. And now he was a junkie, and he needed a fix. Sudden compassion for Paco burned Faye's eyelids. The poor slob of a *pachuco*.

As Faye is already well known to the reader at this nearly mid-way point of the novel, we do not need to be nudged by the author into realizing that he is unstartled, "such things were always happening to him." Nor does Faye's curiously psychiatric relation to the boy gain in convincingness by our being told flatly that "Paco was neurotic." (Surely an understatement!) Indeed Faye is not what he or Mailer thinks he is but a sentimentalist, with his (ouch!) "pimply dreamy kid" and his (OUCH!) eye-scalding "compassion."

In *Advertisements for Myself* there are many indications that Norman Mailer will pull out of his difficulties, which are in part the difficulties of other writers of his age and time. The achievements of the literary past inevitably acquire an excess of prestige by contrast with the present creative stalemate. And since the creative stalemate happens to coincide with a condition of unexampled economic prosperity, it is natural that writers should dream, not only of rewriting the American classics, but of running for President. With his essential humor, sanity, and (yes!) humility, Mailer seems to perceive much of this situation and to give promise of reconciling his appetite for life with his appetite for ideas. But a novel in perhaps a thousand pages? *Raintree County* approached that length, I believe, but *Moby Dick,* in my edition, runs to only 822.

Norman Mailer's Yummy Rump

by Stanley Edgar Hyman

"There are nights when one comes home after a cancerously dull party, full of liquor but not drunk, leaden with boredom, somewhere out in Fitzgerald's long dark night. Writing at such a time is like making love at such a time. It is hopeless, it desecrates one's future, but one does it anyway because at least it is an act. Such writing is almost always unsprung. It is reminiscent of the wallflower who says, 'To hell with inhibitions, I'm going to dance.' The premise is that what comes out is valid because it is the record of a mood. So one records the mood. What a mood. Full of vomit, self-pity, panic, paranoia, megalomania, *merde,* whimpers, excuses, turns of the neck, flips of the wrist, transports. It is the bends of Hell. If you purge it, if you get sleep and tear it up in the morning, it can do no more harm than any other bad debauch."

This is Norman Mailer in *Esquire* not long ago, ostensibly talking about the work of a contemporary, but obviously telling us the genesis of his new novel. Instead of tearing it up in the morning, Mailer published it as *An American Dream. An American Dream* is a dreadful novel, perhaps the worst I have read in many years, since it is infinitely more pretentious than the competition. Mailer's novel is bad in that absolute fashion that makes it unlikely that he could ever have written anything good. Since its awfulness is really indescribable, instead of trying to describe it I will try to communicate its quality by allowing three of its constituents to represent the whole. These are: its plot, its mystique of human smells, and its tropes.

The novel covers several days in the life of the narrator, Stephen Richards Rojack, a New Yorker in his early forties. He was briefly a Congressman, and now makes his living as a professor of existentialist psychology at a city university, where he offers a seminar in Voodoo, and as master of ceremonies on a far-out television interview program; he is the author of one popular book, *The Psychology of the Hangman*. Rojack was a hero in the Second World War, and is in fact "the one intellectual in America's history" with a Distinguished Service Cross. He is separated from his wife, a beautiful rich Roman Catholic of Hapsburg ancestry, Deborah Caughlin Mangaravidi Kelly.

Rojack begins the novel's action by a wrestling match with his wife, occasioned by her boasting of perversities with her lovers, in the course of which he strangles her. He leaves the corpse on the carpet, goes downstairs and buggers the maid, who in her enthusiasm admits to being a Nazi, and tells him that he is absolutely a sexual genius. Then he goes back upstairs, cleans his wife's corpse up a bit, and pitches it out the window.

This piles up traffic on the East River Drive, and one of the cars involved contains Eddie Ganucci, a statesman in the Mafia, and a beautiful blonde nightclub singer named Cherry Melanie, who looks "like a child who has been anointed by the wing of a magical bird," and with whom Rojack promptly falls in love. As soon as the detectives release him, Rojack goes to the club where Cherry sings, outfaces a burly prizefighter, and takes Cherry home to bed.

The next day there is another interview with the detectives, in the course of which Rojack defends himself so skillfully that he is told: "You missed a promising legal career." Then he learns that his wife's murder has been declared a suicide as a result of his father-in-law's influence. He returns to Cherry, who confesses to being a fan of his television program, and expresses her feeling for his talents by biting pieces of skin out of his ear. She tells him that she was raised by an incestuous half-brother and half-sister, after which he succeeds in bringing her to the first orgasm she has ever experienced in genital intercourse.

While they are engaged in mutual congratulations, Cherry's former lover, a gifted Negro singer and "stud" named Shago Martin, walks in on them. He pulls a switchblade on Rojack, but Rojack, unarmed, overcomes him, beats him up, and throws him down the stairs. Rojack then goes to visit his father-in-law, the mysterious tycoon Barney Oswald Kelly, another former lover of

Cherry's. While Rojack is at Kelly's, President Kennedy (called "Jack") telephones to express his condolences. The Nazi maid is now working for Kelly and simultaneously blackmailing him, and she tells Rojack that at the time of her death Deborah was involved with lovers high in American, Soviet, and British espionage circles. "Last night there must have been electricity burning in government offices all over the world," she adds.

Kelly compels Rojack to listen to his life story, spiced with father-daughter incest, and Rojack then demonstrates his courage (he intends "to blow up poor old Freud" by showing that cowardice is the root of neurosis) by walking a dangerous parapet near Kelly's terrace. Kelly tries to push him off the parapet with an umbrella, but Rojack smashes Kelly in the face with the umbrella and departs. He goes back downtown and learns that Shago has been beaten to death by an unidentified assailant in Morningside Park, and Cherry has been beaten to death in her apartment by a confused friend of Shago's. Rojack arrives just in time to hear her last words. He then drives to Las Vegas, where he is highly successful at the dice tables. The book ends with his telephoning Cherry in Heaven; we know it is Heaven because "Marilyn says to say hello."

These are merely a few of the simpler strands in the plot. Synopsis cannot convey the unbelievability of the characters (Kelly, for example, seems based largely on Fu Manchu: he says "me" for "I," but asks "do you know that phrase of Kierkegaard's of course you do—I was in a fear and trembling"). It cannot convey the genteel double standard of the sex (sodomy is for servants), or the windy occultism that accompanies the sex acts (going to bed with Rojack must be like going to bed with Madame Blavatsky). It particularly cannot convey the dreamy unreality of the conversation ("You black ass ego," says Cherry sternly to Shago).

The book is full of mystiques, Rojack has powers of telekinesis and precognition; the deaths of Shago and Cherry seem to be caused by a posthumous curse of Deborah's, which Rojack escaped by walking the parapet; there is a great deal of pajama-party demonology, including an encounter with "the most evil woman ever to live on the Riviera," who justifies the title by keeping a scorpion in a cage.

The most curious of these mystiques is the spirit odors that the characters emanate. Before he cleanses himself by strangling

Deborah, Rojack smells "like the rotten, carious shudder of a de-
cayed tooth." Deborah's smell is compounded of "sweet rot," "burning rubber," and "a bank." The Nazi maid has "a thin high con-
stipated smell," as well she might. A pair of detectives give off,
respectively, "a kind of clammy odor of rut," and "the funk a bully
emits when he heads for a face-to-face meeting." Ganucci exudes
"an essence of disease, some moldering from the tree of death."
Cherry smells "of something sweet and strong," among its elements
"the back seats of cars." The principal detective smells "sour with
use, and also too sweet." Shago's odor is "a poisonous snake of
mood which entered my lungs like marijuana," later "a smell of
full nearness as if we'd been in bed for an hour." Kelly emits "some
whiff of the icy rot and iodine in a piece of marine nerve left to
bleach on the sand," varied by "the stench which comes from de-
votion to the goat."

These phrases should give some idea of Mailer's prose, which is
additionally distinguished by poetic inversions ("Neat and clean
was his blue shirt"), unidiomatic tenses ("Whatever Deborah would
deserve"), and sentences without a fig leaf of syntax ("Enormous,
and stared at one with a clear luminous look, an animal's fright,
some creature with huge eyes.") The similes, however, deserve special attention. Some of them are Homeric, for example, a passage
that begins, "Once, in a rainstorm I witnessed the creation of a
rivulet," and concludes six lines later: "That was how the tears
went down Cherry's face."

Many of the similes are tritely romantic: "narrow and mean as
the eye of a personnel director," "the look of a rock-hard little
jockey recollecting an ugly race," "faint as the ghost of a jewel
box." Others are excessively labored: "as if drunkenness were a
train which rocketed through the dark and I was sitting in a seat
which gave out backward on the view and so receded further and
further from some fire on the horizon: thus came each instant
nearer to the murmur one hears in the tunnel which leads to
death."

Some of the similes seem deranged. "Hot as the gates of an icy
slalom" is one such; others are: "I cried within like a just-cracked
vase might shriek for cement," which is ungrammatical in addition;
and "with the insight of an ice pick the precise thought came to
me." Two woeful herpetological tropes suggest that Mailer has

never seen a snake: Shago's switchblade "opened from his palm like a snake's tongue"; "The umbrella lay like a sleeping snake across my thighs."

Mailer's slovenly misuse of language creates non-existent characters and stories. "Like sitting to dinner in an empty castle with no more for host than a butler and his curse" is the single mysterious reference in the book to The Butler's Curse. "I was close to a strong old man dying now of his overwork" does not mean that an old man is dying near Rojack, in fact there is no old man; it is Mailer trying to say that Rojack feels poorly. Other tropes are notable for their spit-on-the-Harvard-crimson vulgarity: "a delicious pain clean as a mistress' sharp teeth going 'Yummy' in your rump" is perhaps my favorite, although an orgasm "fierce as the demon in the eyes of a bright golden child" has a lot to recommend it.

I do not think that all of this is due to simple ineptness. Some of it surely represents Mailer's immortal longing, to be a *big* fancy writer like Thomas Wolfe. I submit one further simile in evidence: "as if the terrors of men were about as admirable as the droppings of hippopotami." This has everything: turns of the neck, flips of the wrist, transports, *merde,* even an elegant Latinate plural.

Enough. Why didn't Mailer pitch the whole preposterous mess out the window after he read it over? Ask *Esquire* and Dial Press and Dell Books and Warner Brothers, which have guaranteed him half a million dollars for it.

The Energy of New Success

by John W. Aldridge

For a good many years now Norman Mailer has been making a determined effort to exploit all the resources of literary and social outrageousness in order to impress himself in a major way on the life and thought of his time. At no point in the course of this effort has the going been easy for Mailer; in fact, it has been so difficult and personally taxing that one often supposed that his ultimate objective was not the moral reformation of his society but the annihilation of himself. The fight he has carried on has made almost superhuman demands on his will power and his courage; it has caused deep erosion of his ego, even at those moments when his ego has been most insufferably in evidence; and inevitably it has provoked him to follies and excesses that have done him and his work serious harm.

For one thing, it has led him to antagonize large sectors of the reading public and to make powerful enemies among many people who might otherwise have been disposed to help him in a literary way. For another, it has cut down on the quality of his achievement as a novelist by giving almost everything he has written since *The Naked and the Dead* a curiously strained, claustrophobic quality that seemed to speak of the existence of creative ambitions too intense for his creative grasp. One could sense in both *Barbary Shore* and *The Deer Park* that the main current of his energy was trying to go elsewhere, trying to engage certain crucial ideas that were beginning to take shape in his mind, but was being balked by some recalcitrance in his material or some limitation in his language. Deep within those books one felt the pressure of something big growing, a vision or prophecy or simply a hatred that was perhaps too radical and disturbing to find embodiment in the conventional forms of the novel, perhaps too radical and disturbing for Mailer himself, who seemed to be reaching out for reassurance and support even as he was energetically engaged in alienating just about everybody.

For a long time Mailer was driven to seek easy and sensational shortcuts to the fulfillment he appeared unable to find in his work. He tried to gain attention through self-advertisement, challenges of the law, attempts to pass himself off as a New York mayoralty candidate, as the only man with guts enough to defy Sonny Liston to his face, as the man mainly responsible for Kennedy's election to the Presidency. The essays, furthermore, in which he put forth these claims seemed to be the only writing he was able to do, and this struck many people as an open admission that he had at last decided he could not make it in an important way as a novelist and was trying to salvage what was left of his career by peddling his megalomania to *Esquire.*

It was hard to say whether prevailing opinion was right or wrong, whether these were indeed the antics of a man sick for publicity at any price, or the honestly frustrated responses of a writer who for some reason could not mediate successfully between his ambitions and the restrictive literary circumstances of his time. Undoubtedly, they were a little of both. But certain clues to be found in his random utterances and published work slowly began to give greater weight to the second interpretation. The autobiographical passages of *Advertisements for Myself,* in particular, seemed to suggest that although he was indeed sick for publicity, he was not sick for it at any price. He was much too anxious about his career to be willing to risk it by exploiting, solely for publicity reasons, his dubious roles of professional bad boy and clown. If he behaved irresponsibly, he did so for naïve but very different and wholly honorable reasons: because he suffered from a deep-lying dissatisfaction with his position as a serious novelist and was trying in all the wrong ways to break out of the impasse in which he felt himself trapped and meet what seemed to him his first responsibility to himself. It only made his dissatisfaction seem more poignant to recognize, as of course he could not, that it was based on a sadly inflated idea of the kind of position a serious novelist can expect in our day to enjoy.

Very early in his career Mailer fell victim to the notion that large popular success was the fit and natural reward for significant achievement in the novel. He appears to have arrived at this conclusion after long and jealous study of the lives and work of the important novelists of the twenties and thirties, some of whom managed to achieve popularity with the reading public at the same time that they were recognized by the people who mattered as major literary figures. Hemingway, for example, was both great and world-famous, and so, in more modest degree, were Fitzgerald, Steinbeck, and Wolfe. Mailer of course reacted powerfully and personally to the good fortune of these men and from it abstracted a formula for success with which he proceeded, characteristically, to prove himself a failure. It seemed to him that if a novelist were serious enough and good enough, he would inevitably be widely read and widely praised. If he were not widely read and widely praised, that could only mean that he was not good enough. In fact, he could consider himself a total loss unless his books made the bestseller lists and stayed on them a certain generous number of weeks.

It apparently never occurred to Mailer that his idea of literary success was perfectly suitable and applicable to the commercial novelist with his heart set on Book-of-the-Month Club adoption, or that he was drawing a false inference from historical circumstances that could only be considered extraordinary and temporary. The times in which he himself became a novelist were very different from the twenties and thirties, and the whole relationship between the novelist and the reading public had profoundly changed—and changed, according to his own logic, for much the worse. Among the writers with whom he could consider himself in direct competition, only Salinger enjoyed anything like the status of the younger Hemingway or Fitzgerald, and there was much in Salinger's work and reputation at which Mailer might legitimately have sneered. Most of his other contemporaries, furthermore, appeared to have resigned themselves to being more praised or criticized than read, and to having a certain limited status in the literary world while remaining virtually unknown to the general reading public. But Mailer was temperamentally incapable of resigning himself. He took it for granted that his really decisive competition was not with his contemporaries, for whom, on the whole, he had little respect, but with the most distinguished of his predecessors, and he continued to hold out for the kind and degree of popular success he assumed had been theirs.

Thus, one found him in *Advertisements* brooding over Hemingway's career and trying to discover the secret of the master's "strategy," or admiring, among others, Truman Capote because Capote had managed to parlay his pretty eccentricities into a campy kind of celebrity. From the beginning the emphasis was all on the image a writer might, with care and cunning, project, the impression he was able to make on the public through his personality and behavior rather than through his work. Hemingway's career had been exemplary in this regard. For years Hemingway had written nothing "which would bother an eight-year-old or one's grandmother," and yet his reputation was firm because "he knew in advance, with a fine sense of timing, that he would have to campaign for himself, that the best tactic to hide the lockjaw of his shrinking genius was to become the personality of our time." Hence, it followed with a perfect twisted consistency that the present sufferer from lockjaw had only to become a comparable personality in order to achieve a reputation of comparable firmness.

One could concede Mailer the highly debatable point that Hemingway's reputation was by that time firm, and still refute the argument he based upon it. Hemingway may have become the personality of our time, but he did not do so on the strength of his personality alone, nor was he able to use his personality to win acceptance for his poorer work. *To Have and Have Not* and *Across the River and into the Trees* were widely recognized to be inferior novels, and the only effect of the personality was to make their badness seem more pitiable than it might otherwise have seemed. There was never any question, as Mailer appeared to believe, of the public's accepting the bad work because the personality was so attractive. The truth was that the bad work hurt Hemingway so severely that he never fully recovered. He was never again so secure in reputation as he had been just after the appearance of *A Farewell to Arms*. What Mailer chose to ignore was that the original reputation, which alone made the personality possible and tolerable, was based on excellent work. Hemingway won the approval of the public in the first place by confronting them simultaneously with work they could admire and a personality with which they could closely identify. But the personality would have been meaningless and fraudulent without the work, and any firmness Hemingway's reputation might still have had was the result entirely of the respect generally felt for his early excellence, and not of any misunderstanding, willful or otherwise, about the value of his later achievement.

It is of course possible, although unprovable, that Hemingway's personality helped to do what Mailer once said Vance Bourjaily's literary politicking had done: relaxed "the bite of the snob to the point where he or she can open the mouth and sup upon the message." It is even probable that without the personality, Hemingway's reputation, or at least his celebrity, would have been nowhere near so large. An important writer can, provided he has done important work, promote his own fashion in such a way that he will win an earlier and more sympathetic reception for his work than he might have won through the more modest display of merit alone. But in trying to apply Hemingway's example to his own case, Mailer had neglected to follow the rules in two vitally important respects. He had failed to project a personality with which more than a few perverse or disgruntled souls could easily identify, and his work after *The Naked and the Dead* had simply not been good enough or appealing enough to attract a large public following. Hemingway had, after all, enlightened and entertained. He had not only been popular; he had written popularly. Mailer had, for the most part, merely baffled and irritated, at the same time that he had written with a sophistication and from moral assumptions that only a small segment of the public could be expected to share.

Nevertheless, the point seemed to be that Mailer *needed* Hemingway's kind of success and believed that he should have it. He could admit that he might not be personally attractive to a general audience. But he was also convinced that it can be "fatal to one's talent not to have a public with a clear . . . recognition of one's size." Just how the public could be expected to achieve such a recognition without being provided with work of size, he did not explain. He simply had to have such a public in order to keep his talent and his confidence alive. He needed to think extremely well of himself in order to write even half well, and the trouble was that every time he would manage to begin thinking well of himself something would happen to make him think badly.

The autobiographical sections of *Advertisements* were very largely a record of the forces that conspired to deprive Mailer of his self-esteem. First *Barbary Shore,* then *The Deer Park,* failed to win the approval he so desperately required. The former did not make the bestseller lists at all; the latter made them for a tantalizing week or two, then slipped off, if not quite into oblivion, into the next worst thing: middling, lukewarm notoriety. After the failure of *Barbary Shore* he might, he said, have learned "to take [his] return ticket to the minor leagues without weeping too much in the beer"—except that he was plagued by the intuition that he was working his way toward saying something unforgivable, not something badly or opaquely said but something unforgivable. The trouble, it seemed, was not the quality of the communication but the outrageousness of the thing communicated. It was simply too powerfully and painfully honest for human consumption. Thus, he rationalized, and thus he agonized over his failure to achieve a success that, by all logic, he should have despised and probably *would* have despised if he had achieved it.

His difficulties finding a publisher for *The Deer Park* had been another blow, resulting in more serious damage to his self-esteem. He might have done so much so easily if only some publisher had accepted the book enthusiastically when it was first offered, and the reviewers had raved when it first appeared. "For the vitality of my work in the future," he said, "and yes, even the quality of my work, I needed a success and I needed it badly if I was to shed the fatigue I had been carrying since *Barbary Shore*." If *The Deer Park* had managed to be "a powerful best seller (the magical figure had become one hundred thousand copies for me) . . . I would then have won. I would be the first serious writer of my generation to have a best seller twice, and so it would not matter what was said about the book . . . a serious writer is certain to be considered major if he is also a best seller." And to be *considered* major by virtue of one's sales figures was not only the same as *being* major; it was essential to one's *continuing* to be major.

The implications of such statements are so appalling that one is shocked by them out of almost all understanding of the truth they conceal. Yet the truth, however ugly, is undeniable. Success, even of the most blatantly commercial kind, *can* very often make the difference between being recognized and being ignored. The fact that a writer is considered to be important or in some way appealing to large numbers of people can cause him to be singled out for special scrutiny and discovered to have qualities that may in fact *be* important and that might otherwise have been overlooked. Once again it is a matter of relaxing the bite of the snob. Bestsellerdom has often been known in our day to create a large, if temporary, reputation on the strength of very little evidence, just as it has been known to rescue from obscurity a reputation that deserved to be large. For a writer of Mailer's competitive temperament and particularly his early experience of success, it is easy to see how continued success could become a psychological necessity on which the quality of his subsequent performance might very well depend. Having once based his high opinion of himself on the public's high opinion of him, he had no choice but to think less of himself when the public's interest fell off. The fact that Mailer also happened to have become a kind of writer who could no longer please a large public no matter how hard he tried, or thought he wanted to try, did not diminish his need for the benefits to be derived from having pleased. It simply deepened his confusion and frustration.

The whole trouble was that the huge success of his first novel had infected him with the values, if not the skills, of a petty politician. He had pleased his constituents and been elected to office. Now he felt that he had to please them again in order to be reelected. And this he could not do without compromising his ambition to write outrageously and according to his changed ideas of what fiction should be. He may, as he said, have been running for President ever since 1948, but his politics had altered radically in the interval and so apparently had the character of his constituents. He could hardly expect to charm them with his bright promise of 1948. He could not go on writing *The Naked and the Dead* over and over. Yet the books he had written seemed necessarily unpleasant, and those he wanted to write seemed destined to grow more unpleasant the more he hoped that by some miracle their unpleasantness would win him the election. His frustration was such that he appeared to be on the verge of doing almost anything to bring that miracle about except the thing that his needs, as he stated them, made logically imperative: to write quite cynically what the public wanted to read. Since that was unthinkable, the politician in him turned ugly and began to campaign against him. By the time he started writing the fateful *Village Voice* columns, he had acquired the suicidally belligerent habits of a man who understood his own value so little that he felt compelled to seek his image in the outrage of others (I offend; therefore, I am) and convert every public encounter into a potential occasion for challenge and test.

He began to court hostility with as much vigor as he had previously courted popularity, and it was soon obvious that he did so *in order* to destroy in himself every last hope of popularity, of ever being elected President, so that he would be free to get back into some relation of honesty with his deepest and surest creative instincts. For it was only by persuading the public to hate him that he could give up the idea of trying to persuade the public to love him. And he needed to be hated in order to start loving himself once again and resume the lone, aggressively outlaw role that he sensed was his natural one.

Little by little he had left behind his dream of quick success. Now he set out quite deliberately to kill that dream and began for the first time since *The Naked and the Dead* to be honest with himself, not with his work, but with himself. For the first time he admitted that what he wanted more than success was to provoke, incite, and if possible, revolutionize—to do, in short, what he had all along been trying to do without wanting to accept the consequences. Like Henry James after his failure to find success in the theater, he felt freed by failure to write out of his profound and radical intuitions without regard for the feelings of those who had alienated him by their indifference. Ironically, it was from this time on that he began to show signs of becoming the major writer he had been asking the public to take him for. And it was a deeper irony as well as perfectly logical that those signs were most evident in the sections of *Advertisements* in which he lamented most bitterly his lost battle to be accepted as major.

There and in the essays he soon began to publish in *Esquire* and later collected in *The Presidential Papers*—the essays that so many people saw as evidence of his creative failure—he produced by far the best writing he had ever done. In particular, it seemed that at some point in that troubled journey back to himself, at some moment in that bleak period of foiled prospects and compensatory bluster and brag, he had discovered a style, his true style, one entirely unlike any to be found in his earlier novels. Both *Barbary Shore* and *The Deer Park* had suffered badly from verbal constipation. The clean, hard, yet flexible language of *The Naked and the Dead* had given way in those books to something choked and flat, without flexibility or ease. Everything in them came out sounding like a metallic voice announcing the arrival and departure of aircraft—heavy, toneless, and very dead. There was a loin-wrung, post-masturbatory quality about the style of *Barbary Shore,* and *The Deer Park* bore the marks of an act of sheer will working against an enormous inertia of imaginative fatigue and lost hopes. It was not clear at the time why this should be so, but it is clear now in the light of Mailer's subsequent stylistic breakthrough. He was quite simply never a novelist in the true sense after *The Naked and the Dead,* and that book, like most war novels by young men, was as much an accident of experience as it was a creative achievement. But after it Mailer began to have real difficulty projecting his feelings and ideas into an objective dramatic situation. The necessity to create characters and relate them meaningfully to one another obviously forced him to be concerned with problems that did not really interest him and that, therefore, impeded the development of his talent in the direction it appeared naturally to be trying to take. His natural subject was not, it seemed, other people but himself. He did not want to invent; he wanted to confess, to display himself as the sole recorder and protagonist of significant contemporary experience.

So it was that when he came to write *Advertisements* and the *Esquire* essays, Mailer experienced an immense release of inhibitions and was able for the first time to confront his feelings and ideas in their full complexity. He found it possible to make complete use of his resources not only as a highly skilled worker in language but as an intuitive thinker of an at times almost superhuman sensitivity to the psychic realities of his time. And he expressed this sensitivity in a style that combined the mean talk of the hipster and the edgy rhetoric of psychiatry into a prose instrument as lethal as a switchblade. Hence, it would appear that, far from being a symptom of failure, Mailer's excursion into the essay was actually a vital preparation for the moment when his language would at last be adequate to his ambitions, and he would be ready to undertake the major creative breakthrough that his latest novel, *An American Dream,* so clearly represented, a novel in which Mailer for the first time made sustained use of his new style in fiction.

There were, of course, many readers and critics who felt that the book represented not a breakthrough but the final stage of breakdown. It was severely criticized by some very respectable and responsible people, and one could certainly understand why. By conventional standards it was an unpardonably ugly book and, taken in terms of its story, a profoundly silly book, full of grotesque and implausible occurrences and characters who appeared to be uniformly insane. But what the critics failed to comprehend was that it could not be properly judged by standards normally applied to the novel and that, for all its ugliness,(it was essentially a work of humor and self-satire, most humorous in those places where it treated derisively some of its most serious-seeming effects) It was a burlesque treatment of the obscene version of the American Dream that possesses the unconscious mind of America at the present time, and what appeared to be, and patently were, excesses and absurdities were also an integral part of the humorous intent, and perfectly in keeping not only with the psychotic quality of the dream but with (the tradition to which the book seemed most clearly to belong, the tradition of the prose romance, in which fantasy and fact, witchcraft and melodrama, myth, allegory, and realism combine) to produce what Richard Chase has called "a profound poetry of disorder." The book's antecedents were not the novels of Henry James or Jane Austen but the romances of Cooper, Melville, and Hawthorne, and one of Mailer's contributions was to rehabilitate the form of the romance and adapt it to the literary needs of the immediate present. The book, in short, was an examination not of human and social surfaces but of our fantasy life, a vastly hallucinated yet deeply real account of the American dream become in our day the American nightmare.

In it Mailer explored the possibilities for both damnation and salvation to be found in some of the most reprehensible acts known to our society—murder, suicide, incest, fornication, and physical violence. He attempted to dramatize, and always with a clear sense of their comic implications, the various ways a man may sin in order to be saved, consort with Satan in order to attain to God, become holy as well as whole by restoring the primitive psychic circuits that enable him to live in harmony with himself and find his courage, regardless of whether his courage seeks its test in the challenges of love or the temptation to murder, whether he ends by becoming saint or psychopath. He wrote, in short, a radically moral book about radically immoral subjects, a religious book that transcends the conventional limits of blasphemy to expose the struggle toward psychic redemption that is the daily warfare of our secret outlaw selves.

As a piece of fiction the book had, to be sure, outrageous flaws.

Mailer committed every sin known to literature, but like his hero he somehow succeeded in getting away with murder. For the book's defects could do nothing to alter one's impression that it was the product of a devastatingly alive and original creative mind at work in a language capable of responding with seismographic sensitivity to an enormously wide range of impressions. There seemed to be no limit to what Mailer was now able to do with words, particularly in recording the physical and psychological realities of people as they impinged upon the mind of a man constantly flagellating himself to new heights of awareness. In fact, it is possible to say that in it Mailer brought to full development a prose idiom of higher sensitivity to the exact condition of contemporary consciousness than any we have had in fiction since the best work of Faulkner, and that he managed through that idiom to create an image of our time that will undoubtedly be recognized as authoritative for this generation.

Mailer stands alone among his contemporaries in possessing a coherent metaphysics of the human condition as it now exists. He also stands alone in possessing an intellectual force that is at the same time a dynamic and uniquely personal imaginative vision. He alone, therefore, seems likely to possess the power to shift us out of our old comfortable modes of seeing and feeling and cause us to experience the shock of recognition we always experience when we have placed before us realities seen for the first time with the honesty of a truly original talent. If Mailer has not yet become the great novelist he has so long fought to become, he has clearly become a major creative consciousness and conscience, the most annoying, destructive, hateful, but altogether remarkable writer of these undistinguished years.

Interpretation of Dreams

by Leo Bersani

An American Dream has been nearly as widely panned as it has been widely reviewed, but in how many cases has it really been read, or, to put the best construction on it, read in book form rather than in the *Esquire* installments? A dazzling performance, a recklessly generous yet disciplined exercise in self-exposure and self-invention, Mailer's latest novel has had the further distinction of provoking a quaint resurgence of neoclassical canons of taste. The strategy of attack has naturally been not entirely ineffective. It can't, after all, be denied that the novel sins continuously against the rules of propriety and verisimilitude, and the clarities of *bon sens*. So that by ignoring what Mailer has done, his attackers have been able to have quite a time of it showing what he should have done. Elizabeth Hardwick, in *Partisan Review,* announced that *An American Dream* is "a very dirty book—dirty and extremely ugly." And if we look for something closer to a reasoned argument in her review, we find the curious logic that the story "is artless, unmysterious and so there is no pain in it, no triumphant cruelty or instructive evil." It's mysterious to *me* why mystery is necessary for pain, why cruelty should be triumphant (over what? exactly how?) or evil instructive (to make the reader a "better person"?), or indeed what relevance such ideas about the novel have in what purports to be an account of *this* novel. Tom Wolfe, treating us once again to his special blend of *Wham-bang!* interjections and Comp. Lit. pedantry, thinks that Rojack is killed off with too much thinking in the first fourteen and a half pages of the novel, complains of "unreal dialogue," but finally concedes that Mailer may one day be able to "climb into the same ring as James M. Cain." For Joseph Epstein, *An American Dream,* "on any level one chooses to read it"

"Interpretation of Dreams" (review of *An American Dream*) by Leo Bersani. From *Partisan Review* 32, no. 4 (Fall, 1965), 603–8. Copyright © by *Partisan Review*. Reprinted by permission of the author and *Partisan Review*.

(?), is "confused and silly," and (shades of English 223: Nineteenth-Century Realistic Fiction) he condemns Mailer for being "more interested in the novel as a spectacle than as a convincing representation of life, more concerned with projecting personal fantasies than creating verisimilitude."

Philip Rahv, writing in the *New York Review of Books,* manages both to capture Miss Hardwick's moralistic tone (he complains of Rojack's being freed, by plot manipulation, "from paying any sort of price for what he has done") and to echo Mr. Epstein's notions of what a novel is supposed to do (the story lacks "verisimilitude, even in the most literal sense.") Finally, in a plot summary apparently designed to show the uselessness of attempting a critical evaluation of this "dreadful novel," Stanley Edgar Hyman unwittingly demonstrates some of Mailer's marvelous humor and indifference to plot, and shows in addition his own inability to cope with the difficulty of Mailer's language and especially the exuberant inventiveness of his similes.[1] Unfortunately, Mailer's defenders—with the notable exception of Richard Poirier in *Commentary*—seem as anxious as his detractors to get away from the book. John Aldridge, in an apocalyptic reading for *Life* which Mailer had printed in *Partisan Review* to offset Miss Hardwick's scolding comments, speaks of *An American Dream* as "a devil's encyclopedia of our secret visions and desires, an American dream or nightmare"; Mailer, we are told, has created "an image of our time which will undoubtedly stand as authoritative for this generation." And Conrad Knickerbocker, adopting that flattening perspective from which the *Times* reassures its readers that good books, good plays and good movies are never special or particular but are always speaking to all of us about all our problems, praises Mailer for searching for something called "the mana, the magics, submerged and hideous, that move the age."

But the seriousness of *An American Dream* involves a denial of certain kinds of novelistic seriousness, of social probability and relevance, as well as of so-called intellectual depth. It is an intensely private novel, and one key to what has offended or puzzled the reviewers is probably in the way Mailer allows his hero to treat himself, in that peculiar blend of self-concentration and self-deprecation which, in fact, largely accounts for the originality of his language.

1. See above, pp. 104–8.

The expectations of a political novel which might be set up by the joke that begins the story are rapidly destroyed. Mailer in *An American Dream* is somewhat like Balzac in his attitudes toward social maneuvering and power; he seems just as naïvely melodramatic in his notion of what goes on at the top, and the images of political power in both novelists should be immediately recognizable as private mythologies expressing private obsessions and dreams of power ideally demonic. Both are impatient with the specific strategies for gaining and keeping power, as distinct from the excitement of exercising it. Barney Kelly, like Vautrin, is a spooky physical presence who overwhelms Rojack with a wild assortment of suffocating smells, just as Vautrin paralyzes Rastignac and Lucien de Rubempré by shooting bullet-like particles of his fantastic will through the air and into the soft soil of their more passive minds. Mailer, like Balzac, is better at suggesting some of the sexual impulses that perhaps account for the enjoyment of power than at detailing the more prosaic and conscious calculations that pave the way to it. Kelly's success story is brashly improbable (he possessed the stock market by telepathy); what he really wants to talk about with Rojack is the frightening thrill of incest with Bess and her daughter, and later with Deborah, and the most impressive demonstration of his power is in the extraordinary passage where he invites Rojack to "get shitty" with him and Ruta. In his wish to have the three of them "pitch and tear and squat and kick, swill and grovel on the Lucchese bed, fuck until our eyes were out, bury the ghost of Deborah by gorging on her corpse," in his brutal, simultaneous appeal to impulses of anality, homosexuality, necrophilia and cannibalism, the magic of his power is made marvelously concrete by the energy of his indulgence in bodily fantasies, an energy so great that Rojack begins to share the fantasies, to feel "unfamiliar desires."

It is power of this sort that both fascinates and terrifies Rojack; the murder of Deborah and, perhaps more significantly, the story of that murder are his attempts to free himself from it. If Rojack responds like an electric coil to multitudinous "invasions" from the outside world, it is because he is pathologically convinced that what he calls his "center" may be stolen from him at any moment, at the same time that he feeds on this sense of constant threat as a kind of substitute for a sense of self. This fantasy provides what could be called the psychological theme, or obsession, of the novel, and it may or may not, incidentally, throw some light on what has often seemed to be Mailer's facile talent for making himself obnoxious in public. When, for example, we read that Rojack, instead of feeling relief at being left alone for a few moments in the police station, yearns for Roberts' return, "much as if that merciless lack of charity which I had come to depend on in Deborah (as a keel to ballast the empty dread of my stomach) was now provided by the detective," we may at least wonder to what extent Mailer's own sense of himself has depended on his ability to provoke attack. *An American Dream,* at any rate, records a dramatic and exhilarating struggle with that "empty dread," an attempt to fight the vampire complex that makes Rojack both fear and need a world of devouring bitches, telepathic powers and omnipotent smells. The novel, for all its apparently complacent acceptance of magic, is a continuous attack against magic, that is, an attack against fantasies of the self as both all powerful and totally vulnerable.

The strategy of resistance is, inevitably, literary, and the power of *An American Dream* is in its demonstration of verbal tactics which finally make what I have called the psychological theme irrelevant. The "courage" which is made so much of in the novel, and which the reviewers have found lamentably banal as a moral philosophy, is much more of a brilliant and difficult trick than a virtue in the ordinary sense. While it is often merely the bravery born of a superstitious compulsion, as when Rojack forces himself to walk along the parapet of Kelly's terrace, it involves, more profoundly, a willingness to entertain the most extravagant fantasies and hallucinations in order to change their affective coefficient. By taking the risk of abandoning himself to the fantastic suggestiveness of every person, every object, every smell encountered during the thirty-two hours he writes about, Rojack discovers fantasy as a source of imaginative richness in himself instead of fearing it as an ominous signal from mysterious, external powers. He moves, in other words, from fantasy as a psychological illusion about the world to the use of fantasy as a somewhat self-conscious but exuberant display of his own inventive powers. Every menace becomes the occasion for a verbal performance, and his fluttering nervousness about being deprived of his "center" is rather humorously belied by the incredibly dense and diversified self which his language reveals and creates. Nothing in the book (not even Rojack's moving attempt to know love as something sane and decent with Cherry) except the virtuosity of the writing itself indicates a way out of the nightmare Rojack seems to be telling. The nightmare would be nothing more than a nasty story if Mailer, like his critics, had allowed it to separate itself from the virtuosity, from, especially, the metaphorical exuberance which is, I think, a way of mocking and outdoing the dangerous inventiveness of a magic-ridden world. This means, of course, that the *playfulness* of the novel is by no means a frivolous attitude toward "dirty" or "ugly" events, but rather the natural tone of a man for whom events have become strictly literary-novelistic situations to be freely exploited for the sake of a certain style and the self-enjoyment it perhaps unexpectedly provides.

It is, then, irrelevant to complain of improbable situations or unreal dialogue in *An American Dream*. Rojack's playfulness, his verbal exuberance, is the sign of a confident use of power, and it involves an occasionally reckless indifference to the probability of his own experience. The telling of his story becomes *Rojack's* invention as well as Mailer's once his life confronts him as choices to be made about language and novelistic form. The plot of *An American Dream* is, therefore, nothing more than a mode of Rojack's inventive exuberance, and, while it is perhaps understandable that the anecdotal aspect of fiction should trick us most easily into confusions between art and life, we should be admiring the power of extravagance in Rojack's tall story instead of upholding the faded banner of verismilitude. Rojack's experience is largely a pretext for trying his hand at different ways of telling a story: making love to Ruta is a calculated allegory of good and evil, a parody of literary struggles between the Lord and the Devil, but the scene in the police station and Rojack's telephone calls are masterful exercises in the art of realistic dialogue and psychological detail. And much of the novel's humor is in the unexpected shifts from one kind of writing to another: the conversation with Dr. Tharchman moves from intricate, understated satire to an exaggerated display of *humour noir,* and some of the suspense of a spy story is brought in just long enough to make us feel the greater importance of what is more like a ghost story.

This free play of virtuosity in the narrative structure of *An American Dream* also characterizes Rojack's similes, which the reviewers have pounced on with a comical solemnity about stylistic propriety. Mr. Hyman, in his outraged enumeration of the similes he hates most, is only the most hilarious example of all those readers who have declared with absolute seriousness that they have never thought of a pigeon's breast when touching the trigger of a gun, or had an orgasm "fierce as a demon in the eyes of a bright golden child." Novelists themselves have, of course, been known to isolate their metaphors from their style, to test each one for its individual "rightness" or "objective" validity. Flaubert's maniacal search for a perfect equivalence between image and a preexistent "subject" (a fear of style disguised as an idolatry of style) probably accounts, to some degree, for his leaden metaphors and the clumsiness of his rhythms. But Mailer in *An American Dream,* unlike Flaubert, never uses metaphor for the purpose of arresting our attention, of making us stop to admire a tiny verbal island, an exquisite *trouvaille.* Rojack's similes *make* a self of enormous, even fantastic imaginative range, and their power lies in a kind of dialectical reference to, and denial of characters and events in the novel. They change the story, as it is being told, into a challenge to the resources of fantasy; their complexity is not in their farfetched nature, but lies rather in the dramatic burden they carry of transforming oppressive experience into tokens of stylistic play. The plausibility of Rojack's similes is irrelevant; what matters is that he makes us feel his associations as spontaneous, irresistible fantasies, and that we accept his most elaborate verbal constructions as illustrating the elaborateness of immediacy rather than of development toward an idea. For no intellectual strategy could explain the humor or justify the casual difficulty of Rojack's style. It is, in a sense, his very absence of thought (an absence deplored by Mr. Epstein and by Granville Hicks) which creates Rojack's "system" of defense, his refusal to conceptualize sensation and to be reasonable about the accumulation of metaphor which makes of his writing an act of total responsiveness.

An American Dream is an impressively original work, but it shouldn't be necessary to point out that Mailer is not the first novelist to prefer to the conventions of social probability in fiction a more direct form of self-display. The illusion of distinctness between the narrator and the social world he is presumably observing and reporting on is only weakly maintained in Proust and in James's later novels, where we already sense a certain impatience with the mediation of fantasy into "objective" characters and events. In both James and Proust, what seems to be a fascination with the suggestiveness and self-inventive possibilities of language leads to some carelessness about novelistic situations, a tendency to allegorize the world as a rather transparent (rather than hidden) projection of the self. But most of Mailer's critics surely know about all this, and if we are to dismiss the possibility of a deliberate ganging-up on him for past offenses, the irrelevance of what has been said about *An American Dream* must perhaps be explained by the shock and resentment produced by a work that would force us to admit the self-indulgence, the particularity and even, in a certain sense, the irresponsibility of interesting art. Mailer's admirers are already hard at work making him responsible and relevant to all sorts of things, but to read *An American Dream* is, happily, to see the hopelessness of their good intentions. Nothing, after all, could be more typical of the marvelous lightness of imagination than to test, in the most scrupulous detail, the possibility of a grown-up love, built on tenderness and respect, with Cherry, and then to end the whole thing on the frivolous note of that charmingly nonsensical phone call to heaven.

Mailer and the Fitzgerald Tradition

by Richard Foster

I

Since World War II our fiction writers have been evolving a vision of contemporary experience that while firmly based on constituent realities is essentially—perhaps "transcendentally"—affirmative in kind. Martin Green has identified this prevailing thrust of affirmation with what he calls "American rococo": a lavish and loving, if often sharply ironic penchant for detailing the surfaces of contemporary experience. The mode constitutes, as Green writes, "a kind of yea-saying, though very different from the kind Whitman aimed at." [1] Salinger and Nabokov are Green's chief examples. But writers as different as Ellison and Heller, Pynchon and Barth, might be mentioned with equal relevance. With its fondness for surreal collocations of particulars, for excursions into arcane learning and pseudo-learning, for the looser forms of quasi-biography and picaresque, for curious admixtures of high jinks and high seriousness, for uninhibited flights of lyricism and rhetoric, the plenitude of the new mode typically yields fiction fragrant with mystical insights and submerged religiosity. Green has suggested that Fitzgerald is the originator of "American rococo" (p. 228), a perception reinforced by novelist Wright Morris, who sees in Fitzgerald's work the characteristically American subject of "nostalgia" for the timeless, the innocent and the ideal transmuted by the existential thrust of his imagination, as it worked on his personal experience and observation, into an "absurdist" vision of contemporaneity:

"Mailer and the Fitzgerald Tradition" by Richard Foster. From *Novel* 1, no. 3 (Spring, 1968), 219–30. Copyright © 1968 by *Novel*. Reprinted by permission of the author and the publisher.

1. *Re-appraisals: Some Commonsense Readings in American Literature* (London, 1963), p. 215.

It is fitting that Fitzgerald, the aesthete of nostalgia, of the escape clause without question, should be the first American to formulate his own philosophy of the absurd. . . . Different from the philosophers themselves, he lived and died of it. He had come, alone and prematurely, on a fact that was not yet fashionable: he had come on the experience rather than the cliché.[2]

It is as if Fitzgerald's lifework of novels, stories and essays had rediscovered for his time a vision of that "curiously American 'existentialism'" noted in Ralph Waldo Emerson by Green (p. 53). My argument here, based on such recognitions as these, is that no American among the inter-war generation of writers has greater relevance to the best of our novelists writing now than F. Scott Fitzgerald.

Jack Goodman, an editor for Simon and Schuster who read Norman Mailer's *The Deer Park* on its ill-fated rounds of the publishers, described its author in his report as "a sort of post-Kinsey F. Scott Fitzgerald." This shrewd perception, which puts a major writer of the moment into significant relation with his literary past, supports just the critical argument I have been advancing. For Mailer is at once the most intrinsically relevant and the most inventively original of Fitzgerald's inheritors, and thus a most valuable writer in whom to study the reaches of Fitzgerald's tradition both intensively and, as it were, from the inside.

When asked during his *Paris Review* interview to name the writers to whom he owes most, Mailer responded first and most surprisingly with the name of E. M. Forster. The names that came next were perhaps less surprising: "I have been influenced by—well, Farrell to begin with. Dos Passos, Steinbeck (I am trying to do it chronologically), Hemingway, and later Fitzgerald—much, much later. And Thomas Wolfe, of course." The positioning and means of qualifying this admission of debt to Fitzgerald seem to place a special if somewhat reluctantly avowed emphasis on him. Hemingway is the writer most frequently cited in Mailer's prose, of course, and usually with admiration. But Fitzgerald, who turns up only a little less frequently, he often treats with condescension, sometimes even with scorn. (Though in his introduction to his recently published collection of short fiction Mailer speaks of Fitzgerald as "another favorite" in the short story game.) And yet in the impor-

2. "The Function of Nostalgia," *F. Scott Fitzgerald: The Man and His Work,* ed. Alfred Kazin (Cleveland and New York, 1951), pp. 26–27.

tant ways Mailer's fiction is much more like Fitzgerald's than like Hemingway's. The kinds of men and women inhabiting their fictional worlds, and the archetypal relationships obtaining between them—the women as promissory images of value and possibility, the men as agents of motive and choice—are clearly similar. Like modern versions of Spenserian knights, their heroes move through mazes of sexual ambiguity inhabited by true and false goddesses, by restorative earth-mothers and half-mad Cassandras, by tyrantesses and simple girls, who lead or mislead them in their uncertain quests for fulfillment or aliveness or goodness. "Mate the absurd with apocalyptic," Mailer once said of his own imagination's susceptibility, "and I am captive." This self-description could as easily have been Fitzgerald's as Mailer's. But it could never have been Hemingway's. Questions of "influence" aside, the least one could say about the relation between Fitzgerald and Mailer is that *The Deer Park* and *An American Dream* seem to derive from a sensibility with much the same essentials as that which produced *The Great Gatsby, Tender Is the Night,* and *The Last Tycoon.*

Tender Is the Night has perhaps the most obvious relevance to Mailer's work, shedding its rich light directly on *The Deer Park,* Mailer's most ambitious novel to date. But then, *The Last Tycoon,* with its thematic mixture of politics, Hollywood, and the compulsions of personal power, and *The Great Gatsby,* with its subtle and complex narrator-hero relationship, have their clear relevance to *The Deer Park,* too. And they illuminate as well *Barbary Shore* and *An American Dream*—the former a kind of half-paralyzed reduction of the dynamics of Fitzgerald's vision to garrulous absurdity, the latter a propulsive translation of the same elements into rawly neural and muscular events. Fitzgerald's fiction contains secondary stretches which look toward whole books like *Barbary Shore* or *The Deer Park*—the story "May Day," for example, or parts of *Tender Is the Night* where Dick Diver's crack-up is gauged by his either intensely witnessing or being helplessly absorbed into scenes of the debility of his world. His notes for *The Last Tycoon,* furthermore, and the remains of his several false starts on *Tender Is the Night,* show an imagination haunted by the theme of crime as a reflexive response to a world corroded by unnatural sexual hostility and traumatic moral displacement. In the light of such Fitzgerald materials *An American Dream* seems startlingly to be the kind of novel Fitzgerald might have conceived had he lived through the Second

World War and the McCarthy era into the Cold War years of Korea
and Eisenhower, Cuba and Kennedy.

These striking likenesses and continuities extend to the non-fiction. For both writers the conventional distinction between fiction
and fact, or between fiction and something like "journalism," was
likely to vanish under the stress of creative intensity. Though both
have viewed themselves primarily as writers of fiction, both have
also been naturally adept at vividly personal essays on the contemporary scene. But this non-fiction feeds back, for both writers, into
their fiction, and is in fact hardly distinguishable from it in either
substance or art. Fitzgerald's mainly lyric essays on the birth and
death of the Twenties are sustained versions of the typifying medi-
tations and sketches on the times that appear in his stories and
novels. In Mailer's essays public men and contemporary events are
imaginatively transformed into characters and conflicts of fictional
fullness and independence, and in such novels as *Barbary Shore* and
The Deer Park, contemporary ideological matter is given a gener-
ously discursive as well as dramatic embodiment. In a passage that
might well have been written by Fitzgerald, who tended in the long
run to equate artistic achievement with the moral aliveness of the
artist as a human being rather than with the sophistication of his
skills as a craftsman, Mailer once expressed the conviction that for
the writer "keeping in shape" morally and intellectually is much
more important than "craft":

> Craft is very little finally. But if you're continually worrying about
> whether you're growing or deteriorating as a man, whether your
> integrity is turning soft or firming itself, why then it's in that slow
> war, that slow rearguard battle you fight against diminishing talent
> that you stay in shape as a writer. . . .[3]

But "the moment you borrow other writers' styles of thought, you
need craft to shore up the walls." And then he went on to justify
the practice of journalism—which is not "an essential betrayal of
the chalice of your literary art"—as an important existential means
of humanly and morally "keeping in shape." "Temples," he con-
cluded roundly, "are for women." It is notable that while Fitzgerald
regretted some of his shoddy work as a potboiling fiction writer, he
seems never to have scorned his journalistic essays on the times.

3. See above, p. 38.

The contemporary essays of both writers, always highly personal, tend to take the form of quasi-autobiography, even confession, with the authors speaking as representative men who have been carried by circumstances and sensibility into the existential center of the life of their times. This is the nature of Fitzgerald's "Crack-Up" series, that uniquely lyrical "trilogy of depression," as he once called it, which records one man's overexpenditure of selfhood and personality, in an era of such extremes, to the point of "emotional bankruptcy." Mailer's confessional *Advertisements for Myself*, with its record of quick artistic and popular success followed by subsequent disappointment and deflation, its dialectic of vain confidence and abject self-ridicule, has much in it about the experience and meaning of "crack-up"—the dissipation of intense ambition, energy, and conviction into drink, dope, distraction, and a sick liver. Close to the end of *Advertisements*, following a free-swinging evaluation of his American contemporaries ("the talent in the room") and just preceding an exhibit of fragments from a huge, hopefully apocalyptic, and still unachieved multivolume novel-in-progress, he writes, and with Fitzgerald's name affixed to the passage like an authenticating seal, a "Last Advertisement for Myself Before the Way Out," part of which follows:

> When I come to assess myself, and try to measure what chance I have of writing that big book I have again in me, I do not know in all simple bitterness if I can make it. . . . I had the freak of luck to start high on the mountain, and go down sharp while others were passing me. So I saw their faces as they learned to climb, and what faces they were! . . .
> Still! There is the fault of others, and the fault of oneself, and I have my debts to pay. Fitzgerald was an indifferent caretaker of his talent, and I have been a cheap gambler with mine. As I add up the accounts, I cannot like myself too much, for I was cowardly when I should have been good, and too brave on many a bad chance, and I spent my first thirty years abusing my body, and the last six in forced marches on my brain, and so I am more stupid today than I ought to be, my memory is half-gone, and my mind is slow; from fear and vanity I paid out too much for what I managed to learn. When I sit down, soon after this book is done, to pick up again on my novel, I do not know if I can do it, for if the first sixty pages are not at all bad, I may still have wasted too much of myself, and if I have—what a loss. How poor to go to death with no more than the notes of good intention. *It is the actions of men*

and not their intentions which make history—the best sentence
I've ever written—but I would hate to face eternity with that for
my flag, since I am still at this formal middle of my life a creator
of sentiments larger than my work.

The exhaustion of a creative gift of personality by the sheer
weight of unformed reality which it confronts Mailer conceives in
much the same way Fitzgerald did—as an inevitable overexpenditure and final bankruptcy of vital spirits:

> Every man has a different point where he gets close to his being.
> Sooner or later everything that stands between him and his being—
> what the psychologists call defenses—is used up, because men have
> to work through their lives; just being a man they have to stand
> up in all the situations where a woman can lie down. Just on the
> simplest level . . . where a woman can cry a man has to stand.
> And for that reason, men are often used more completely than
> women. They have more rights and more powers, and also they
> are used more.

Such fated exhaustion of masculine power, grace, and faith is the
substance of one kind of modern tragedy. And in most of the work
of both writers this inherently tragic matter is characteristically dis-
tanced or conserved by being rendered in an essentially comic perspective. Fitzgerald's heroic Gatsby and Monroe Stahr, for
example, are defeated as much by internal dilutions of absurdity
as they are by the external counterforce of their fates. Mailer's
heroes, Sergius O'Shaugnessy of *The Deer Park* and Steve Rojack of
An American Dream, for example, may touch tragedy, but they survive its consequences by eschewing greatness for the knowledge that
comes with the acceptance of absurdity. Fitzgerald completed the
imaginative measurement of his own limits as a man by creating at
the bottom end of his career the oaf-slob Pat Hobby, who as
a dumb and barbarized screen hack radically counterbalanced
the bright Phoebus of young aspirations—the romantic self-image of
youth, Amory Blaine. And when a few years ago, in a somewhat
Fitzgeraldian surge of ambition for fulfillment in action and dollars,
Mailer tried to force himself on Sonny Liston as impresario-magi-
cian for the second Patterson-Liston fight only to find himself
humiliated and psychically deflated, he wrote—as he might also
have written of his abortive mayoralty campaign in New York—
"I had not begun to have the strength this morning to be so very

good as I had wanted to be. Once more I had tried to become a hero, and had ended as an eccentric."

Fitzgerald might well have been astonished, even offended, by much of Mailer's material, just as Henry James probably would have been by Fitzgerald's. But his probable surprise that such a writer as Mailer could be identified as one of his heirs perhaps confirms, by a kind of test of exception, both the continuities between them and the paradoxical principle that a writer's finished achievement can change in time. Mailer's characterization of America as "the country in which the dynamic myth of the Renaissance—that every man was potentially extraordinary—knew its most passionate persistence, . . . the land where people still believed in heroes: George Washington; Billy the Kid; Lincoln; Jefferson; Mark Twain, Jack London, Hemingway; Joe Louis, Dempsey, Gentleman Jim . . ." is almost pure Fitzgerald, or Fitzgerald essentialized. And so is this passage—which could be a gloss of *Tender Is the Night* or *The Last Tycoon*—on the surreal forms which "the dream" reflexively generates in order to survive when history approaches the limits of natural possibility:

> And when the West was filled, the expansion turned inward, became part of an agitated, overexcited, superheated dream life. The film studios threw up their searchlights as the frontier was finally sealed, and the romantic possibilities of the old conquest of land turned into a vertical myth, trapped within the skull, of a new kind of heroic life, each choosing his own archetype of a neo-renaissance man, be it Barrymore, Cagney, Flynn, Bogart, Brando, or Sinatra. . . .

And in such passages as the following, where the impetus of the Fitzgerald vision begins to transcend Fitzgerald's experience, we are aware of passing beyond him without really leaving him behind:

> And this myth, that each of us was born free, to wander, to have adventure and to grow on the waves of the violent, the perfumed, the unexpected, had a force which could not be tamed no matter how the nation's regulators . . . would brick-in the modern life . . . ; the myth would not die. . . . It was as if the message in the labyrinth of the genes would insist that violence was locked with creativity, and adventure was the secret of love.

In the last of these passages, all of which are from Mailer's long *Esquire* piece on the 1960 Democratic convention, Mailer takes his

sweeping prospect into a new historical dimension, the age pre-
figured in the pattern of developing strife between fascist temperament and communist will which lurks behind the landscape of general breakdown in *Tender Is the Night* and *The Last Tycoon*. This
new age is our own, with its multiple covert totalitarianisms, its prevailing violence, its proliferation of techniques of mass dehuman-
ization. Though their conscious minds and wills repelled its orgiastic solicitations, the coming age had already begun to express itself
in the chaotic passions and self-destructive instincts of the disinte-
grating Dick Diver and Monroe Stahr, and indeed in Fitzgerald
himself. Mailer is not only a post-Kinsey, but a post-Hiroshima
Fitzgerald as well.

II

If Mailer's work constitutes an imaginative advancing of Fitzgerald's kind of vision in response to the exigent facts and imperatives of recent history, what remains constant within the pattern of
change is the two writers' strong and very similarly constituted
idealism of temperament. The extraordinary and creative people in
Fitzgerald's fiction are impelled to give to and transform others, to
recreate the world around them. And Fitzgerald, like one of his
own protagonists, was a self-confessed "schoolmarm," a title amply
justified by his numerous and charming letters of moral and social
advice to his daughter "Scottie" and other young people, such as
Andrew Turnbull, and by the charmingly pedantic and elaborate
"College of One" which he conducted for the cultural enrichment
of his last love Sheilah Graham. In 1934 he proposed to Dean
Christian Gauss of Princeton, and with utter seriousness, that he
give a series of lectures there "on the actual business of creative
fiction." "The lectures I've not planned but they would be in general the history of say: 1. What constitutes the Creative Temperament. 2. What Creative Material Is. 3. Its Organization. And so
forth and so on." Critics and scholars interested in Fitzgerald will
regret that these lectures were never composed. But Dean Gauss decided, quite understandably, that it would not work. Fitzgerald had
hardly more success with Scribner's than he did with Dean Gauss
and the proposed lectures. One of his most enthusiastically conceived projects was his idea, proffered in 1922, for an inexpensive

"Scribner library" drawn from the massive and quite distinguished Scribner backlists.[4] The "Scribner library," which did not come to fruition during Fitzgerald's lifetime, is now, of course, one of the staples of the paperback publishing industry, with reprints of Fitzgerald's own work making a large contribution to it.

In 1936 Fitzgerald wrote to Asa Bushnell, Princeton's athletics manager and a former college clubmate, about his idea for a new library on the campus: a reproduction of the old building on the spot where it had been demolished, with specialized underground book galleries radiating outward from it toward the appropriate buildings, each gallery "a sort of subway, served . . . by electric trucks, and passing a series of alcoves lit overhead by skylights paralleling the present walks. . . ." "Is this a crazy idea?" Fitzgerald had queried at the beginning of his letter. A little, perhaps. But it is craziness of the same creative sort that caused Norman Mailer to build a model for a revolutionary vertical city of the future to be composed of variously intersecting dwellings, ramps and causeways, like the open skeleton of a vast mountain rising thousands of feet in the air; or to propose jousting tournaments in Central Park, skyscraper climbing, "free-style fighting societies," and an "Adventurers' Corps," as new means of forestalling delinquency among America's urban youth. If Mailer's projects are a little "crazier" than Fitzgerald's, the difference in degree is perhaps due to the effects of exacerbated historical circumstances on a similarly romantic moral sensibility. For both men such gestures of reform and recreation are heuristic symbols of the possibilities for significant human life in the present. And for both men those possibilities are characteristically envisioned not in images of individual retreat and isolation but rather in images of human communion in a viable society.

This appetite for solutions to problems pertaining to the general human good not only signifies the temperament of the idealist, but also that of the hero, or the idealist in action. Fitzgerald's Amory Blaine, waiting for maturity and a sign of his mission, is a potential hero, and Anthony Patch is a failed hero. Gatsby is an unrecognized hero, as unrecognized in his own eyes as in the world's. Dick Diver, born on the threshold of a changing world, is a traditional hero, both gifted and knowing, whose powers are finally exhausted by the apocalyptic energies of a new age. Monroe Stahr, the same

4. *The Letters of F. Scott Fitzgerald*, ed. Andrew Turnbull (New York, 1963), pp. 155–157.

kind of hero, has been left yet further behind by history—noble, proud, and creative, he is thus vulnerable and doomed. As Fitzgerald's career develops, then, his choice of protagonists tends to shift from aspiring and representative types like Amory Blaine to active and exemplary ones like Dick Diver. An analogous pattern of development can be seen in Mailer, but with the crucial difference that as his protagonists become increasingly active and exemplary they also become more deracinated and anarchic. If *The Deer Park* is Mailer's *The Great Gatsby, An American Dream* is his *Tender Is the Night.* And if Sergius O'Shaugnessy of *The Deer Park* is Mailer's composite equivalent of questioning observer Carraway and self-creating Gatsby, existential anarch Steve Rojack of *An American Dream* is his bourgeois Dr. Diver in background, taste, and intellectual seriousness. Yet O'Shaugnessy, instead of achieving selfhood and heroic stature by total dedication to some "dream," waits, watches, and stumbles half-absurdly toward unconventional self-creation through the exhilarations of good orgasms and mediocre bullfighting. And Rojack, instead of blessing a world that has destroyed him, prefigures new possibilities of salvation by committing spontaneous acts of violence and passion.

But there are some lively images of the traditional hero in Mailer's work. They live primarily in his non-fiction, however, and from that immediately "real" context they have the effect of confirming the positive, and often covertly traditional moral significance of his anti-heroes. The *Paris Review* interviewer of the fearsome Mr. Mailer remarked on the hospitality and easy civility of his host, describing his effect as that of "a kind of secular prince"—a phrase that Fitzgerald might have applied to Gatsby, Diver, or Monroe Stahr. It is Fitzgerald's name, in fact, that sounds the keynote of Mailer's most elaborate and memorable portrait of a contemporary hero, John F. Kennedy, in his brilliant *Esquire* tapestry of the 1960 Democratic convention:

> Then the demonstration. Well-run, bigger than Johnson's, jazzier.
> . . . Besides, the personnel had something of the *élan,* those paper
> hats designed to look like straw boaters with Kennedy's face on
> the crown, and small photographs of him on the ribbon, those hats
> which had come to symbolize the crack speed of the Kennedy team,
> that Madison Avenue cachet which one finds in bars like P. J.
> Clarke's, the elegance always giving its subtle echo of the Twenties
> so that the raccoon coats seem more numerous than their real count,

and the colored waistcoats are measured by the charm they would have drawn from Scott Fitzgerald's eye [*sic*]. But there, it occurred to one for the first time that Kennedy's middle name was just that, Fitzgerald, and the tone of his crack lieutenants, the unstated style, was true Scott. The legend of Fitzgerald had an army at last. . . .

Next follows the Stevenson nominating speech by Eugene McCarthy, and the responding demonstration, which Mailer sees as nostalgic yearning for the Thirties. But through this mass purgation and its aftermath of weariness, "Fitz's army held," and Kennedy is at last nominated.

Mailer's evocations of Kennedy as nominee, candidate, and president are studded with effects of style and imagery that echo Fitzgerald's portraiture of his own heroes. Kennedy is a resurgent image of "Renaissance man, . . . handsome as a prince in the unstated aristocracy of the American dream." The First Lady of the young President-to-be is, like Nicole Warren for Dick Diver, "queen of the arts, . . . our Muse if she chose to be." Kennedy is a "hero" because by sheer beauty and glamor and force of personality he draws to himself the love and commitment of others even as he stands aloof and apart from them. And he is the *"existential* hero" because in his magnetism and his mystery, he has the capability of becoming the gathered thrust of a whole people's new and powerful and undirected life-energy into an uncharted future. For this reason, the election itself is an existential venture in ultimate and perhaps fearful choosing between the known and the unknown. The pre-election polls show Kennedy the winner. And yet, writes Mailer in this striking echo of Fitzgerald:

> no one in America could plan the new direction until the last vote was counted by the last heeler in the last ambivalent ward, no one indeed could know until then what had happened the night before, what had happened at three o'clock in the morning on that long dark night of America's search for a security cheaper than her soul.

Ambivalence is the keynote here, an ambivalence expressing the substantive ambiguity of new historical realities. At the end of *The Great Gatsby* Nick Carraway summons the vision of an "orgiastic future" (Fitzgerald had written "orgastic"—"the adjective," he protested to Maxwell Perkins on receiving proof and noticing the change, "for 'orgasm' and it expresses exactly the intended ecstasy") toward which the American psyche is naturally drawn. In *Tender Is the Night* and *The Last Tycoon,* where the Apollonian sensibility of earlier Fitzgerald seems to be giving way to opposing forms and impulses, the inchoate future is coalescing into a lurid historical present. Order is capitulating to anarchy, intellect to passion, love to sexuality—"Surely some revelation is at hand. . . ." In Fitzgerald's late work, as his traditional idealism moves closer to its inevitable demise, the final instinct of his heroes is virtually to court and further their threatened destruction, as if they sense that from the death of their own worn-out life-forms fresh life may be released.

Mailer shows a similar ambivalence of vision, similar in the way a white design on a black ground is like the same design in black on white. In *Advertisements for Myself* he writes of "authority and nihilism stalking each other in the orgiastic hollow of this century." And he exhibits this pattern of contemporary experience everywhere in both his imaginative writing and his personal life—between which two there is as little substantive distinction to be made as there was in Fitzgerald's case. This tentative prophet of anarchy as a way of personal salvation nevertheless proposed, in 1960, to run for Mayor of New York, whereupon, "with the same diabolical care one often reserves for the best of one's ambitions," he proceeded to destroy the possibility by various means, including the stabbing of his wife at a party. And in the eleventh Presidential Paper, called "Death," that funniest, most complex, and perhaps most profound of his essays, he tells us how the topside of his psyche made him want to promote shining, clean-cut boxer Floyd Patterson as the triumphant champion of lonely adolescents, unsung romantics with a heroic vision, martyrs to principle ("He was the artist . . . an archetype of the underdog, an impoverished prince"); and how he gave way finally, like Patterson himself and all who identified with his cause, to the dark, chthonic undertow of brutal actuality represented by Sonny Liston and his world, "where you had no dream but making it, where you trusted no one because your knowledge of evil was too quick to its presence in everyone." In his famous essay on "The White Negro" and its succeeding addenda, Mailer, like Yeats, not only defines but woos and invites his personal image of the "rough beast" of this apocalyptic time—the hypersexual hipster anarch. Yet in an interview in the same volume he eloquently defends chastity and true love and attacks promiscuity, masturbation, the use of contraceptives, and modern atheistic rationalism, as forms of sacrilege.

Speaking almost as a conservative guardian of traditional values in the arts, Mailer writes an essay on Jean Genet in which he condemns the surrealist impulse in modern literature for artistic vanity and moral nihilism. Yet in another essay he is exhilarated by Samuel Beckett's *Waiting for Godot* as a powerful articulation of humane awareness for our moment in history:

> I feel the hints, the clues, the whispers of a new time coming. There is a universal rebellion in the air, and the power of the two colossal super-states may be, yes, may just be ebbing, may be failing in energy even more rapidly than we are failing in energy, and if that is so, the frantic search for potent Change may break into the open with all its violence, its confusion, its ugliness and horror, and yet like all Change, the violence is better without than within, better as individual actions than as the collective murders of society, and if we have courage enough, there is beauty beneath. . . .

This passage has its relevant modern analogues in Yeats, in Lawrence, even in Eliot. But the directness, almost the "realism" with which history's dark message is read in the social and political "facts" of the contemporary moment, and the casual, almost slangy way in which not despair but acceptance, confidence, even a kind of "gaiety," declares itself as the final meaning of this dark night of knowledge, gives its author, in the end, a closer affinity with Fitzgerald's vision than with anyone else's.

It is a doubleness of vision, then, rather than an inconsistency or even an ambivalence, that characterizes the imaginative responses of Mailer and Fitzgerald to history's drift from tradition and order toward anarchy and chaos. Paradoxically, because they welcome life they must also welcome such diseases, violences, and deaths as make more life possible. In an essay called "Fitzgerald and the Future," an early commentator once defined Fitzgerald's chief theme as the search for selfhood in a world where the dead Puritan norm of identity had been replaced by no viable successor. Because there were no sound models to follow, the strong creative impulse in Fitzgerald's protagonists lacked an adequate object, became formless, and thus turned destructive. "To destroy," wrote the critic, "is the oldest and easiest way of asserting one's Self. If there is no traditional philosophy of individualism worth accepting, if there is no social aim to give definition to young lives, there will come, along with the breakdown of old values, a moral inner compulsion to self-destruction, so that the many will be shattered in the hope that the one will remain." [5] This critic, detecting the "doubleness" of Fitzgerald's moral vision, has failed to understand the significance of that doubleness. Because so much recent American fiction is an extension of Fitzgerald's tradition, we can now see more readily that this doubleness is the mark of an "existential" vision different and more complex than the critic has realized. We can hypothesize, moreover, that this doubleness is the substance of a continuing and inherently American interpretation of modern experience which has its first full flowering in our fiction with Fitzgerald.

III

In his *Paris Review* interview Mailer speaks of the tension in himself between a conscious Marxist conviction and an unconscious fascination with "murder, suicide, orgy, psychosis, all the themes I discuss in *Advertisements*." [6] This tension, which produced *Barbary Shore,* is not unlike the conflict between conviction and compulsion that must have moved Fitzgerald while writing *Tender Is the Night*. Mailer is describing how, existentially, a work of art deeply rooted in the dynamics of present history comes into being, and what existential reality is like to an idealistic sensibility which is also highly attuned to those dynamics. Not much later in the interview he speaks of how, while working on the last draft of *The Deer Park,* he evolved the notion of an "existential God" whose being and fate is identical with the being and fate of man. Though he reports having later read some of the European existentialist thinkers, he claims to have had little knowledge of them at the time, and observes that, anyway, they lack the "intimations of eternity" which as a contemporary American alive to his experiential moment he discerns, "like new continents" on our "psychic maps." Fitzgerald, despite his smattering of Spengler, was similarly innocent of philosophy. And though he was in no other respect the "intellectual" that Mailer has always been, his stories and essays and novels show that in spite of his sense of the collapse of history it was in the nature of his temperament and sensibility to catch

5. Weller Embler, "F. Scott Fitzgerald and the Future," *F. Scott Fitzgerald: The Man and His Work, ed. cit.,* p. 219.
6. See above, p. 29.

glimpses of some of those very gods and continents, some of the same glimpses that show in certain philosophers—proto-Existentialist, perhaps, in a specially American way—whose thought nourished deeply on the American experience: Alfred North Whitehead, William James, and of course Emerson.

In 1840 Emerson wrote the following:

> The way of life is wonderful; it is by abandonment. The great moments of history are the facilities of performance through the strength of ideas, as the works of genius and religion. "A man," said Oliver Cromwell, "never rises so high as when he knows not whither he is going." Dreams and drunkenness, the use of opium and alcohol are the semblance and counterfeit of this oracular genius, and hence their dangerous attraction for men. For the like reason they ask the aid of wild passions, as in gaming and war, to ape in some manner these flames and generosities of the heart.

These concluding sentences of the essay "Circles" describe man's generic need to thrust toward a consciousness, a knowledge, a self-realization that lies beyond the boundaries of permitted and understood experience. It is a need symbolically embodied in the very nature of America's historical experiment, and variously expressed by its chief writers from the beginnings of American literature to the present. It is Emerson's mature theme, and it is Melville's, Dickinson's, Whitman's. As the creative counterforce beneath his conventional sensibility, it emerged as the life-energy, too, of Henry James's imagination. And after James it is Fitzgerald's.

It is the affirmativeness of Fitzgerald's confrontation of failure, reductive truth, and the harsh laughter of the absurd—his continually renewed expansiveness and positiveness in the face of "reality," the style of his courage—that is so movingly and engagingly "American." "I see," wrote Fitzgerald in 1936 in defense of "The Crack-Up," "that an unfriendly critic might damn the series as the whining of a spoilt baby, but in that case so is most poetry the complaints of the eternally youthful thing that persists in the writer. . . ." In the few years of life that remained to him he was to produce many good things, not the least of which, written when he was himself near the bottom of the pit of failure, were his late letters to his daughter "Scottie." In one of them he writes with approval of her connection of the Louisiana Purchase with Fred Astaire lifting his foot "for the world's pleasure," and in the same breath wishes her "to be among the best of your race," unwasted by trivial aims: "To be useful and proud—is that too much to ask?" And Mailer writes, near the end of his odd, funny, poignant, utterly serious Patterson-Liston piece on the psychodynamics of failure and death, "To believe the impossible may be won creates a strength from which the impossible may indeed be attacked." "To be useful and proud . . ."; "To believe the impossible may be won . . ."—this pattern of affirmative and idealistic impulses reflexively renewed or reborn in the face of disillusioning experience, plus the contemporaneous American subject matter which is the characteristic substance of their imaginative visions, not only connects Fitzgerald and Mailer importantly, but puts both of them in the main stream of American writers for whom the beauties and ambiguities of the "American dream" have been the inescapable motifs.

The Americanness of Norman Mailer

by Michael Cowan

One of the most revealing critical debates surrounding Norman Mailer's writings has had to do with his Americanness—the extent to which he has been a hapless reflector or even victim of America's prevailing middle-class mores, and the extent to which he has been a successful and self-conscious critic of, conscience for, and even prophet to his country and times. One of the most recent expressions of the first view is Kate Millett's suggestion, in *Sexual Politics,* that "Sexual congress in a Mailer novel is always a matter of strenuous endeavor, rather like mountain-climbing—a straining ever upward after achievement. In this, as in so many ways, Mailer is authentically American." [1] Alan Trachtenberg, on the other hand, has said that *The Armies of the Night* could have been written only by "a writer steeped in American life, with all his wits about him," and that Mailer's "extremities of style are directly in response to extremities and disproportions and incongruities" in the American experience. [2]

In fact, Mailer believes that one of a writer's highest goals is to "clarify a nation's vision of itself" (*CC,* 98). [3] As he implies at the end of *The Armies of the Night,* he has continually judged his own career as a writer by his ability to challenge Americans to reaffirm that their nation is "the land where a new kind of man was born from the idea that God was present in every man not only as com-

1. *Sexual Politics,* Kate Millett (Garden City, New York: Doubleday, 1970), p. 14.
2. "Mailer on the Steps of the Pentagon," *The Nation,* Vol. 206, no. 22 (May 27, 1968), 701–2.
3. Abbreviations and pagination refer to the following works: *ADV—Advertisements for Myself; AM—An American Dream; ARM—The Armies of the Night; BS—Barbary Shore; CC—Cannibals and Christians; DP—The Deer Park; FIRE—Of a Fire on the Moon; MI—Miami and the Siege of Chicago; ND—The Naked and the Dead; PP—The Presidential Papers; WHY—Why Are We in Vietnam?*

passion but as power, and so the country belonged to the people; for the will of the people—if the locks of their life could be given the art to turn—was then the will of God" (*ARM*, 288).

Mailer's view of the underlying pattern of American history is not particularly original, but it places him firmly in line with many major American writers from Emerson and Melville to Faulkner: the belief that American development is the product of a confrontation with virgin nature on a vast scale; the rapid and accelerating rate of social and psychological change that results from the American attempt to fill such large natural space with a burgeoning machine technology; the heterogenous background of the Americans—immigrants all—partly melting into a new composite American, partly exacerbating social tensions as they whirl around the white Protestant center. The "revolution of consciousness" he calls for in *Advertisements for Myself* is primarily a call for a psyche capable of confronting its own wilderness of possibilities. The American, working from a sense of large territorial possibilities, feels a vast potential for remaking himself, for becoming a "new man." But in experimenting with many possible "new selves," he begins to lose a clear sense of possessing any stable self. The goal of the American novelist, Mailer believes, is not only to dramatize this schizophrenia in the national psyche—to remain true to a vision of the essential doubleness at the heart of the American dream—but to affirm that the creative implications of this doubleness are ultimately more worthy of faith than the destructive implications. Like Faulkner in his Nobel Prize address, Mailer still clings to the hope that, although "one must balance every moment between the angel in oneself and the swine" (*MI*, 93), the angel still has the possibility of winning out—though only if one first faces the swine as courageously as he can. Mailer proposes that an American's best chance for salvation depends on treating the conflict at the center of the national psyche as an epic battle.

In light of such concerns, it should not be surprising that, of all nineteenth-century American writers, the one from whom Mailer most obviously draws strength and lessons is Herman Melville. No doubt one reason for his appeal to Mailer lies in the immensity of Mailer's literary ambitions. In *Advertisements for Myself*, Mailer proclaims his own ambition "to write a novel which Dostoevsky and Marx; Joyce and Freud; Stendhal, Tolstoy, Proust and Spengler; Faulkner, and even old moldering Hemingway might come to read, for it would carry what they had to tell another part of the way" (*ADV*, 477); and echoing Ishmael's own statement, he speaks of this novel as "a descendant of Moby Dick which will call for such time, strength, cash and patience that I do not know if I have it all to give, and so will . . . avoid the dream" (*ADV*, 156).

Mailer's proclamation prompted F. W. Dupee to argue that "the attraction of *Moby Dick* to Mailer . . . seem to consist largely in its bulk, profundity, and prestige. It is to him . . . an image of literary power rather than a work to be admired, learned from and then returned to its place of honor." [4] In fact, however, Mailer's response to *Moby Dick* has been more intricate and thoughtful than Dupee suggests. Another reason for Mailer's attraction to Melville is implied in his discussion of the backgrounds of modern American literature in his *Esquire* essay on "Some Children of the Goddess":

> Tolstoy and Dostoevsky divided the central terrain of the modern novel between them. Tolstoy's concern was with men-in-the-world, and indeed the panorama of his book carries to us an image of a huge landscape peopled with figures who changed that landscape, whereas the bulk of Dostoevsky's work could take place in ten closed rooms: it is not society but a series of individuals we remember, each illuminated by the terror of exploring the mystery of themselves. . . . One can point to *Moby Dick* as a perfect example of a novel in the second category—a book whose action depends upon the voyage of Ahab into his obsession. . . . (*CC*, 128).

Mailer's own response to the inward voyage of the self into its own obsession is traceable in his fictional protagonists, and certainly in the self-image that he presents in *Advertisements* and other works. Whatever sense of himself that Mailer has gleaned from Hemingway or Malraux or other "artists of action," he has certainly discovered an equally powerful model in the oceanic depths of *Moby Dick*.

The decor of Mailer's Brooklyn Heights duplex apartment, as described by a Playboy interviewer in 1968, is perhaps one way in which Mailer has responded to this model: "Nautical items abound, from the brass ship's clock over the kitchen and the dismantled engine-room telegraph beside the big bookcases to the glass-and-wood gable forecastle, which Mailer built above the kitchen and bedrooms and which can be reached only by climbing ropes, trapezes or deck ladders." Mailer's appeal to the sense of

4. See above, pp. 96–103.

adventurousness symbolized by a voyaging ship has often extended beyond his own residence. In an article for the New York *Times* he proposes cities reaching into the clouds whose buildings "could begin to look a little less like armored tanks and more like clipper ships" and whose airborne residents could "feel the dignity of sailors on a four-master at sea . . . returned to that mixture of awe and elation, of dignity and self-respect and a hint of dread, that sense of zest which a man must have known working his way out along a yardarm in a stiff breeze at sea" (*CC,* 237). It is just these sorts of complex feelings that Stephen Rojack experiences as he walks around the parapet of Barney Kelly's penthouse apartment: "as used up as a sailor who has been tied for hours in the rigging of a four-master beating through a storm" (*AM,* 259). Mailer's characteristic advocacy of Americans' need for adventurous voyages into the dangerous frontier world of the self seems, by Mailer's own statements, to find a strong counterpart in Melville.

We are told in *The Naked and the Dead* that Robert Hearn's senior essay, for which he "has been given a magna" at Harvard, is entitled *A Study of the Cosmic Urge in Herman Melville* (*ND,* 345). The world that Hearn attempts unsuccessfully to come to terms with on Anopopei (perhaps this is why Mailer gives him a magna rather than a summa) is a wild landscape dominated by the mania of a commander and the presence of an unconquerable leviathan. "The biggest influence on *Naked,*" Mailer remarked in 1951, "was *Moby Dick* . . . I was sure everyone would know. I had Ahab in it, and I suppose the mountain was Moby Dick." [5] It is unwise to press too hard for precise parallels between the two novels. Hearn, for example, may resemble Ishmael in his intellectual background, his speculative habits, and the ennui that drives him onto the uncharted sea of war, but in his confrontation of Cummings or Croft, he comes closer to expressing what Melville calls the "unaided virtue" of Starbuck. Cummings and Croft share the role of Ahab. And the heterogeneous backgrounds and values of Croft's patrol make it a paler version of the *Pequod*'s crew. Like Melville's whalers, each soldier of the patrol finds himself on a mission that comes to involve not only a primal struggle with social authority or a non-human wilderness but a nightmarish war with the ambiguities and divisions of his own inner nature.

5. Harvey Breit, *The Writer's Art* (Cleveland and New York: World, 1956), p. 200.

The central symbol of these ambiguities and dangers is Mount Anaka itself, which, like Moby Dick, casts its awesome presence over the entire novel, inspiring men to conquest but confronting them with naked ambiguities about themselves and their world. Anaka is unreachable not only physically but intellectually; like Moby Dick or the doubloon that Ahab nails to the *Pequod*'s mast, the mountain is always viewed partially. And as in Melville's novel, the varying and even conflicting meanings that individual characters read into Anaka tell as much about themselves as about the mountain. To Gallagher, for example, "the mountain seemed wise and powerful, and terrifying in its size. Gallagher stared at it in absorption, caught by a sense of beauty he could not express. The idea, the vision he always held of something finer and neater and more beautiful than the moil in which he lived trembled now, pitched almost to a climax of words . . . but it passed and he was left with a troubled joy, an echo of rapture (*ND*, 447). Roth fears the mountain—it seems to him "so open, so high"—and prefers even the suffocating jungle "to these naked ridges, these gaunt alien vaults of stone and sky. . . . The jungle was filled with all kinds of dangers but they did not seem so severe now. . . . But here, one misstep and it would be death. It was better to live in a cellar than to walk a tightrope" (*ND*, 638). Hearn finds that the mountain "roused his awe and then his fear. It was too immense, too powerful. He suffered a faint sharp thrill as he watched the mist eddy about the peak. He imagined the ocean actually driving against a rockbound coast, and despite himself strained his ears as though he could hear the sound of such a titanic struggle" (*ND*, 497). To Croft too "the mountain looked like a rocky coast and the murky sky seemed to be an ocean shattering its foam upon the shore." But Croft finds Anaka more compelling than does Hearn:

> The mountain and the cloud and the sky were purer, more intense, in their gelid silent struggle than any ocean and any shore he had ever seen. The rocks gathered themselves in the darkness, huddled together against the fury of the water. The context seemed an infinite distance away, and he felt a thrill of anticipation at the thought that by the following night they might be on the peak. Again, he felt a crude ecstasy. He could not have given the reason, but the mountain tormented him, fascinated him, beckoned him, held an answer to something he wanted. It was so pure, so austere (*ND*, 497).

Whereas Hearn is more impressed with the dangers and ambiguities
suggested in his mind by Anaka—"It was the kind of shore upon
which huge ships would founder, smash apart, and sink in a few
minutes" (*ND,* 498)—Croft is more compelled by the intensity and
purity of its challenge to his own powers: "he led the platoon up
the mountain without hesitation. . . . Despite all the exertion of
the preceding days, he was restless and impatient now, driven forward by a demanding tension in himself. . . . He was continually
eager to press on to the next rise, anxious to see what was beyond.
The sheer mass of the mountain inflamed him" (*ND,* 635). And his
failure to conquer Anaka is important not for what it tells him
about his physical limitations but for what it has revealed to him
about his inner nature: "Deep inside himself, Croft was relieved
that he had not been able to climb the mountain . . . [and] was
rested by the unadmitted knowledge that he had found a limit to
his hunger" (*ND,* 701).

As *The Naked and the Dead* suggests, Mailer mines *Moby Dick*
not only for major analogues to the adventures that he has constantly stressed as an essential component of America's psychic and
social health but, equally important, for a major symbol of the
ambiguities and dangers that attend such excursions. Significantly,
since Mailer has taken on the mantle of "Historian," he has found
Melville's book also a useful reference point for determining how
far his countrymen have departed from their "organic" heritage.
Observing the 1964 Republican convention, he is reminded of the
degeneration that security-minded Americans have allowed to take
place in the cultural tradition of which Melville was a part:

> The American mind had gone from Hawthorne and Emerson to
> the Frug, the Bounce, and Walking the Dog, from *The Flowering
> of New England* to the cerebrality of professional football in
> which a quarterback must have not only heart, courage, strength
> and grace but a mind like an I.B.M. computer. It marks the turn
> we have taken from the Renaissance. There too was the ideal of a
> hero with heart, courage, strength, and grace, but he was expected
> to possess the mind of a passionate artist. Now the best heroes
> were—in the sense of the Renaissance—mindless. . . . (*CC,* 28–29).

This "mindlessness" to which the American imagination has degenerated shows itself in the degeneration of America's major symbols of power. By the time Moby Dick has reached the rudderless
world of D.J. in *Why Are We in Vietnam?,* he has become merely

the occasion for sophomoric wordplay: "Herman Melville go hump Moby and wash his Dick" (*WHY*, 26). Whereas the American Renaissance's major symbol of power, Moby Dick, combined not only essential ambiguity with dignifying epic drama, contemporary America's major symbols of power, such as the Pentagon, have become not only faceless but utterly without dramatic personality, have become, in fact, "anonymous" signs of the failure of the adventurous symbolizing imagination in American public life. As Mailer treats it in *The Armies of the Night*, the Pentagon becomes almost a travesty on Melville's mighty leviathan:

> the strength of the Pentagon is subtle . . . it is doubtful if there was ever another building in the world so huge in ground plan and so without variation. . . . The Pentagon, architecturally, was as undifferentiated as a jellyfish or a cluster of barnacles. One could chip away at any part of the interior without locating a nervous center. . . . High church of the corporation, the Pentagon spoke exclusively of mass man and his civilization; every aspect of the building was anonymous, monotonous, massive, interchangeable.
>
> For [the Mobilization Committee's] revolutionary explorers, the strangeness of their situation must have been comparable to a reconnaissance of the moon. . . . It was impossible to locate the symbolic loins of the building—paradigm of the modern world indeed, they could explore every inch of their foe and know nothing about him. . . . (*ARM*, 226–29).

It may seem somewhat ludicrous to compare the Pentagon to the great whale's "pasteboard mask" through which Ahab wants obsessively to strike or to see in its facelessness the ultimate unknowability that Ishmael sees in the whale ("Dissect him how I may, then, I but go skin deep; I know him not, and never will. But if I know not even the tail of this whale, how understand his head? much more, how comprehend his face, when face he has none"). But Mailer feels the same incongruity. The easiest way into the Pentagon, he reminds us, is through its shopping center and cafeteria, and he finds "something absurd" in this possibility. "To attack here was to lose some of one's symbolic momentum—a consideration which might be comic or unpleasant in a shooting war, but in a symbolic war was not necessarily comic at all" (*ARM*, 229–30). The decline in the power of the epic symbol is thus not only a reflection of a degeneration of national value but a terrifying reminder of how difficult it is for a contemporary American writer to create an image that again will move his countrymen to heroic action. Mailer is reminded again of this challenge when he visits the Vehicle Assembly Building at Cape Kennedy where Apollo 11 is being built. His first tentative attempt at surrounding the vehicle in epic hyperbole is challenged by the official language in which the vehicle is encased: "VAB—it could be the name of a drink or a deodorant, or it could be suds for the washer. But it was not a name for this warehouse of the gods. . . . Nothing fit anything any longer. The art of communication had become the function, and the machine was the work of art. What a fall for the ego of the artist. What a climb to capture the language again!" (*FIRE*, 56).

But this imaginatively degenerated world is all that Mailer has. Loving America too much to leave it, he must dig for redemptive metaphors in his native soil. He is thus obviously pleased that, in contrast to the lack of real drama that a super-plastic Miami offers him in 1968, bloody, stockyard-smelling Chicago "gave America its last chance at straight-out drama" and thus provides potential "salvation of the schizophrenic soul." Watching the overwhelming battle at the Chicago Hilton between the protesters and the police, Mailer searches for a mighty image appropriate to the dramatic occasion and finds one in *Moby Dick*:

> it was as if the war had finally begun, and this was therefore a great and solemn moment, as if indeed even the gods of history had come together from each side to choose the very front of the Hilton Hotel before the television cameras of the world and the eyes of the campaign workers and the delegates' wives, yes, there before the eyes of half the principals at the convention was this drama played, as if the military spine of a great liberal party had finally separated itself from the skin, as if, no metaphor large enough to suffice, the Democratic Party had here broken in two before the eyes of a nation like Melville's whale charging right out of the sea (*MI*, 172).

What is interesting about this passage is not merely that Mailer is searching for an epic symbol with which to give weight yet another time to the dialectic of American life, but that he has self-consciously chosen to do so by means of a traditional symbol transformed for his own purposes. Melville's Leviathan, as Mailer treats him, is no longer merely a natural force against which the American must wage his epic and perhaps tragic frontier wars. It has become a symbol of the split at the center of the American's sense of identity. Moby Dick is not merely a frontier threat, but a humanized resource from the past that the American imagination can use in its never-ending struggle to redeem the present. Without denying the existential value of remaining true to the "perpetual climax of the present," Mailer affirms also that such a present is not a break with but outgrowth of the past, and that the frontiers of the modern consciousness require not only existential resources but in addition the creative adaptation of tools offered by a historical tradition.

In charting Mailer's implicit quest for a usable past as a literary tool, we could profitably compare him not only to Melville but to writers like Hawthorne or Faulkner. In all of these writers, an essentially romantic sensibility proposes that high tragedy is more worthy of the human spirit than a divine comedy turned facile, that the individual can often show more dignity in suffering the defeat of his greatest dreams than in winning mundane victories, that guilt is as essential an ingredient as pride to the mature man's self-respect and sense of essential identity. If anything, this traditional stance has become more marked in Mailer's non-fiction since the early sixties. By the time he writes *Armies,* with his penchant for unresolvable oxymorons, he is referring to himself as a "radical conservative" and emphasizing the agony of his attempt to become "some natural aristocrat from these damned democratic states" (*ARM,* 41). Asserting his kinship with Robert Lowell and other *"Grands conservateurs"* of America's noblest traditions, Mailer has claimed ownership of a hard-won ironic detachment from which he can approach the apocalyptic aspirations of, say, the march on the Pentagon with the sad and yet humanizing understanding that this has not been the first time—and will undoubtedly not be the last—that Americans have gone all-out for apocalypse: that the dream of revolutionary adventure is itself an essential defining characteristic of the American tradition. In fact, it is this link with the past that gives the event much of its resonance:

> As Lowell and Mailer reached the ridge and took a turn to the right to come down from Washington Monument toward the length of the long reflecting pool which led between two long groves of trees near the banks to the steps of Lincoln Memorial, out from that direction came the clear bitter-sweet excitation of a military trumpet resounding in the near distance, one peal which

seemed to go all the way back through a galaxy of bugles to the cries of the Civil War and the first trumpet note to blow the attack. The ghosts of old battles were wheeling like clouds over Washington today (*ARM,* 91).

The *enfant terrible* of *Advertisements,* crying for a "revolution of consciousness," has increasingly given way to the brooding "historian," "reporter," and "detective" who, in *Miami,* argues that "we will be fighting for forty years" (*MI,* 223).

While in Washington to participate in the march on the Pentagon, Mailer stays at the Hay-Adams hotel and, in the course of pondering his emerging mission as Historian, finds himself wondering if "the Adams in the name of his hotel bore any relation to Henry" (*ARM,* 54). While we need not make much of his aside, it is interesting to speculate briefly on the kinship of these two historian sons of Harvard, particularly between the Mailer from *Armies* to *Of a Fire* and the Adams of *The Education.* It is in *Armies* that Mailer first dons the third-person narrative guise used by Adams in *The Education,* and for much the same reason. As Alan Trachtenberg remarks, "the implausible assault upon the Pentagon . . . becomes the perfect vehicle to bring Mailer's own inner experience into focus, and Mailer himself, 'a comic hero,' a 'figure of monumental disproportions,' becomes the perfect figure through which 'to recapture the precise feel of the ambiguity of the event and its monumental disproportions.' Much like Henry Adams in his *Education,* Mailer here discovers an aptness between his own posture in the world and the crazy configurations of the world itself." [6]

Like Adams, Mailer has increasingly treated his work as the rather ironic story of an education whose value as preparation for succeeding in or at least understanding a rapidly changing modern world is at best ambiguous. Whereas Adams claims to be an eighteenth-century child trying to prepare in the nineteenth century for a twentieth-century civilization, Mailer seems a nineteenth-century romantic (with a trace of the puritan) trying to straddle the twentieth century in order to seize a twenty-first century that has arrived before its time. Like Adams, Mailer sees history as an accelerating movement from unity to multiplicity. What could be more Adamslike than Mailer's statement in *Of a Fire on the Moon* that:

> It was the first century in history which presented to sane and sober minds the fair chance that the century might not reach the

6. "Mailer on the Steps of the Pentagon," p. 701.

end of its span. It was a world half convinced of the future death of our species yet half aroused by the apocalyptic notion that an exceptional future still lay before us. So it was a century which moved with the most magnificent display of power into directions it could not comprehend. The itch was to accelerate—the metaphysical direction unknown (*FIRE*, 48).

Like Adams, Mailer—if with less elegance and historical experience —probes the past for a base from which to triangulate the future. Both writers proceed primarily by manipulating the ambiguities and shifting meanings of an immense series of dualities and by couching these dualities in sweeping and even melodramatic terms. Like *The Education,* Mailer's most recent work is in important ways a poet's search for a metaphorical structure that will at least bring the illusion of order to the multiplying contradictions of modern experience.

The kinship of both writers is most strongly marked in *Of a Fire on the Moon.* Mailer's meditation on the meaning of Apollo 11 is framed usefully by Adams' comments in the last chapter of *The Education.* Approaching New York in 1905 by boat, Adams finds the view of the technologically wondrous city:

more striking than ever—wonderful—unlike anything man had ever seen—and like nothing he ever much cared to see. The outline of the city became frantic in its effort to explain something that defied meaning. Power seemed to have outgrown its servitude and to have asserted its freedom. The cylinder had exploded, and thrown great masses of stone and steam against the sky. The city had the air and movement of hysteria, and the citizens were crying, in every accent of anger and alarm, that the new forces must at any cost be brought under control. . . . He was beyond measure curious to see whether the conflict of forces would produce the new man [who could control them], since no other energies seemed left on earth to breed. The new man could be only a child born of contact between the new and the old energies.

It is in much the same spirit of distaste and guarded respect that Mailer observes the "bomb" that he believes Apollo 11 to be. And out of much the same curiosity that leads Adams to formulate "A Dynamic Theory of History," Mailer begins to formulate "a psychology of astronauts" to help explain the "new men" who must guide the bomb's powers.

As preparation for this task, Mailer rather wryly takes on the

kind of role that Adams finds for himself in the latter part of
the *Education*—that of a senior American statesman and philosopher whom the world has by-passed and who therefore must make
a virtue out of being an important if detached observer of the
rapidly changing scene. If Adams "felt nothing in common with
the world as it promised to be," he believed "he could at least
act as an audience." Mailer describes himself in similar terms: "He
has learned to live with questions. Of course, as always, he has little
to do with the immediate spirit of the time. . . . He has never had
less sense of possessing the age. He feels in fact little more than
a decent spirit, somewhat shunted to the side. It is the best possible
position for detective work." This role of "somewhat disembodied
spirit" has an important artistic virtue for Mailer: "he was conceivably in superb shape to study the flight of Apollo 11 to the
moon. For he was detached this season from the imperial demands
of his ego. . . . He felt like a spirit of some just-consumed essence
of the past. . . ." (*FIRE*, 6).

A philosophical but playful spirit from the past, Mailer probes
the meaning of American technology at the Manned Spacecraft
Center and at Cape Kennedy in much the way that Adams probes
the implications of the dynamo at the Chicago, Paris, and St. Louis
Expositions. Viewing the dynamo as "a symbol of infinity," Adams
treats it as the most appropriate symbol of the age's moral values:
"Before the end, one began to pray to it. . . . Among the thousand
symbols of ultimate energy, the dynamo was not so human as some,
but it was the most expressive." Similarly, Mailer describes the
Vehicle Assembly Building as "the antechamber of a new Creation":

> he came to recognize that whatever was in store, a Leviathan was
> most certainly ready to ascend the heavens—whether for good or
> ill he might never know—but he was standing at least in the first
> cathedral of the age of technology, and he might as well recognize
> that the world would change, that the world had changed, even
> as he had thought to be pushing and shoving on it with *his* mighty
> ego. And it had changed in ways he did not recognize, had never
> anticipated, and could possibly not comprehend now. The change
> was mightier than he had counted on, the full brawn of the rocket
> in this cavernous womb of an immensity, this giant cathedral of a
> machine designed to put together another machine which would
> voyage through space. Yes, this emergence of a ship to travel the

ether was no event he could measure by any philosophy he had been able to put together in his brain (*FIRE,* 55).

Facing the force of the dynamo and its problematic relationship to the force of the Virgin, Adams argues that he can search for a means of measurement only by becoming "a pilgrim of power." Mailer adopts the same strategy: "The first step in comprehension was to absorb. . . . He would be, perforce, an acolyte to technology."

As a reluctant acolyte, Mailer forces himself to treat the Apollo 11 not merely as a dynamo but as the moral equivalent to the Virgin of Mont St. Michel and Chartres. Describing the spotlighted rocket on the night before the launch, he wryly suggests that "she looked like a shrine with the lights upon her. In the distance she glowed for all the world like some white stone Madonna in the mountains, welcoming footsore travelers at dusk" (*FIRE,* 59). He sees white Protestant America, long deprived of a Madonna, as hopefully investing the rocket with all the powers of comfort and cure for their alienation: "all over the South . . . they would be praying for America tonight—thoughts of America served to replace the tender sense of the Virgin in Protestant hearts."

American technology, then, has attempted to harness the forces of nature which Melville had symbolized by Moby Dick, and Mailer is willing as detached observer to leave ambiguous the question of whether the launching of Apollo 11 shows man taming nature or nature's revenge on man—further, whether the rocket is a "Sainted Leviathan"—Moby Dick canonized by the American dream—or "a Medusa's head" whose only powers are those of death (*FIRE,* 84). The rocket launch is thus the latest and one of the most dramatic of America's frontier encounters with the wilderness, and Mailer, as grimacing "acolyte to technology," identifies himself with all Americans who feel compelled to continually search for their identity by means of such ambiguous confrontations: "A tiny part of him was like a penitent who had prayed in the wilderness for sixteen days, and was now expecting a sign. Would the sign reveal much or little?" (*FIRE,* 98)

The response to Mailer's question is appropriately less an answer than an image. As the rocket rises, the worlds of the Dynamo, the Virgin, and Moby Dick—of technology, imagination, and nature— merge into a new, powerful, but intensely ambiguous symbol of the American dream. The launch is immensely "more dramatic" than he has anticipated:

> For the flames were enormous. No one could be prepared for that. . . . Two mighty torches of flame like the wings of a yellow bird of fire flew over a field, covered a field with brilliant yellow bloomings of flame, and in the midst of it, white as a ghost, white as the white of Melville's Moby Dick, white as the shrine of the Madonna in half the churches of the world, this slim angelic mysterious ship of stages rose without sound out of its incarnation of flame and began to ascend slowly into the sky, slow as Melville's Leviathan might swim, slowly as we might swim upward in a dream looking for the air. And still no sound.
>
> Then it came . . . an apocalyptic fury of sound equal to some conception of the sound of your death in the road of a drowning hour, a nightmare of sound, and he heard himself saying, 'Oh, my God! oh, my God! oh, my God! oh, my God! oh, my God! oh, my God! . . . and [had] a poor moment of vertigo at the thought that man now had something with which to speak to God. . . . (*FIRE*, 99–100).

If the flight of Apollo 11 has renewed once again a feeling for the cosmic implications of the American enterprise, it has once again pointed to the overwhelming nightmares that the enterprise inevitably carries with it, and Mailer can even suggest that the God who directs this modern Pequod may be a colossal Ahab gone monomaniacal: "the Power guiding us . . . was looking to the day when all of mankind would yet be part of one machine . . . an instrument of divine endeavor put together by a Father to whom one might no longer be able to pray since the ardors of His embattled voyage could have driven Him mad" (*FIRE*, 152). But the terror of such a possibility seems ultimately less important to Mailer than the sheer drama it creates. For the feeling of high drama reassures him that he is once again in an epic arena where the divided halves of the American psyche can meet in potentially creative combat: "It was somehow superior to see the astronauts and the flight of Apollo 11 as the instrument of . . . celestial or satanic endeavors, than as . . . a sublimation of aggressive and intolerably inhuman desires. . . . Aquarius preferred the . . . assumption that we were the indispensable instruments of a monumental vision with whom we had begun a trip" (*FIRE*, 151–52).

As a Brooklyn-born "Nijinsky of ambivalence," Mailer, like Whit-

man, has been exasperatingly eager to contradict himself in order
to keep open a multitude of possible approaches to modern American experience. His major works are hymns to incompletion and
openness and rarely conclude so much as continually begin: Mikey
Lovett flees with his "little secret," Sergius O'Shaugnessy begins a
search for "new circuits," *Advertisements* catches the narrator on
"the way out," Steven Rojack heads for Guatemala, D.J. lights out
for Vietnam, and *Armies* and *Miami* seem calls to arms rather than
final battles. Characteristically, the return of Apollo 11's astronauts
to earth suggests to Mailer less the completion of a mission than
the birth of a new line of thought, one embodying his desire along
with that of Emerson's American Scholar to "see every trifle bristling
with the polarity that ranges it instantly on an eternal law." At the
conclusion of *Of a Fire on the Moon,* the polarity embodies itself
in the small fragment of moon rock brought back by the astronauts
from the lunar wilderness. Though Mailer has typically treated the
moon as the symbolic home of cancer, madness, and the sickness
unto death, and though the fragment is separated from him by
a sterile technological casing, he finds the rock giving off to his
imagination, like a blade of Whitman's grass, the smell of innocent
new life:

> he liked the moon rock, and thought—his vanity finally unquench-
> able—that she liked him. . . . there was something young about
> her, tender as the smell of the cleanest hay, it was like the subtle
> lift of love which comes up from the cradle of the newborn . . .
> and so he had his sign, sentimental beyond measure, his poor dull
> sense had something he could trust (*FIRE,* 472).

Many critics have found such analogical leaps unconvincing. Such
opinions, however, have not dampened Mailer's zealous and constant search among the common as well as spectacular materials of
his nation for new launching pads. No matter how impressive or
awkward Mailer's soaring through the painful but stimulating ambiguities of contemporary American life and thought, the irrepressi-
bility of his flight is itself a demonstration of the Americanness of
his dream.

What Mailer Has Done

by Richard Gilman

In Norman Mailer's hyperbolic world it will no doubt seem like a putdown to say that his new book [*The Armies of the Night*] is a fine, exciting piece of work, flawed but immensely interesting, a literary act whose significance is certain to grow. Mailer never lets us forget that he wants it all: all the kudos, all the marbles, honorary degrees in every field, a status that can best be described in a phrase from the adolescence he has never wholly shaken off: King of the Hill. All estimation of him is affected by his having always wanted, in the worst way, to *count,* the ferocity with which he attacks everything that stands in the way of his being seen to count having its roots in the fact that, as he says in this book, "the one personality he finds absolutely insupportable [is] the nice Jewish boy from Brooklyn."

That a nice Jewish boy from Brooklyn simply can't be a representative American figure, much less a mover and shaker, is the principle of much of Mailer's acrobatics and histrionic movements. He has willed himself into pertinence and power, and it is one of the most fascinating and instructive episodes of our recent cultural history. More than any other of our writers Mailer has intervened in the age so that he has come to count, more securely as time goes on, and if it isn't exactly in the way he wants, if it still seems ridiculous to call him the *best* American writer, he nevertheless matters in a way that only a man with so mighty and precarious an ego as his could find disappointing. He long ago made it out of niceness and Jewishness and Brooklyn; with this book he makes it into a central area of the American present, where all the rough force of his imagination, his brilliant gifts of observation, his ravishing if

"What Mailer Has Done" by Richard Gilman (review of *The Armies of the Night*). From *The New Republic* 158, no. 23 (June 8, 1968), 27–31. Copyright © 1968 by Harrison-Blaine of New Jersey, Inc. Reprinted by permission of *The New Republic.*

often calculated honesty, his daring and his *chutzpah* are able to flourish on the steady ground of a newly coherent subject and theme and to issue in a work more fully *in our interests* than any he has ever done.

Mailer's subject, as it has always been in some measure, is himself, but this time a self balanced between objective events and private consciousness in a riper way than ever before. And his theme is just that relation of antipathy but also fertile interdependence between the self and history, the ego and actuality, which he has always strenuously sought—with greater suggestiveness than substance it's often seemed—to make the arena and justification of his work. In writing about his participation in the anti-Vietnam demonstrations in Washington last October (most particularly the march on the Pentagon), Mailer has finally succeeded in laying hands on the novelistic character he has never quite been master of before, and at the same time succeeded in finding a superbly viable form for his scattered, imperfect and often greatly discordant gifts.

I don't think it's been clearly enough seen how Mailer's talents and strengths have for the most part been disjunctive if not wholly contradictory. Such contradiction may be a mainstay of his energy, but it's also an element of his fretful anarchy. His rather old-fashioned novelist's inquisitiveness about the behavior of men in society has, for example, often been diverted by his utopianism, his extra-literary hunger for things to change and change *now*, in palpable ways rather than in the imaginary, alternative ways, in which most artist-novelists deal. His ambition for guruhood, prophetic status, has run up against his violent need for immediate action. His reportorial gifts have been charged with novelistic daring but also corrupted by novelistic license. And his sense of writing as the expression and progress of personality, less a rigorous art than a style of public appearance, a way of counting, has kept him from achieving the full mastery of language, the hardwon grace of a conquest by which previously nonexistent realities are brought into being, that we associate with writers we call great.

In *The Armies of the Night* Mailer's talents come more than ever into working agreement and, moreover, move to ameliorate his deficiencies. Antinomies are revolved: the artist who has to invent and the observer who has to prey on facts merge into the same person; the transcendencies of art and the imminences of action move toward each other's replenishment; the excesses of personality find a

new and strangely valuable use in the face of the opaque excesses
(and history has come to be almost nothing but excesses) of our
public days and years.

This is the central, rather wonderful achievement of the book,
that in it history and personality confront each other with a new
sense of liberation. By introducing his ego more directly into history than he ever has before, by taking events which were fast dis-
appearing under the perversions and omissions of ordinary journalism as well as through the inertia we all feel in the face of what is
over with, by taking these events and revivifying them, reinstating
them in the present, Mailer has opened up new possibilities for the
literary imagination and new room for us to breathe in the crush
of actuality.

I don't think anyone who is more purely an artist than Mailer
could have brought this off; but neither could any kind of journalist,
no matter how superior. This is the conjunction of Mailer's special
being—half artist-half activist, half inventor-half borrower—with
what the times require: an end, for certain purposes, of literary
aloofness on the one hand and of the myth of "objective" description on the other. With a speed approaching light's, history thrusts
itself upon us, no longer the special province of "history-making"
people, no longer the mysterious work of blind forces or, alternatively, of scientifically ascertainable "laws." History is indeed what
we make it, and Mailer, by making himself the chief character of a
"novel" whose truth doesn't have to be invented and by making
history reveal an "esthetic" dimension has helped bridge gaps of
long standing, has brought some ordinarily sundered things together
in a revelatory book whose nearest counterpart in our literature,
for all the obvious differences, is Henry Adams' *Education.*

How well Mailer's ego serves him now! He begins his education
and the book with an account of his reluctant agreement to participate in the demonstrations. In these pages, the notorious literary
personality, with its disarming shifts between megalomania and self-
deprecation, is fully on display. He speaks (in the third person, as
he does throughout the book) of the "living tomb of his legend,"
tells how "he hated to put in time with losers," writes grandly of
how the "architecture of his personality bore resemblance to some
provincial cathedral which warring orders of the church might have

designed separately over several centuries," reveals that "a party lacked flavor for him unless someone very rich or social was present," and tells us about his "illusion of genius," the "wild man in himself," the "absolute egomaniac" and the "snob of the worst sort."

All this has two functions: to "humanize" the character who is going to participate in history, and to push his sense of self to its limits, so that history will have the most formidable, because most representative opponent. Much of Mailer's appeal has always lain in his stance vis-à-vis the powers that be; the Jimmy Cagney of literature, he has especially been a model for youth, who have always admired him perhaps more for being a welterweight taking on heavies than for being a heavyweight himself. And as Mailer moves on into the actual events of those four days in Washington this cocky stance —the self as the equal of all large intimidating public opponents, yet also the self aware of its small size and internal divisions—becomes a representative posture for all of us. More than ever, Mailer's embattled ego is seen to be the troubled, sacrificial, rash and unconquerable champion for all of ours.

The ego fluctuates wildly. He arrives in Washington in a sober mood: "Like most New Yorkers he usually felt small in Washington. The capital invariably seemed to take the measure of men like him." But the "wild man" he harbors pushes forward and takes over. At a party given by a liberal academic couple, in whose home he smells "the scent of the void which comes off a Xerox copy," he manages to affront his hostess. At a rally later at the Ambassador Theatre he outrages nearly everybody by what is to be reported in the press as his drunken behavior. He is indeed somewhat drunk, but not without wit or point to his actions, and his account of the evening is a sustained triumph of autobiographical writing.

But autobiography of a particularly intense and unconventional kind. Into this report of a public meeting, his part in which had months before been corrupted into "history" by *Time* magazine and the daily press, Mailer introduces the most personal matters: his having missed the urinal in a dark men's room; his resentment at having been replaced as M.C., his strongly ambivalent attitude towards the audience. And into this candid and irreverent autobiography he sweeps the other participants—Paul Goodman, Dwight Macdonald, Robert Lowell—writing about them in a form of high and liberating gossip, infusing particularity and personality and queer informing detail into their remote public biographies, their status as names.

Macdonald, "the operative definition of the gregarious," "gesticulated awkwardly, squinted at his text, laughed at his own jokes, looked like a giant stork, whinnied, shrilled and was often inaudible." Lowell, towards whom Mailer positions himself through much of the book in a remarkably frank species of testing, a weighing of their very different personalities and backgrounds, stands "with a glint of the oldest Yankee light winging off like a mad laser from his eye," gives off "at times the unwilling haunted saintliness of a man who was repaying the moral debts of ten generations of ancestors," moves with a slouch the "languid grandeurs" of which testify to generations of primacy in Boston and at Harvard, and provides Mailer with one of the book's central themes and preoccupations.

For in seeking a shape for the relationship of the self to the historical events of that weekend in Washington, and to the historical realities that had led up to it, Mailer has understood how his own self has to be employed as both battleground and partial perspective, how other selves such as Lowell's, products of an almost wholly different background from his, an America of complex traditions, austere moralities, rooted political conscience, elegance, personal diffidence combined with patrician standards for public behavior—the textbook older American *style*—have to be taken into the picture so that it might be seen what a confluence of varied egos and personalities occurred at that point in Washington, within history, facing it and making it. Lowell (the New England style), Paul Goodman (the wholly liberated urban Jewish style) and the multifarious styles of the older liberals and young dissidents and radicals who made up the bulk of the demonstrators: something congruent and crucial to our American understanding rose from their incongruity and widely separated motives, their having come from so many starting-points to that time and place.

As the demonstrators gather for the march on the Pentagon, Mailer moves brilliantly between analyses of his own immediate feelings, descriptions of the look and feel of the crowd, and a grand, lyrical sociology. As the tension rises he finds himself going beyond the play-acting which has subtly characterized his participation up to now, "as if some final cherished rare innocence of childhood still preserved intact in him was brought finally to the surface and there expired, so he lost at that instant the last secret delight in life as a game where finally you never got hurt if you played the game well enough."

He looks at the young rebels, who have started from points well beyond his own romantic and fundamentally "cultured" view:

> A generation of the American young had come along different from five previous generations of the middle class. The new generation believed in technology, more than any before it, but the generation also believed in LSD, in witches, in tribal knowledge, in orgy and revolution. It had no respect whatsoever for the unassailable knowledge of the next step; belief was reserved for the revelatory mystery of the happening where you did not know what was going to happen next; that was what was good about it. Their radicalism was in their hate for the authority—the authority was the manifest of evil to this generation. It was the authority who had covered the land with those suburbs where they stifled as children while watching the adventures of the West in the movies, while looking at the guardians of dull genial celebrity on television; they had had their minds jabbed, poked and twitched and probed and finally galvanized into surrealistic modes of response by commercials cutting into dramatic narratives, and parents flipping from network to network—they were forced willy-nilly to build their idea of the space-time continuum (and therefore their nervous system) on the jumps and cracks and leaps and breaks which every phenomenon from the medium seemed to contain within it.

The balance he maintains, the breadth of his vision here, his capacity to see history whole while being immersed in its unfolding and while in the act of *rewriting* it (always a keen temptation to tendentiousness)—these, I think, are the result of his novelist's patience and sophistication holding his ideological horses in check. The young are "villains" too:

> Mailer was haunted by the nightmare that the evils of the present not only exploited the present, but consumed the past, and gave every promise of demolishing whole territories of the future. The same villains who, promiscuously, wantonly, heedlessly, had gorged on LSD and consumed God knows what essential marrows of history, wearing indeed the history of all eras on their back as trophies of this gluttony, were now going forth (conscience-struck?) to make war on those other villains, corporation-land villains, who were destroying the promise of the present in their self-righteousness and

greed and secret lust (often unknown in themselves) for some sexo-
technological variety of neofascism. Mailer's final allegiance, however, was to the villains who were hippies.

The March proceeds. In a superb passage, one in which all the
strands of personality and public stance, self and community, politics and feeling are brought reinforcingly together, Mailer moves
to appropriate and give utterance to a passionate, coherent moment
within the chaos and cross-purposes of life in this country in our
time:

> . . . the sense of America divided on this day now liberated some
> undiscovered patriotism in Mailer so that he felt a sharp searing
> love for his country in this moment and on this day, crossing
> some divide in his own mind wider than the Potomac, a love so
> lacerated he felt as if a marriage were being torn and children
> lost—never does one love so much as then, obviously, then,—and
> an odor of wood smoke, from where you knew not, was also in the
> air, a smoke of dignity and some calm heroism. . . . Mailer knew
> for the first time why men in the front line of a battle are almost
> always ready to die: there is a promise of some swift transit—one's
> soul feels clean . . . walking with Lowell and Macdonald, he felt
> as if he stepped through some crossing in the reaches of space
> between this moment, the French Revolution, and the Civil War,
> as if the ghosts of the Union Dead accompanied them now to the
> Bastille. . . .

And now, as culmination:

> . . . he was arrested, he had succeeded in that, and without a
> club on his head, the mountain air in his lungs as thin and fierce
> as smoke, yes, the livid air of tension on this livid side promised
> a few events of more interest than the routine wait to be free, yes
> he was more than a visitor, he was in the land of the enemy now,
> he would get to see their face.

From this point, about half way through, the intensity slackens
somewhat, the writing growing rather more abstract, the thought
more general. "Prisoner of his own egotism, some large part of the
March had ended for him with his own arrest." Yet the book remains steadily interesting. Into the account of his two days in jail
Mailer inserts passages of political and intellectual autobiography,
opinions on many social matters, a theory and position paper on the
Vietnam war (together with a remarkable, bold insight into how
this most "obscene" of wars has paradoxically provided him and

countless other Americans with "new energy"), obiter dicta on American phenomena, all of which are sustained and given resonance by the foundation of extraordinary pertinence and the atmosphere of intimate, incorruptible dialogue that have been established.

In the last quarter of the book Mailer turns from "History as a Novel" to "The Novel as History." What he means by these phrases isn't always clear, nor are his claims for what he's done convincing in the way he intends. In dividing his book this way—the first long section composing a history in the form of fiction, that is to say as a true "tale" with characters, a plot, a narrative, etc., the second making up a novel in the form of history, *i.e.,* actual events treated as though they exemplify fictional structures and procedures, an "esthetic," as Mailer says—he hasn't succeeded in nailing down the distinctions he's after. One senses something only half right in his argument that only "the instincts of the novelist" can get at the "mystery" of such historical events as the Washington demonstration and in his proposition that because such history is so largely "interior" the "novel must replace history at precisely that point where experience is sufficiently emotional, spiritual, psychical, moral, existential, or supernatural to expose the fact that the historian in pursuing the experience would be obliged to quit the clearly demarcated limits of historical inquiry."

The trouble lies in Mailer's notion of "novel" and "novelist." The idea has always ruled him—and is, I think, the source of his erratic and inconclusive performance as an imaginative writer—of the novelist as someone whose gifts of intuition and prophecy enable him to see more deeply than other men into society or human organizations. From this follows the notion that novels are superior reports on social or psychic or moral phenomena and that fiction is therefore a superior way of agitating for change and helping bring it about. I think this a rather outdated conception of fiction and that his possession of it, along with his retention of the Hemingwayian policy of style as performance, has kept Mailer on certain wrong, if for him inevitable, tracks. Novels, the best ones, have very little to do anymore with such uses (what they once had to do with them was, for that matter, largely in the realm of pretext); novelists who are artists expect nothing to change, do not imagine that their work can safeguard or resurrect men, have no interest in being *acknowledged* legislators. The novel remains, through all its present travail, a medium for the creation of new kinds of truth and pleasure.

What Mailer has done is not to have written a novel in the form of history or history in the form of a novel, not to have produced any startlingly new forms, but to have rescued history from abstraction and aridity by approaching it with certain "novelistic" instruments at the ready and in a certain large, general "novelistic" spirit. They are rather old-fashioned things, constituents of an older idea of fiction, the kind of qualities we associate with Balzac and Zola and Maugham and textbook notions of the novel. A more advanced novelist than Mailer, one less interested in getting at social or political reality, wouldn't have been able to bring it off; that Mailer is only imperfectly a novelist, that his passion for moving and shaking the actual has prevented him from fully inhabiting imaginary kingdoms, is the underlying, paradoxical strength of this book.

The important thing is that Mailer has refused to leave history, actuality, to historians and journalists. Writing *as he can,* as part-inventor, part-observer, part-intervener, writing with gusto and vigor and an almost unprecedented kind of honesty, writing very badly at times (among dozens of examples, these: "they sensed quickly that they now shared one enclave to the hilt"; "On the *a fortiori* evidence, then, they were young men with souls of interesting dimension"; "psychedelic newspapers consider themselves removed from any fetish with factology") but writing always with a steady aim: to do for our present situation and, by implication, all our communal pasts and futures, what our traditional instrumentalities of knowledge and transcription haven't been able to do—place our public acts and lives in a human context—Mailer has put us all in his debt. In the light of that, whether or not he's the best writer in America, the best novelist or the best journalist would seem to be considerations out of a different sort of game.

The Ups and Downs of Mailer

by Richard Poirier

For well over a decade now, Norman Mailer has been obsessed with what he takes to be the deepening schizophrenia of America. He was probing the issue in 1954, when he complained that David Reisman did not seem "to have the faintest idea that there is an unconscious direction to society as well as to the individual, and that, just as many phenomena proceed in society at two levels, so a particular man or as easily all Americans can believe consciously that they are superior to advertising while in fact they suffer an unconscious slavery which influences them considerably." By 1968 and *The Armies of the Night,* when every schoolboy had heard that the media were mind snatchers, Mailer had pushed beyond; he had by then reshuffled some rather tired sociological abstractions into an allegorical morality play. "Any man or woman who was devoutly Christian and worked for the American Corporation," he claimed, "had been caught in the unseen vise whose pressure could split their mind from their soul. For the center of Christianity was a mystery, a son of God, and the center of the corporation was a detestation of mystery, a worship of technology."

These few sentences offer a brief but telling illustration of a habit, conspicuous in *Of a Fire on the Moon,* that makes Mailer, often the most exciting of contemporary American writers, sometimes the most fudging one. His mind, lurching into its metaphors, lets itself be taken for a ride, and if he weren't at the same time involved with rowdy stuff, these inveterate literary excursions, these trippings out on the lines of his own hyperboles would give him even more of a Jamesian tinge than he already has. Note how the designation, "any devoutly Christian" man or woman, is distended into some-

"The Ups and Downs of Mailer" by Richard Poirier (review of *Of a Fire on the Moon*). From *The New Republic* 164, no. 4 (January 23, 1971), 23–26. Copyright © 1971 by Harrison-Blaine of New Jersey, Inc. Reprinted by permission of *The New Republic.*

thing called "the center of Christianity" (a phenomenon even harder
to locate on the tattered theological map of this nation than the
devout Christians). His proposition thus bloated, Mailer can then
propose a struggle on a national scale between "mystery" (as if that,
or the suffering of Christ, were a notable feature of Christianity in
America) with the so-called corporation, which has meanwhile become synonymous with "technology."

Out of such legerdemain great novels may be written, even the
plays of Shakespeare, but not when, as here, the materials at hand
are so free floating. And to write history in Mailer's style requires
even more strenuous efforts with language than does the writing of
a novel or a play. Having more claims to preexistent forms of
reality than novels do, history will give up the shape it has assumed
to some other shape only under enormous stylistic (or scholarly)
pressure. In the absence of such pressure, we're left to contemplate
only the failure of the efforts to exert it, to study the drama of
confrontation between a doughty self and resistant historical forces.

Mailer is not satisfied with any such retrenchment of our interest,
however. His books are about Mailer, to be sure, about the man
as he writes history as well as about the man who tried to participate
in its making. But they are meant also to reveal the true nature of
the historical events and issues with which he has involved himself.
Similarly, while his metaphors do reveal the workings of his mind,
in its probing, contradictory, fluid movement, they also, he would
insist, expose the reality of America. He'll settle for nothing less. It's
a heroic ambition, but except in the special circumstances of *Armies*,
where the nature of his participation in events is beautifully syn-
chronized with his writing about them, the ambition is seldom
achieved. Mailer is more often than not the overreacher of his times.

His metaphoric and melodramatic versions of society and history
are of course full of revelations; they tell us more than would a
Mailer gone sane and sedate. While not denying that, I'm trying
to locate the particular cost, in this latest book, of some of his now
settled ways of performing. It might be said that a writer more
"responsible" than he would also be potentially freer. There is
nothing more seductively entrapping than a repetitive commitment
to one's own inventions. It is not the weak, but rather the exceptionally strong writer, a Mailer or a Faulkner or a Hemingway, who

finds himself eventually constrained by the persuasiveness of his own fictions, his own metaphors, his own stylistic manners. These come to dominate his mind, to tether the imagination far more than the "reality" they were meant to displace.

Of a Fire on the Moon suffers precisely because he has come to believe so staunchly in the orthodoxy of what he has already written, to believe so literally in his own metaphors, and in the efficacy of his peculiar management of them. They are almost invariably laid down in pairs, for example, in a dualism, like "mystery" and "technology." Each side is imagined tied to the other in a continual struggle. As a consequence, these tensed pairings express for him the schizophrenia he finds in the country and, as a responsible part of it, in himself. But they do much more than that: their interaction is a stay against the complete disruption of the American community and of communication among its parts. In this respect, as in others, Mailer's style is a conservative rather than a radical instrument. The induced give-and-take between the factions is a necessary alternative to a more dreadful possibility: a drawing apart of the factions, the end of any dialectical relationship between them. The consequences would be either the one-dimensionality which is the condition predicted for us in *Of a Fire on the Moon,* or revolution, the dread eventuality in *Armies.* Revolution for Mailer would mean that he could no longer live *within* his dualisms, no longer partake of the characteristics of both sides; he would have to opt for a fragment of the country and of himself, and in the choice would be final madness. This commitment to necessary oppositions, both as a form of writing and as a form of society, has so far been given its most eloquent expression in *Armies* where the language shuttles back and forth over the various conflicting elements, political and stylistic, with almost unflagging assurance—but in the moon book the shuttling becomes mechanical.

To put it crudely, the first and last sections of *Of a Fire on the Moon* are given to the Mailer who is a theoretical champion of imagination, mystery, and the language of Shakespeare; the long middle section to Mailer who studied hard and can now hold his own in the world of space technology. Anyone familiar with Mailer's work, and especially with the dualisms that have dominated it with so few modifications since the mid-fifties, will find that the new book offers few surprises. Following are some examples of the dualisms to which Mailer had already committed himself and which have in turn committed him to some of the literary and political positions of the new book.

Hip and Square. This famous division of national styles, now fifteen years old, is especially operative in Mailer's observations about corporation executives who, at news briefings, show the injurious evidence of living "the double life of Americans."

God and the Devil. There are many carry-overs from *An American Dream,* also a kind of moon book (its hero has "a frightened romance with the phases of the moon"); and in both works God and the Devil are repeatedly said to be in competition for the contributory energies of man. Cherry guesses in the novel what Mailer guesses here: maybe the "Devil gets most of the best messages we think we're sending up."

The Human Body and the Machine. Quite awhile before Mailer pictured Neil Armstrong, "sitting in the commander's seat, space suit on, helmet on, plugged into electrical and environmental umbilicals" as "a machine himself in the links of the networks," he claimed in "The Twelfth Presidential Paper," echoing Reich, that the biological organism is in some sort of struggle with technological forces and already in part possessed by them.

Language and Technologese. The language of Shakespeare, which finds no place in the Mission Control Center outside Houston, had already been nearly silenced in the Dallas of *Why Are We in Vietnam?* by the programmed rant pouring out of the electrified mind of disc jockeys, and by the nomenclatures, much like NASA's, of Corporations and rifle catalogues.

Odors and Deodorants. Odors have always been Mailer's sign of funky life, of natural decay. It is supposedly our link to that "earlier human," now ourselves, to whom he offers an anticipatory eulogy at the end of this book, a human "so much closer to an animal" than are the predicted "pilot men of an electrical and interplanetary world." Odors were already being phased out in *Armies,* however, by "totalitarianism, the deodorant of nature."

Obscenity and Concepts. Perhaps more important than odors to Mailer as a writer is the possible demise of the verbal equivalent of odors, blasphemies and dirty words. Since World War II, obscenity has lost those enlivening powers that Mailer wistfully remembers in *Armies* as part of the language of his buddies: "all the gifts of the American language came out in the happy play of obscenity upon concept, which enabled one to come back to concept again."

This latter remark offers an important further clue to Mailer's mostly successful play with the dualities of the earlier book. By abrasions, one side of any division does help in *Armies* to enliven the other. Mailer is to be found somewhere between them, his opinions oscillating with his style, his own "conceptual" talk continually corrected by sudden, slangy intrusions. His political position cannot be distinguished from his stylistic one in this area. He thinks of his love for the Southern boys who served with him, but whose sons now stand against him, guarding the Pentagon, and he has just come from the Washington home, where he was gracious if ill at ease, of the kind of liberal, bureaucratic, technocratic, concept-ridden Wasps who will be his new "buddies" in this new army. Making it one of the most anxiously, sadly patriotic books in our literature, Mailer's perplexities in *Armies* are as culturally and stylistically rewarding to his writing as are any of the comparable perplexities of Yeats.

Yet roughly the same position operates to his disadvantage in *Of a Fire on the Moon,* which is, I think, a quite messy performance. Everything he wrote before made it likely that he would have to write about the moon shot; but what was not required of him was that he meet the challenge with techniques used in earlier and lesser confrontations. The landing on the moon raised for him an old question: what will finally be left to the literary imagination by the exploitations of science? In combination with every political, financial, and industrial institution in America, science has empowered technology to the point where it can invade the very symbol of romance and dream. Such big words, such a tired issue—it's really a factitious and phoney issue, I suspect. The real issue is how well it, like any myth or fiction, can be explored, especially by a writer who has already locked himself into those metaphors, those dualisms, those large turns of mind which dictated that this was the question he would want to ask.

It's to the point that the best parts of the book are the ones most freed of Mailer's larger ambitions. Some part of him seemingly wants less to reinstate magic and romance than, deeply, to get away from the lure of them, like Rojack at the end of *An American*

Dream who "wanted to be free of magic, the tongue of the Devil, the dread of the Lord . . . to be some sort of rational man again, nailed tight to details." His most impressive performances are descriptive ones, which isn't to join the tiresome chorus of those who step away from the difficulties of his achievement by saying that he is a great journalist and a lesser novelist. The distinction, not much good to begin with, is trivializing in the case of a writer who reveals here a genius for even the quickest characterizations (Frank McGee is said to have a "personality all reminiscent . . . of a coach of a rifle team"), for casual but packed analogies that Lowell might envy ("what if the moon were as quiet as the fisherman when he lays the fly on the water"), for Proustian social observation (as in his account of an evening at the Houston home of European friends). And he is sometimes close to Lawrence in his capacity for imaginative drifts and extensions, all the while being moved forward by what seem to be the accidental associations of language. Not in his intellectual superstructurings, but in these more open evidences of his powers as a writer is assurance enough that the Machine has not yet collapsed the language or stilled the imagination. His magnificent description, the product of intense research, of the cratered face of the moon excels anything made available in words or pictures by the machined men of the Apollo flights.

The book is messed up by ambitions in excess of what is done brilliantly. Too much of it is put on loan to one dualism or another: technology and intuition, the Sanitary-Lobe and the Wild-Lobe nesting together in every American, technological reality and the reality of death, Von Braun as a man of opposites, NASA as having in it the sound of Nazi even though technology and Nazism may be inimical to one another, the space program as insane or noble, "a search for the good, or the agent of diabolisms yet unglimpsed." On and on it goes. Faced with what seems to me the inescapable fact that the astronauts, differences among them waived, are by nature as well as conditioning rather flat-minded fellows, Mailer is momentarily bewildered. What to do with material so unyielding, so uniform? Old ways of facing new problems produce old questions and answers, but he goes ahead anyway; divide and conquer. Divide the material, argue the differences, reach a kind of stalemate and call it a "mystery."

It is by such means that the book gets hooked on the subject of dreams. After all, the only life other than the irredeemably evident one that Mailer can propose for men of such rectitude has to be in the unconscious. Besides, giving them a double life, however spurious, lets him speculate that to dwell, as they do, "in the very center of technological reality . . . yet to inhabit—if only in one's dreams —that other world where death, metaphysics and the unanswerable questions of eternity must reside, was to suggest natures so divided that they could have been the most miserable and unbalanced of men if they did not contain in their huge contradictions some of the profound and accelerating opposites of the century itself."

Having decided to create a division in the astronauts by populating their unconscious, he must then up the ante still more: their unconscious can't be individuated; it must instead contain the historical, metaphysical, and social components Mailer needs for the on-going rhetoric of his book. Obviously he wouldn't allow their dreams to be the result of anything so merely personal as sublimation. While he can't supply it, he must therefore call for a theory of dreams beyond Freud, thus showing, if only for a moment, his alignment with a kind of intellectual who thinks that questions not answered by Freud or Marx have not yet even been asked. But there's more to come. Once he's escalated his terms to this point, Mailer is scarcely going to settle for the idea that the voyage itself represents merely a larger, corporate effort at the sublimation "of aggressive and intolerably inhuman desires." Even as he allows that possibility, he prefers to divide the matter more ostentatiously: the astronauts and their flight may be the instrument of "celestial and satanic endeavors."

I don't think I am being unfair in schematizing what might be called the incremental technique of Mailer's writing. But why, it still has to be asked, must he engage in these banal acts of cosmic division? Their function is best understood, and made altogether less debilitating, I suspect, if the reader takes them less as part of the substance of the book than its necessary fuel, its lubricant even. They get him moving, get him involved and boosted to a level of intensity where he will then be able to produce the masterful straight stuff in the book, like his description of the Vehicle Assembly Building at Cape Canaveral. He even admits to the opportunistic side of his practices: "It was somehow superior," he explains, to think of the flight in cosmic rather than in less exalting terms, and when he wants to claim that the trip is meant to "reveal some secret in the buried tendencies of our history," he has to agree in the next paragraph that "such remarks are large, they are grand, they roll off into the murk of metaphysical storm." (Been reading Melville lately?) The book is tricked out with such near disclaimers, near apologies for its own inflations.

I'm not necessarily opposed to inflation, as what admirer of *King Lear* could be, or to sophomoric explanations that Mailer is showing what it's like to take a space trip in the mind. I don't even object to what Mailer at one point proposes as the justification for the scale of his enterprise: "a first reconnaissance into the possibility of restoring magic, psyche, and the spirits of the underworld to the spookiest venture in history, a landing on the moon, an event whose technologese had been so complete that the word 'spook' probably did not appear in twenty million words of NASA prose." It's simply that in this book Mailer proves less a Prospero of *The Tempest* than a Glendower of *Henry IV,* though a Glendower shrewd enough to anticipate the riposte to his claim that he "can call spirits from the vasty deep": "Why, so can I, or so can any man;/But will they come when you do call them?"

I suppose it could be said that the book is meant to demonstrate why there will never be now in America the revolution feared in *Armies.* The Wasps have won by default, those "Faustian, barbaric, draconian, progress-oriented, and root-destroying people." They are coming into control of evolution, and the literary imagination, with all the odors and obscenities that nourish it, is at last obsolete, with this book itself as one of its final records, as Christopher Lehmann-Haupt has suggested. The last chapter almost says as much. It's more likely, though, that only Mailer's standard routines have become obsolete. I think they probably have. Besides, the points where he is not doing his routines show that he still can, in his own phrase, "climb to capture the language again." He and not the space program, not Technology, is responsible for making the climb harder than it need be by carrying intellectual luggage that is always heavy, usually excess, and now manifestly a hindrance.

Chronology of Important Dates

1923   Mailer born at Long Branch, New Jersey, January 31.

1927   Moves with family to Eastern Parkway, Brooklyn.

1939   Enters Harvard.

1941   Wins *Story* magazine contest with "The Greatest Thing in the World."

1942   Writes a play called "The Naked and the Dead" about his summer work in a Boston state mental hospital. After graduation from Harvard in 1943 as a major in aeronautical engineering, he rewrites the play as a novel, *A Transit to Narcissus,* which fails to find a publisher.

1944   In January, drafted into the U. S. Army. In March, marries Beatrice Silverman and is inducted. His wife joins the Waves.

1946   Discharged from the 112th Cavalry after serving in the Philippine campaign at Leyte, the invasion of Luzon, Manila, and the occupation of Japan.

1947   Finishes *The Naked and the Dead* in October after fifteen months' work; gives the novel to his publisher and leaves three days later with his wife for study at the Sorbonne on the G. I. Bill; begins *Barbary Shore* in Paris.

1948   Returns from Paris; *The Naked and the Dead* published; makes speeches in support of Henry Wallace's candidacy for President.

1949   March: Separates himself from Wallace and the Progressive Party; goes to Hollywood as a scriptwriter and begins to work on *Barbary Shore* again; daughter Susan born.

1950   Returns to the East, where he continues work on *Barbary Shore* in New York, Provincetown, and Putney, Vermont.

1951   *Barbary Shore* published; works in New York on short stories.

1952   "The Man Who Studied Yoga" published; divorced from first
          wife.

1954   Marries Adele Morales; writes a series of articles on the
          United States and Russia for *Dissent*; helps found the *Village
          Voice* and later writes a column; problems in the revision and
          censorship of *The Deer Park*.

1955   *The Deer Park* published.

1956–57   Stops writing his column for the *Village Voice* and spends
          several months in Paris; daughter Danielle born.

1958   Writes "The Time of Her Time."

1959   *Advertisements for Myself* published; daughter Elizabeth
          Anne born.

1960   Begins a monthly column for *Esquire*; April 25: receives
          award from the National Academy of Arts and Letters; sum-
          mer: conducts his own defense and is acquitted in Province-
          town trial for interfering with police; November 14: arrested
          at Birdland for complaining about the bill, acquitted; No-
          vember 19: stabs wife after a party at their New York apart-
          ment; November 22: committed to Bellevue for observation,
          released after seventeen days; December: writes two short
          stories: "The Killer: A Story," "Truth and Being: Nothing
          and Time."

1961   January 31: indicted on two counts of felonious assault and
          one count of possession of a deadly weapon; February 3:
          pleads not guilty; February 7: curtain rung down at New
          York YMHA while he reads his poetry because an official
          believes it to be pornographic; March 10: pleads guilty to
          third degree assault; May 10: put on probation.

1962   Divorced from second wife; marries Lady Jean Campbell;
          Deaths for the Ladies and Other Disasters (poems) published;
          daughter Kate born.

1963   Divorced from third wife; marries Beverly Bentley; November
          8: *The Presidential Papers* published (originally announced
          as *The Devil Revisited*).

1964   *An American Dream* serialized in *Esquire* (January–July); son
          Michael Burks born.

1965   *An American Dream* published.

1966   *Cannibals and Christians* published; son Stephen McLeod born.

1967   January 7: *Wild 90* (film) shown; January 31: first performance of *The Deer Park* (play); *The Deer Park* in play form published; *Why Are We in Vietnam?* and *The Short Fiction of Norman Mailer* published; October: participates in March on the Pentagon.

1968   *The Armies of the Night* published; covers the Republican and Democratic presidential conventions; *Miami and the Siege of Chicago* published; first showing of *Beyond the Law* (film).

1969   April 15: announces candidacy for the Democratic nomination for Mayor of New York and comes in fourth in a field of five; films *Maidstone*; goes to Houston and Cape Kennedy to cover the moon shot.

1970   *Of a Fire on the Moon* published; May 5: begins a three-day sentence in Washington, D. C., for his arrest in the Pentagon March.

1971   *The Prisoner of Sex,* "King of the Hill," and *Maidstone, a Mystery* (film script, essay on film, and production description) published. December: first performance of *D.J.*, a one-act play based on *Why Are We in Vietnam?;* birth of daughter Maggie Alexandra (with Carol Stevens).

1972   *Existential Errands* published.

Notes on the Editor and Contributors

LEO BRAUDY, editor of this volume, teaches English at Columbia University. He is the author of *Narrative Form in History and Fiction: Hume, Fielding, and Gibbon* and *Jean Renoir: The World of His Films.*

JOHN W. ALDRIDGE is Professor of English at the University of Minnesota. The author of *After the Lost Generation, In Search of Heresy,* and *A Time to Murder and Create,* he will be writing a biography of Mailer with permission to make first use of all available materials.

JAMES BALDWIN, the novelist and essayist, is the author of *Go Tell It on the Mountain, The Fire Next Time,* and *Another Country.* His latest works are the novel, *Tell Me How Long the Train's Been Gone,* and *A Rap on Race,* with Margaret Mead.

LEO BERSANI is the author of *Balzac to Beckett* and *Marcel Proust: The Fictions of Life and Art.*

MICHAEL COWAN teaches English at the University of California, Santa Cruz. He is the author of *City of the West: Emerson, America, and the Urban Metaphor.*

F. W. DUPEE, now retired from teaching English at Columbia University, is the author of *Henry James* and the co-editor of *Selected Letters of E. E. Cummings.*

RICHARD FOSTER teaches English at Macalester College. He is the author of a University of Minnesota pamphlet on Norman Mailer as well as *The New Romantics: A Reappraisal of the New Criticism.*

RICHARD GILMAN teaches at the Yale School of Drama and is the cultural editor of *The New Republic.* He is the author of *The Confusion of Realms* and *Common and Uncommon Masks.*

STANLEY EDGAR HYMAN (d. 1970) is the author of *The Armed Vision* and *The Tangled Bank.*

STEVEN MARCUS is Professor of English at Columbia University. He is the author of *Dickens: From Pickwick to Dombey* and *The Other Victorians.*

RICHARD POIRIER is Professor of English at Rutgers University. His latest book is *The Performing Self,* which includes a discussion of Norman

Mailer. He is presently working on a book about Mailer that will appear in the Modern Masters series.

GEORGE SCHRADER is Professor of Philosophy at Yale University and the editor of *Existential Philosophers: Kierkegaard to Merleau-Ponty.*

DIANA TRILLING, the literary and social critic, is the author of *Claremont Essays* and contributes frequent essays to a wide variety of journals.

Selected Bibliography

Works by Norman Mailer

Advertisements for Myself (essays, short stories, poetry with a running commentary). New York: G.P. Putnam's Sons, 1959; pb.: Berkley Books.

An American Dream (novel). New York: The Dial Press, Inc., 1965; pb.: Dell.

The Armies of the Night (nonfiction). New York: New American Library, 1968; pb.: Signet.

Barbary Shore (novel). New York: Holt, Rinehart & Winston, Inc., 1951; pb.: Grosset Universal Library (introduction by Norman Podhoretz); Signet.

The Bullfight, a Photographic Narrative with Text by Norman Mailer. New York: C.B.S. Legacy Collection Book, distributed by The Macmillan Company, 1967.

Cannibals and Christians (essays). New York: Dial, 1966; pb.: Dell.

Deaths for the Ladies, and Other Disasters (poems). New York: G. P. Putnam's Sons, 1962; pb.: Grove Press; Signet.

The Deer Park (novel). New York: G. P. Putnam's Sons, 1955; The Dial Press, Inc., 1967; pb.: Berkley Books; Signet.

The Deer Park (play). New York: The Dial Press, Inc., 1967; pb.: Dell.

Existential Errands (essays). Boston: Little, Brown and Company, 1972.

The Idol and the Octopus (essays). New York: Dell, 1968 (pb.).

"The King of the Hill" (essay). New York: Signet, 1971 (pb.).

The Naked and the Dead (novel). New York: Holt, Rinehart, & Winston, Inc., 1948; Modern Library; pb.: Signet.

Maidstone, a Mystery (movie script, essay). New York: Signet, 1971 (pb.).

Miami and the Siege of Chicago (nonfiction). New York: New American Library, 1968; pb.: Signet.

Of a Fire on the Moon (nonfiction). Boston: Little, Brown and Company, 1970; pb.: Signet.

The Presidential Papers (essays). New York: G. P. Putnam's Sons, 1963; pb.: Berkley.

The Prisoner of Sex (essay). Boston: Little, Brown and Company, 1971, pb.: Signet.

The Short Fiction of Norman Mailer. New York: Dell, 1967 (pb.).

The White Negro (essay). San Francisco: City Lights, 1957 (pb.).

Why Are We in Vietnam? (novel). New York: G. P. Putnam's Sons, 1967; pb.: Berkley.

Books about Norman Mailer

Aldridge, John W. *After the Lost Generation.* New York: McGraw-Hill Book Company, 1951. ("Mailer, Burns, and Shaw: The Naked Zero")

Eisinger, Chester E. *Fiction of the Forties.* Chicago: University of Chicago Press, 1963.

Flaherty, Joe. *Managing Mailer.* New York: Coward-McCann, Inc., 1970. (An account of Mailer's 1969 campaign for Mayor of New York that gives some of the flavor and facts of the campaign, strained through a bombastic style that the author, Mailer's campaign manager, no doubt thinks is an homage to his candidate.)

Foster, Richard. *Norman Mailer.* Minneapolis: University of Minnesota Press, 1968. (An excellent pamphlet.)

Geismar, Maxwell. *American Moderns: From Rebellion to Conformity.* New York: Hill & Wang, Inc., 1958. ("Norman Mailer: The Bohemian of the National Letters")

Gelmis, Joseph. *The Film Director as Superstar.* Garden City, New York: Doubleday & Company, Inc., 1970. (Contains an extensive interview with Mailer about his movie-making, centering on *Maidstone.*)

Harper, Howard M., Jr. *Desperate Faith: A Study of Bellow, Salinger, Mailer, Baldwin and Updike.* Chapel Hill, N. C.: University of North Carolina Press, 1967.

Hassan, Ihab. *Radical Innocence.* Princeton, N. J.: Princeton University Press, 1961. ("Encounter with Necessity: Styron, Swados, Mailer")

Howe, Irving. *A World More Attractive.* New York: Horizon Press, 1963. ("A Quest for Peril: Norman Mailer")

Kaufmann, Donald L. *Norman Mailer: The Countdown (The First Twenty Years),* preface by Harry T. Moore. Carbondale, Ill.: University of Southern Illinois Press, 1969.

Kazin, Alfred. *Contemporaries.* Boston: Little, Brown and Company, 1962. ("How Good Is Norman Mailer?")

Langbaum, Robert. *The Modern Spirit.* New York: Oxford University Press, 1970. ("Mailer's New Style")

Leeds, Barry H. *The Structured Vision of Norman Mailer.* New York: New York University Press, 1969.

Manso, Peter. *Running Against the Machine.* Garden City, N. Y.: Doubleday & Company, Inc., 1969. (A compilation of position papers and speeches made during Mailer's campaign for the mayoralty nomination.)

Millett, Kate. *Sexual Politics.* Garden City, New York: Doubleday & Company, Inc., 1970. (Mailer responds to Millett's section on Henry Miller, D. H. Lawrence, Jean Genet, and himself in *The Prisoner of Sex.*)

Noble, David W. *The Eternal Adam and the New World Garden: The Central Myth in the American Novel Since 1930.* New York: George Braziller, Inc., 1968.

Podhoretz, Norman. *Doings and Undoings.* New York: Farrar, Straus & Giroux, Inc., 1964. ("The Embattled Vision of Norman Mailer," an excellent essay first printed in *Partisan Review* in 1959.)

Rahv, Philip. *The Myth and the Powerhouse.* Boston: Farrar, Straus & Giroux, 1966. ("Crime without Punishment," a good negative view of *An American Dream.*)

Tanner, Tony. *City of Words.* London: Jonathan Cape, Ltd., 1971. ("On the Parapet: A Study of the Novels of Norman Mailer," a very interesting essay that deals in part with Mailer's language.)

Vidal, Gore. *Rocking the Boat.* Boston: Little, Brown and Company, 1962. ("Norman Mailer: The Angels Are White," a combination personal memoir and review of *Advertisements for Myself.*)

Weinberg, Helen. *The New Novel in America: the Kafkan Mode in Contemporary Fiction.* Ithaca, N. Y.: Cornell University Press, 1970. (Perhaps the most interesting of the academic omnibus studies.)

Widmer, Kingsley. *The Literary Rebel,* preface by Harry T. Moore. Carbondale, Ill.: University of Southern Illinois Press, 1965. ("Several American Perplexes," dealing with Mailer and Paul Goodman, should be read in the light of Mailer's attack on Goodman in *The Armies of the Night.*)

Articles and Reviews about Norman Mailer

Aaron, Jonathan, "Existentialist Sheriff," *The New Journal* 1, no. 5 (December 10, 1967), 6–7. (Mailer at Yale reading a pre-publication section of *The Armies of the Night* to an at-first-hostile audience.)

Aldridge, John W. "From Vietnam to Obscenity," *Harper's* 236, no. 1413 (February, 1968), 91–97. (A long review of *Why Are We in Vietnam?* that concentrates on Mailer's use of obscenity.)

Auchincloss, Louis. "The Novel as a Forum," *New York Times Book Review* (October 24, 1965), p. 2. (An attack on the excessively ideological content of *An American Dream* that associates Mailer with Zola and in opposition to James.)

Braudy, Leo. "Advertisements for a Dwarf Alter-ego," *The New Journal* 1, no. 13 (May 12, 1968), 7–9. (Review of *The Armies of the Night*.)

————. "Baldwin and the White Man's Guilt," *The Phoenix* (March 3, 1963), pp. 1–3. (An account of the controversy between Mailer and Baldwin over *The White Negro*.)

————. Review of *Maidstone, a Mystery*, *New York Times Book Review* (December 21, 1971), pp. 2–3, 25.

Canby, Vincent. "When Irish Eyes Are Smiling, It's Norman Mailer," *New York Times Drama Section* (October 27, 1968), p. 15. (Interview and article dealing with the filming of *Beyond the Law*.)

Carroll, Paul. "An Interview with Norman Mailer," *Playboy* 15, no. 1 (January, 1968), 69–84.

Decter, Midge. "Mailer's Campaign," *Commentary* 37, no. 2 (February, 1964), 83–85. (A review of *The Presidential Papers*.)

DeMott, Benjamin. "Docket No. 15883," *The American Scholar* 30, no. 2 (Spring, 1961), 232–37. (On Mailer's arrest for stabbing his second wife, Adele.)

Dickstein, Morris. Review of *Of a Fire on the Moon*, *New York Times Book Review* (January 10, 1971), p. 1.

Dienstfrey, Harris. "The Fiction of Norman Mailer," *On Contemporary Literature*, ed. Richard Kostelanetz. New York: Avon Books, 1964.

Hardwick, Elizabeth. "Bad Boy," *Partisan Review*, 32, no. 2 (Spring, 1965), 291–94. (An attack on *An American Dream* that Mailer attempted to counter by printing John W. Aldridge's *Life* review as an advertisement.)

Healey, Robert C. "Novelists of the War: A Bunch of Dispossessed," in *Fifty Years of the American Novel*, ed. Harold C. Gardiner. New York: Charles Scribner's Sons, 1951.

Hesla, David. "The Two Roles of Norman Mailer," *Adversity and Grace*, ed. Nathan A. Scott, Jr. Chicago: University of Chicago Press, 1967.

Kael, Pauline. "Celebrities Make Spectacles of Themselves," *The New Yorker* 43, no. 48 (January 20, 1968), 90–95. (Review of *Wild 90*.)

Kerr, Walter. "Evil: Plainly a Fun Thing," *New York Times Drama Sec-*

tion (February 12, 1967), pp. 1, 7. (Review-article about the play version of *The Deer Park*.)

Macdonald, Dwight. "Our Farflung Correspondents: Mailer v. Massachusetts," *The New Yorker* 36, no. 34 (October 8, 1960), 154–66. (A jovial account of Mailer's successful attempt to serve as his own lawyer when charged with drunkenness and disorderly conduct by the Provincetown police.)

Maddison, Michael. "Prospect of Commitment," *Political Quarterly* 32, no. 4 (October, 1961), 353–62. (A provocative comparison between Mailer and Ionesco on the one hand and Brecht on the other dealing with the problem of ideology in literature.)

Martien, Norman. "Norman Mailer at Graduate School," *New American Review,* no. 1, pp. 233–41. (Mailer on a college-speaking tour.)

Matz, Charles. "Mailer's Opera," *Opera News* 34, no. 17 (February 21, 1970), 14–16. (The writing of a libretto for *An American Dream*.)

Mudrick, Marvin. "Mailer and Styron: Guests of the Establishment," *Hudson Review* 17, no. 3 (Autumn, 1964), 346–66.

Nichols, Dudley. "Secret Places of the Groin," *The Nation* 181, no. 19 (November 5, 1955), 393–95. (A noted Hollywood scriptwriter questions the "reality" of *The Deer Park*.)

Poirier, Richard. "Morbid-Mindedness," *Commentary* 39, no. 6 (June, 1965), 91–94. (A review of *An American Dream* that discusses the uses of melodrama and romance.)

Richardson, Jack. "The Aesthetics of Norman Mailer," *New York Review of Books* (May 8, 1969), pp. 3–4. (A review of *Miami and the Siege of Chicago* that makes some interesting remarks about Mailer's style.)

Richler, Mordecai. "Norman Mailer," *Encounter* 25, no. 1 (July, 1965), 61–64. (A generally negative review of *An American Dream* with a sympathetic sketch of Mailer lecturing in London.)

Roddy, Joseph. "The Latest Model Mailer," *Look* 33, no. 11 (May 27, 1969), pp. 22–28. (An excellent profile of Mailer built around the filming of *Maidstone*.)

Schroth, Raymond A., S. J. "Mailer and His Gods," *Commonweal* 90, no. 8 (May 9, 1969), 226–29. (Argues that the theological strain in Mailer's work has been "most successfully synthesized" with his life and art in *The Armies of the Night*.)

Schulz, Max F. "Mailer's Divine Comedy," *Contemporary Literature* 9, no. 1 (Winter, 1968), 36–57. (An examination of Mailer's use of allegory.)

Shaw, Peter. "The Tough Guy Intellectual," *Critical Quarterly* 8, no. 1

(Spring, 1966), 13–28. (An excellent article that discusses the tradition of the intellectual *naïf* in America.)

————. Review of *Miami and the Siege of Chicago, Commentary* 46, no. 6 (December, 1968), 93–96.

Solotaroff, Robert. "Down Mailer's Way," *Chicago Review* 19, no. 3 (June, 1967), 11–25.

Steiner, George. "Naked But Not Dead," *Encounter* 17, no. 6 (December, 1961), pp. 67–70. (Review of *Advertisements for Myself*.)

Swados, Harvey. "Must Writers Be Characters?" *Saturday Review* 43, no. 40 (October 1, 1960), pp. 12–14, 50. (A discussion of American writers centering on the problem of self-display, which, Swados argues, always encourages non-literary discussion.)

Toback, James. "Norman Mailer Today," *Commentary* 44, no. 4 (October, 1967), 68–76.

Trachtenberg, Alan. "Mailer on the Steps of the Pentagon," *The Nation* 206, no. 22 (May 27, 1968), 701–2.

Volpe, Edmond L. "James Jones–Norman Mailer," *Contemporary American Novelists,* ed. Harry T. Moore. Carbondale, Ill.: University of Southern Illinois Press, 1964.

Weber, Brom. "A Fear of Dying: Norman Mailer's *An American Dream,*" *Hollins Critic* 2, no. 3 (June, 1965), 1–11.

Willingham, Calder. "The Way It Isn't Done: Notes on the Distress of Norman Mailer," *Esquire* 60, no. 6 (December, 1963), 306–8. (An indictment of Mailer's literary bad manners in "Some Children of the Goddess" and an attempt to answer his attacks on his fellow writers.)

Winn, Janet. "Capote, Mailer and Miss Parker," *The New Republic* 140, no. 6 (February 9, 1959), 27–28. (An account of the three appearing on a television talk show together.)

Wolfe, Tom. "Son of Crime and Punishment," *Book Week* (March 14, 1965). (A review of *An American Dream* comparing its conception and execution to that of Dostoevsky's novel.)

Wood, Margery. "Norman Mailer and Nathalie Sarraute: A Comparison of Existentialist Novels," *Minnesota Review* 6, no. 1 (Spring, 1966), 67–72. (Concentrates on *An American Dream*.)